The Power of Inaction

A volume in the series

Cornell Studies in Political Economy
edited by Peter J. Katzenstein

A list of titles in this series is available at www.cornellpress.cornell.edu.

The Power of Inaction
Bank Bailouts in Comparison

Cornelia Woll

Cornell University Press
Ithaca and London

First published 2014 by Cornell University Press
Printed in the United States of America

Library of Congress Cataloging-in-Publication Data

Woll, Cornelia, author.
   The power of inaction: bank bailouts in comparison / Cornelia Woll.
      pages cm. — (Cornell studies in political economy)
   Includes bibliographical references and index.
   ISBN 978-0-8014-5235-2 (cloth: alk. paper)
   1. Bank failures—Government policy. 2. Bailouts
(Government policy) I. Title.
   HG1725.W654   2014
   332.1—dc23   2013042835

Cornell University Press strives to use environmentally responsible
suppliers and materials to the fullest extent possible in the publishing
of its books. Such materials include vegetable-based, low-VOC inks
and acid-free papers that are recycled, totally chlorine-free, or partly
composed of nonwood fibers. For further information, visit our website
at www.cornellpress.cornell.edu.

Cloth printing   10 9 8 7 6 5 4 3 2 1

To my family

Contents

Figures and Tables

Abbreviations

AFEP	Association française des entreprises privées
AIG	American International Group
BCCI	Bank of Credit and Commerce International
BdB	Bundesverband deutscher Banken
BVR	Bundesverband der Volks- und Raiffeisenbanken
CAP	US Capital Assistance Program
CBFSAI	Central Bank and Financial Services Authority of Ireland
CDS	credit default swaps
CEO	chief executive officer
CPP	US Capital Purchase Plan
DBA	Danish Bankers Association
DG	Directorate-General
DSGV	Deutscher Sparkassen- und Giroverband
EAA	Erste Abwicklungsanstalt
ECB	European Central Bank
EMU	Economic and Monetary Union
EU	European Union
Fannie Mae	Federal National Mortgage Association
FBF	Fédération bancaire française
FDIC	Federal Deposit Insurance Corporation
FDICIA	Federal Deposit Insurance Corporate Improvement Act
FHFA	Federal Housing Finance Agency
FMS-WM	FMS Wertmanagement
FMSA	Bundesanstalt für Finanzmarktstabilisierung
Freddie Mac	Federal Home Loan Mortgage Corporation
FSA	Financial Services Authority
FSCS	Financial Services Compensation Scheme

HBOS	Halifax Bank of Scotland
HRE	Hypo Real Estate
IFSC	International Financial Service Centre
IMF	International Monetary Fund
Indymac	Independent National Mortgage Corporation
KfW	Kreditanstalt für Wiederaufbau
LB	Landesbank
LikoBank	Liquiditäts-Konsortialbank
LTCM	Long-Term Capital Management
MEDEF	Mouvement des entreprises de France
NAMA	National Asset Management Agency
OeCAG	Österreichische Clearingbank AG
OIAG	Österreichische Industrieholding AG
PCAR	Prudential Capital Assessment Review
PwC	PricewaterhouseCoopers
SFEF	Société de financement de l'économie française
SIGTARP	Special Inspector General for the TARP
SoFFin	Sonderfonds Finanzmarktstabilisierung
SPPE	Société de prise de participation de l'Etat
TARP	Troubled Asset Relief Program
UKFI	United Kingdom Financial Investments

Bailout Games

Nothing to be done.

—Samuel Beckett, *Waiting for Godot*

How could the US government let Lehman Brothers fail? Few questions have been discussed as often in recent economic history, with as much fervor or bewilderment. Following the collapse of the investment bank on 15 September 2008, the financial crisis that had built up for more than a year rippled through the global economy with breathtaking speed, destroying $700 billion in value from retirement plans, government pension funds, and other investment portfolios in just one day, and over $11 trillion during the duration of the entire crisis.[1] Banks everywhere found themselves in great difficulties as liquidity dried up completely, and the financial industry in many countries came to a near collapse. The picture was very similar in other countries with substantial financial industries. To avoid repeating the experience of Lehman's failure, governments rushed to stabilize their banking sectors through bailout schemes, most of them devised in the fall of 2008.

This book compares these bank rescue schemes and makes a very simple point: it is impossible to understand government action without looking at the collective action of the financial industry at the time of near collapse. Turning the opening question around, one needs to ask: How could the US financial industry let Lehman Brothers fail?

Clearly, US financial institutions were all negatively affected by the bankruptcy of their competitor. The rationale for the public bank bailouts that followed was precisely the systemic risk caused by the failure of individual firms. Presumably, the stability of the sector as a whole rather than the financial health of these individual firms was what mattered for

---

1. Financial Crisis Inquiry Commission, *The Financial Crisis Inquiry Report*, 339.

the governments committing public money to save an ailing financial institution. Should the financial industry not have been equally concerned about preserving this stability, which crucially affects the operations of all other firms? According to Federal Reserve Chairman Ben Bernanke, a scholar of the Great Depression, the pressure that was put on financial firms in the aftermath of Lehman's failure was the worst in history: "Out of the 13 most important financial institutions in the United States, 12 were at risk of failure within a period of a week or two."[2] Was it not in the interest of these institutions to avoid the shockwaves sent by Lehman Brothers' bankruptcy?

What might seem like a rather theoretical and scholarly question was in fact the question posed to the CEO's of America's major banks, gathered together by the US secretary of the treasury Henry Paulson on Friday evening, 12 September 2008. Based on a proposal from the Federal Reserve Bank of New York, the administration asked the financial industry to establish a private sector liquidation consortium in order to facilitate an acquisition, similar to the rescue engineered for the hedge fund Long Term Capital Management (LTCM) in 1998. As a contingency, they were asked to come up with an alternative, to find another workable solution to deal with the effects of Lehman's failure.[3] Haunted by the criticism of the public guarantee provided for Bear Stearns several months earlier, the US government argued that it could no longer commit public funds for saving the financial industry. "We did the last one," Paulson told the bankers in the room, "you are doing this one."[4]

To push the financial industry to find a collective solution, he insisted that there would be no government support, "not a penny."[5] The message from the US administration was met with incredulity. "We must be responsible for our own balance sheets and now we are responsible for others?" Lloyd Blankfein, CEO and chairman of Goldman Sachs asked. Paulson remembers how troublesome this realization was for businesses priding themselves as free marketeers. "At what point were the interests of individual firms overridden by the needs of the many? It was the classic question of collective action."[6] According to H. Rodgin Cohen, a Wall Street lawyer and Lehman's legal counsel at the time, the "not a penny" posture was a political strategy. Indeed, the Fed's internal liquidation consortium plan contemplated a financial commitment from the government that was not divulged. Cohen's impression was that the government was "playing a game of chicken or poker."[7]

2. Cited in ibid., 345.
3. Baxter, *Too Big to Fail*, 3–4.
4. Cited in Wessel, *In FED We Trust*, 16.
5. Cited in Financial Crisis Inquiry Commission, *The Financial Crisis Inquiry Report*, 334.
6. Paulson, *On the Brink*, 198.
7. Financial Crisis Inquiry Commission, *The Financial Crisis Inquiry Report*, 334.

A giant and collective game of chicken, indeed! Like the car game that became a household example in game theory, both parties appeared to be driving at full speed at each other in a single lane that crosses a bridge. In such games, where both acknowledge that the worst possible outcome is a crash—the collapse of the economy—the one who yields first, loses. If the government saves Lehman Brothers, it will commit important amounts of taxpayer money and create substantial moral hazard, which may lead to further rescues becoming necessary in the future. If the industry saves Lehman Brothers', it will have to collectively carry the costs, at a time where almost all of them had considerable difficulties themselves. Both parties had a strong incentive not to yield. Although discussions concerning a consortium did make some progress, neither party was ready to cover the most important portion of the risk emanating from Lehman's situation. Despite the general agreement that a failure would be disastrous, neither chickened out. At 1:45 a.m. on Monday, 15 September 2008, Lehman Brothers filed for bankruptcy and financial markets crashed and burned, like speeding cars would when meeting in the middle of the bridge.

Perspectives on Financial Power

In the aftermath of the Lehman failure, governments stopped taking chances. As stock markets plummeted and liquidity dried up, it became evident that markets were not prepared for the failure of systemic institutions, as many had hoped. The negative effects of one failure went far beyond the contagion optimistic analysts had assumed. Within less than a month, most industrialized countries reinforced liquidity provisions and developed bailouts schemes to save institutions from collapsing and to prop up their financial systems. Although some exchanges did take place at the international level, the arrangements were all a decidedly national exercise in crisis management. What is more, their details and institutional setups displayed great variation, despite the fact that they were trying to address similar problems.

In all countries, the political decisions to rescue the banking sector were heavily criticized. With extraordinary amounts of public money committed to saving a sector that had reaped considerable profits in recent decades, few observers were sympathetic to the need for public intervention. Bank bailouts became one of the most scrutinized public policies, with an endless number of inquiry reports written, oversight committees put into place, and media attention focused on explaining who got what, when, and why. In many of the public, popular, and scholarly accounts of bank bailouts, the political influence of the financial industry is singled out as a major culprit for seemingly biased decisions. But what exactly did the financial industry influence? What was the nature of power finance wielded over the fate of the economy and the crisis management in 2008, which affected the lives of so many?

Three main approaches to answering this question exist in early analyses of the crisis in the popular and the academic literature. The first focuses on lobbying and the privileged interactions between the financial industry and public authorities. The second examines institutional constraints as fundamental conditions for public intervention. The third focuses on the symbiotic relationship between finance and the state, and highlights how meaning structures shape government action, or in this case, contributed to complacency.

The first strand most closely focuses on individual strategies of financial institutions and their interaction with governments through lobbying activities. Relying on a public choice perspective where political decisions are traded against resources such as financial support or other favors, analysts in this tradition argue that bailouts were granted because public officials were bought off by the excessively wealthy financial sector. The triggers for intervention are calls by financial donors or constituents for a bailout, not any fundamental concern about financial stability. Such analysts portray the rhetoric accompanying bailouts as the dramatization of the actual risk, as insistence on a "perfect storm" simply to help legitimate intervention.[8] Analytically, authors focus on resources and links between financial representatives and public officials that would help to explain easy access.[9] Others employ a less exchange-focused perspective but nonetheless study the networks between financial and political elites,[10] as well as their joint training and exchange of knowledge. Both lead to converging world views on financial regulation, or "cultural capture."[11] Whatever the precise angle, studies in the first strand are motivated by a desire to understand the interactions between the financial industry and public authorities in order to understand the evolution of regulation and the degree of capture the sector has over the government.[12]

The second strand focuses on institutional constraints rather than individual interactions. Starting from the recognition that institutional choices shape the interests and limit the options of the central stakeholders, institutional analyses focus on the variation in socioeconomic orders to explain industry preferences and government choices. Policymakers in the United States, for instance, expected Europeans to move more readily toward support schemes for the banking sector, because the percentage of bank

8. Ritholtz, *Bailout Nation*; Reinhart, "A Year of Living Dangerously."

9. Acemoglu et al., *The Value of Political Connections in the United States*; Braun and Raddatz, "Banking on Politics"; Igan, Mishra, and Tressel, "A Fistful of Dollars."

10. Seabrooke and Tsingou, *Revolving Doors and Linked Ecologies in the World Economy.*

11. Kwak, "Cultural Capture and the Financial Crisis"; see also Johnson and Kwak, *13 Bankers.*

12. Cf. Baker, "Restraining Regulatory Capture?"; Carpenter and Moss, *Preventing Regulatory Capture.*

intermediation was much higher in Europe than in the United States. This belief mirrors the academic literature. According to Weber and Schmitz, varieties of capitalism are decisive in explaining bailout efforts.[13] In the varieties of capitalism literature, the emphasis is on the role of finance and its relationship to the so-called "real" economy,[14] while the law and finance literature focuses on the legal origins of divergent financial systems.[15] Both strands tend to distinguish between at least two types of financial systems: a bank-based one and a capital-market-based one.[16] The power of financial institutions over government derives from this institutional setting, since banks control very closely the access to funding in the first case and are much more subject to market pressures in the second one.[17] Although we may analyze how the financial industry shapes these different institutions and transforms it through European integration,[18] the central claim of the institutional perspective is that the different settings determine the interests and choices of individual actors. Once an institutional order is stabilized, it confers structural power to those that hold key positions within each arrangement.

The third strand focuses on the joint production of knowledge that defines the stakeholders of financial regulation and their interests. In this strand individual initiatives or institutional features count for little in understanding the influence of the financial industry over policy; instead, by becoming part of a network all relevant stakeholders produce the features through which its behavior is governed. Some refer to this highly intertwined network as the "Wall Street–Treasury complex"[19] or more generally the "state-finance nexus."[20] Politically, the achievement of this network is to move financial regulation from direct state intervention to a decentralized, self-regulated, and market-based approach.[21] But much of this transformation cannot be understood as the conscious maneuvering of strategic actors. At the microlevel, it also relies on the knowledge regimes that govern finance, which the stakeholders in the network help to produce. Building on insights from social theory, in particular Foucault's governmentality,[22] Giddens's structuration theory,[23] and science and technology studies, a series of authors have tried to explain how financial integration and regulation evolves by focusing on the

---

13. Weber and Schmitz, "Varieties of Helping Capitalism."

14. Hall and Soskice, *Varieties of Capitalism: Institutional Foundations of Comparative Advantage*; Crouch and Streeck, *The Political Economy of Modern Capitalism*; Zysman, *Governments, Markets, and Growth.*

15. La Porta et al., "Law and Finance"; Malmendier, "Law and Finance 'at the Origin'."

16. Demirgüç-Kunt and Levine, "Bank-based and Market-based Financial Systems"; Allen and Gale, *Comparing Financial Systems.*

17. Rajan and Zingales, *Saving Capitalism from the Capitalists.*

18. Mügge, *Widen the Market, Narrow the Competition*; Fioretos, *Creative Reconstructions.*

19. Bhagwati, "The Capital Myth."

20. Harvey, *The Enigma of Capital.*

21. Underhill and Zang, "Setting the Rules"; Abdelal, "Writing the Rules of Global Finance."

22. Burchell, Gordon, and Miller, *The Foucault Effect.*

23. Giddens, *The Constitution of Society.*

technologies used to govern it.[24] According to the third strand, the power of finance is best understood as productive power, which operates by shaping the actors' self-understanding and interests, both on the government side and within the financial industry.

Assembling a disparate set of authors and schools, the three perspectives distinguish themselves by their treatment of agency in the exercise of power. The first perspective provides a very active and intentional take on individual interactions. The second maintains that institutional structures circumscribe individual strategies, at least for some period of time until agents are able to adjust institutions. In the third perspective, individual strategies are subordinated to constitutive processes that no actor in particular controls entirely. The influence of the financial sector is diffuse and unfolds over the long term, but it is no less decisive.

By studying the bank bailout packages of six countries—the United States, the United Kingdom, Germany, France, Ireland, and Denmark—this book argues that the first perspective is insufficient to understand variations across countries. The resources of the financial industry and the proximity they have with policymakers are substantial everywhere. It does not make a difference whether these connections rely on campaign funding, revolving doors, joint schooling, or other networks. How these resources are used and when they matter seems to depend on other features that go beyond the pure contacts between the industry and public authorities.

The institutional perspective provides important insights into these features, as does the focus on the productive power of the state-finance nexus. However, both are somewhat indeterminate and provide only a vague sense of agency—and thus political responsibility—for decision making during the crisis. Understanding decision making requires analyzing the responses of public authorities and the financial industry against the backdrop of existing structural constraints.

In particular, the world views and meanings developed in finance in the years leading up to the crisis contained a major structural challenge: the units of analysis that informed the governance of the sector were inconsistent. While regulation was most often designed to channel and proscribe the actions of individual firms and the incentives they face, the justification for intervention in times of crisis is collective: systemic risk.[25] We therefore need to study under which conditions the financial industry responds jointly, integrating this collective challenge, and when they insist only on their individual costs and benefits. The theoretical objective of this book is to show that collective action—and thus the conditions that facilitate or hinder joint responses—matters for government choices in support of the financial sector. In particular, this book illustrates how collective strategies can affect the costs of bank support schemes.

---

24. MacKenzie, *An Engine, Not a Camera*; Cetina and Preda, *The Sociology of Financial Markets*; Callon, Millo, and Muniesa, *Market Devices*; Lépinay, *Codes of Finance*.
25. Cf. Woll, "The Morality of Rescuing Banks."

For the analysis of business-government relations, the insights of the case studies run counter to superficial analysis of the lobbying power of finance. What matters most are not what financial institutions did to influence policymakers, it is what they did *not* do. Given their structural importance, their knowledge of market conditions, and of the shape of their own balance sheets, financial institutions are necessarily an important interlocutor for public officials in times of crisis. For governments everywhere, the participation and contribution of the financial industry to its own rescue was an implicit or explicit concern. The most unbalanced arrangements arose where the financial industry was capable of refusing to participate. The industry's capacity for collective inaction is key to understanding the precise arrangement in each country, and the biases that can result. Inverse to Mancur Olson's logic of collective action,[26] the financial industry can collectively benefit from doing nothing in times during which government guarantees payment of the bill. In a game of chicken, when one party is a collective entity, the unwillingness or incapacity to organize collective action is the winning strategy.

As the tense negotiations in the context of Lehman's failure illustrate, the US financial industry collectively signaled that it was unable or unwilling to find a workable solution for the fate of its competitor. With hindsight, Merrill Lynch CEO John Thain only regretted that they did not "grab [the government representatives] and shake them that they can't let this happen."[27] Despite acknowledging that Lehman's bankruptcy was the single biggest mistake of the whole financial crisis, the major US financial institutions maintained that from their side, there was nothing to be done.

Comparing Bank Rescue Schemes

Bank bailouts led to public expenditures of €1.6 trillion (13 percent of GDP) in the European Union (EU) in the first three years of the crisis and $837 billion (5.47 percent of GDP) in the United States. Initial commitments were roughly three times higher in the EU and four times higher in the United States.[28] Moreover, the crisis led to a median output loss of 25 percent of GDP and a median increase in public debt of 24 percent of GDP, over a three-year period.[29] It is rare to be able to study policies of such massive size and impact, undertaken almost simultaneously across a number of countries in rather similar contexts.

---

26. Olson, *The Logic of Collective Action.*
27. Cited in Financial Crisis Inquiry Commission, *The Financial Crisis Inquiry Report,* 342.
28. Based on data from Stolz and Wedow, "Extraordinary Measures in Extraordinary Times"; European Commission, "The Effects of Temporary State Aid Rules Adopted in the Context of the Financial and Economic Crisis."
29. Laeven and Valencia, "Resolution of Banking Crisis."

And yet despite similar challenges, bank bailouts did not all look alike. A small number of countries pledged well beyond 100 percent of their national income on stabilizing the banking sector, which led to sovereign debt crises in Iceland, Ireland, and Spain. Others initially committed comparable sums, but used only a fraction, in particular, Denmark. Although much of the final assessment will depend on accounting rules and hindsight, it appears that several bailouts have in fact contributed positively to the public budget (e.g., France and Denmark), while others incurred substantial net costs: most notably Ireland, Latvia, Portugal, the United Kingdom, and Germany, when expressed as a percentage of GDP, and possibly the United States when considered in absolute numbers.

Despite the fact that ideas were transferred across boundaries in international negotiations and that the European Commission imposed some general guidelines on its member states in the EU, the bailout packages were not all equally constraining for participating financial institutions. Conditions attached to aid varied, and the pricing of government support ranged from favorable—in the United States—to quite unattractive—in the United Kingdom. Moreover, bailout schemes were managed through rather distinct institutional setups: while many countries chose to administer bailout scheme through government offices or central banks, others set up special entities. In some countries, these special entities were not just public but functioned as public-private partnerships, in particular, in Denmark, France, and Austria.

The overview of national responses shows the degree of variation between national schemes. However, it is difficult to interpret differences among this relatively small set of countries without going into some further detail concerning the challenges policymakers in each case faced. To gain analytical leverage, this book builds on six country studies. Following the distinctions employed in the institutionalist literature, the cases are studied in pairs that we would expect to display similar patterns. Each set of most similar cases nonetheless display marked differences. These differences, I will argue, are rooted in the organization and collective capacity of the financial sector or, in one case, the government's response to the industry's strategy. Put differently, I do not claim to be able to explain the overall variation in crisis management across countries, which depends on a multitude of factors. However, I can show that the organization and political activity of the banking sector makes a difference in cases that should have otherwise turned out more similar.

The United States and the United Kingdom are liberal market economies with two very important financial markets: Wall Street and the City of London. Germany and France are coordinated market economies within the Eurozone, with large banking markets and a stronger tradition in bank-based financial systems, where banks are central in the allocation of credit. Denmark and Ireland, finally, are small open economies, highly depended on international financial markets. Both experienced an extraordinary growth of bond markets over the last decade, relative to the size of their economies,

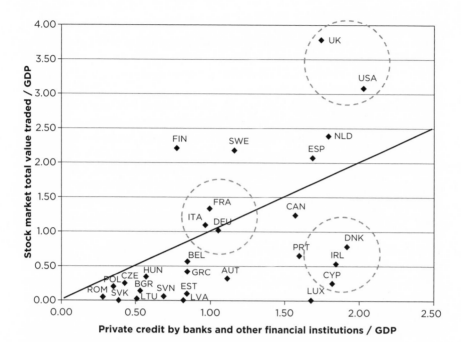

Figure 1.1 Stock market activity versus bank credit
Source: Based on data from Beck, Demirgüç-Kunt, and Levine, "Financial Institutions and Markets across Countries and over Time-data and Analysis," 2009.
Note: The y-axis indicates total value of domestic equities traded on domestic exchanges in 2007, divided by GDP. It measures market trading relative to economic activity and thus reflects the degree of liquidity stock markets provide to the economy. The bank credit ratio equals the value of credit from deposit money banks and other financial institutions to the private sector in 2007 as share of GDP. The line indicates an even ratio between stock markets and bank credit.

and a steep rise in housing market prices that burst as a bubble in the second half of the 2000s.

As the institutionalist literature highlights, the role of banks in the financial system is important for the impact of their failure on the economy more generally. As a consequence, we would expect the influence of banks to vary with changes in the financial structure. A failure of the banking system is all the more consequential if large parts of the financing of the economy depend on banks rather than capital markets.

Since no single indicator captures this distinction well across countries, it is helpful to consider both the size of stock market activities and private credit provided by banks.[30] Figure 1.1 shows how stock market activity as a

30. For discussion see Allen and Gale, *Comparing Financial Systems*; Beck, Demirgüç-Kunt, and Levine, "Financial Institutions and Markets Across Countries and over Time-data and Analysis"; Levine, "Bank-based or Market-based Financial Systems."

share of GDP compares to the bank credit ratio. We can see that the United States and the United Kingdom stand out with respect to both activities but capital markets are even more prominent than banks. France and Germany as well as Italy have sizable stock market activities and credit allocation, but both roughly equivalent to national output.

Besides a focus on financial structure, the comparison between the liberal market economies and the two continental countries allows an examination of the effect of tradition and ideology, in particular vis-à-vis state control over banks. While the United States and the United Kingdom are typically characterized as the primary examples of a hands-off approach, both France and Germany have long traditions of direct state intervention in the banking sector. Tellingly, government ownership in the largest ten banks was 17.26 percent in France and 36.36 percent in Germany in 1995, while it was nonexistent in both the United Kingdom and the United States. Both Ireland and Denmark had comparatively low rates with 4.48 percent and 8.87 percent respectively. Although these figures decreased considerably in the decade that followed, one may think that the decision for government to take equity in large banks has had some precedent in continental Europe, while the United States and the United Kingdom found themselves in largely unfamiliar territory.[31]

To return to financial structure, Ireland and Denmark's domestic equity traded on domestic stock markets is only slightly lower then the continental European countries, but they rely remarkably on bank credit, which is almost twice the size of GDP. In addition, and this is not captured in the figure, both depend highly on international markets, and the financial industry outweighs the size of the country. It is true that the size of the financial industry relative to the size of the country is bigger in Ireland than in Denmark. Total assets in Irish resident banks are about 7 times the size of the Irish GDP compared to 2 times for Denmark. Yet, when comparing the size of the retail clearing banks, which ended up being the object of the government support schemes, total assets for Ireland amount to only 3 times GDP. In other words, by excluding the activities carried out by money market mutual funds operating out of Dublin's International Financial Service Centre (IFSC), one can see that the real economic weight of the Irish financial industry does not deviate dramatically from Denmark's. Moreover, we will see that Irish crisis management was not concerned with the money market mutual funds, but indeed with the retail clearing banks. In addition to economic challenges, country size also matters for political organization, and in particular the capacity of economic actors to engage in compromise to support their national

---

31. Barth, Caprio Jr., and Levine, "Bank Regulation and Supervision"; Andrianova, Demetriades, and Shortland, "Is Government Ownership of Banks Really Harmful to Growth?"

economies.[32] It is therefore important to control for size when comparing socioeconomic orders.

Finally, a word about a country that has also managed a costly bank bailout, but is absent from this study: Iceland. It is difficult to get a precise sense of the costs of the Icelandic intervention, because comparative data are difficult to come by.[33] Moreover, Iceland is in many cases unique, since the collapse of its banking sector was linked in great part to an extreme overextension of financial operations abroad and borrowing in foreign currencies. Through the tremendous imbalances that were created, the Icelandic Central Bank could not possibly act as an effective lender of last resort, that is, one capable of providing liquidity in the relevant currency, which made even fundamentally solvent banks extremely vulnerable.[34] Because of the central role of currency imbalances in the unraveling of the Icelandic crisis, it does not seem a good fit for comparison with government bailout plans in other countries.

However, the Icelandic difficulties bring into focus one fundamental difference between the Irish and the Danish case. While Ireland is a member of the Eurozone, Denmark is not. This may work in two ways. One possibility is that pressure on Ireland to organize its bailout in ways compatible with European guidelines is stronger, that is, that it has less room for maneuver than Denmark. Moreover, Denmark has the possibility to complement its government efforts by liquidity provision through its central bank. Inversely, one may argue that conditions were more difficult for Denmark, because it was not sheltered through the Economic and Monetary Union (EMU). According to Buiter and Sibert, Denmark was as close to the brink as Iceland in 2008: "Iceland's circumstances were extreme, but there are other countries suffering from milder versions of the same fundamental" vulnerability of being "(1) a small country with a (2) large internationally exposed banking sector, (3) its own currency and (4) limited fiscal spare capacity relative to the size of the possible size of the banking sector solvency gap."[35] In countries like Switzerland, Sweden, and Denmark illiquidity can become fatal more quickly than in Ireland, Belgium, the Netherlands, and Luxemburg, which have a reliable lender of last resort, even if they share the same limited fiscal spare capacity.

It is important to keep the monetary policy difference in mind in the Irish-Danish comparison and relate findings back to the US-UK comparison, which both have their own central banks, and the German-French comparison, which are both members of the Eurozone. The within-pair difference in

32. Katzenstein, *Small States in World Markets.*
33. In particular, data on expenditures have to grapple with the problem that both the value of the Icelandic krona and of Icelandic GDP deteriorated with such speed that it is difficult to establish a reference value.
34. Buiter and Sibert, *The Icelandic Banking Crisis and What to Do About It.*
35. Ibid., 2.

terms of monetary policy can thus be analyzed in a second step when return-ing to the overall conclusions from the paired comparison.

In the empirical chapters that follow, I will examine the evolution of bail-out schemes and the business-government relationships underpinning them. A first puzzle is why two liberal capital markets developed markedly different approaches to supporting their banking sectors. While the United States de-signed a bank-friendly bailout for its large financial institutions, the United Kingdom intervened forcefully, both by nationalizations and through forced recapitalization at very unattractive rates. In continental Europe, France proposed a bailout scheme developed in close interaction with the banking industry, which was characterized by favorable conditions for the participat-ing institutions and a rather positive overall result. By contrast, the German government failed in its attempt to engineer a coordinated industry solution and had to rely on public support for institutions that became increasingly costly to unwind. Ireland and Denmark began rather similarly with support plans based on guarantees, which committed excessive amounts of resources to ensuring financial stability. But while Ireland was drawn into a sovereign debt crisis through its unsuccessful banking crisis management, Denmark succeeded in developing a public-private solution that ended up costing only a fraction of the Irish expenditures. These differences, I will argue, result from the collective action capacity of the financial sector and the govern-ment responses to the industry's responses.

Methodology

A number of studies have analyzed bailouts quantitatively, either through-out history[36] or by concentrating on the recent crisis only.[37] Although such overviews help to clarify the most striking differences and glean the evo-lution of bank support, they do not provide a detailed understanding of the stakes and the realm of options governments faced. What is more, one needs to be cautious with the conclusions arising from quantitative analysis because of the malleability of the data. Figures about costs and government intervention are not always as reliable as one would wish for in a quantitative analysis.

First of all, the statistical overviews prepared by organizations such as the European Commission or the International Monetary Fund are preceded by extensive bargaining over categorization and accounting methods. Estimates

36. Honohan and Laeven, *Systemic Financial Crises*; Klingebiel and Laeven, "Managing the Real and Fiscal Effects of Banking Crises; Laeven and Valencia, "Systemic Banking Crises"; Rosas, *Curbing Bailouts*.

37. Panetta et al., "An Assessment of Financial Sector Rescue Programmes"; Schmitz, Weber, and Posch, "EU Bank Packages"; Weber and Schmitz, "Varieties of Helping Capitalism."

of costs and expenditures vary considerably depending on the decisions made about the different categories. One early data set, for example, listed US bailout expenditures as of June 2009 at €825 billion (or $1.15 trillion), but mentioned that these figures *excluded* the capital injections to Fannie Mae and Freddie Mac and the $700 billion TARP package.[38] It is difficult to understand the logic of such choices, and one wonders what actually is counted in the data that are available.

Second, the numbers published continue to be updated or corrected. To cite just one anecdote, German finance minister Wolfgang Schäuble discovered in the fall of 2011 that the bailout costs incurred by the German government were actually €55 billion less than previously announced! An accounting misinterpretation by the agency in charge of unwinding Hypo Real Estate had overstated the liabilities of the bank in 2010 and 2011.[39] While we may expect accounting errors of such staggering proportions to be rare, the event illustrates that one should be cautions not to overestimate the reliability of individual figures.

The analysis therefore moves from an initial overview of the size and nature of bailout measures to a qualitative analysis of the political decision-making process in the United States, the United Kingdom, France, Germany, Ireland, and Denmark. The qualitative analysis is based on the analysis of policy documents, the reports of national accounting offices, parliamentary oversight committees, and special investigators, as well as outside consultant analyses and newspaper accounts. Because of the high media attention and central importance of the policy decisions, many of the key participants testified at length about their actions and motivations, and many of the cited accounts of negotiation details come from these publically available documents.

In addition, and to put the primary documents into perspective, I have conducted more than thirty interviews with representatives of the governments, agency administrators, and the banking sector representatives.[40] The interviews help me reconstruct the evolution of the stakes and the negotiation positions of the actors involved. However, the interview material contains biases.[41] Due to the importance of these issues, the actors most centrally concerned are heads of government, ministers, the governors of the central banks, and the leading management of the banks, which are all notoriously difficult to contact for research interviews. Fortunately, many high-ranking

38. Panetta et al., "An Assessment of Financial Sector Rescue Programmes, 13.
39. Wiesmann, "Bank's €55bn Debt Error a 'Misunderstanding.'"
40. Further details and a complete list of interviews can be found in the annex.
41. I have obtained more interviews in the public sector than in the private sector, and most of the high-ranking officials I have been able to meet have moved out of the positions they held at the time, as the ones still active tend to be concerned about the publicity that might arise from information they give to scholars or journalists. Finally, the number of interviews is distributed unevenly across cases, and I have not spoken with actors at the same hierarchical level in all countries. This implies that the interview material can only serve as a complement to the primary policy documents available.

officials have subsequently published their accounts of the financial crisis, which in many cases helps to fill in missing information.[42] Moreover, media attention to bank bailouts was such that very detailed accounts exist of the most central negotiations, sometimes even in book-length format.[43] The qualitative analysis thus builds on the combination of accounts from interviews, memoirs, and primary and secondary literature, which are all used to cross-check the information given in any one of the individual sources.

Conclusion

This book provides an analysis of business-government relations during bank bailouts, focusing on the ways in which the financial industry was able to exercise power. It highlights the inadequacy of a common perception that bailouts are a direct result of lobbying from financial institutions. Both the structural power and the productive power of finance need to be taken into account to get a more accurate picture of the influence the industry actually wielded. However, the business-government relations that developed in the context of bailouts are surprising to scholars from the institutionalist perspective. The United States and the United Kingdom, two liberal countries with the world's largest financial centers, developed strikingly different approaches to supporting their financial industries. Germany, which is often cited as the archetypical coordinated market economy, was unable to develop a coherent private-sector arrangement because of a divided banking structure. France set up an arrangement in which the six major banks executed central tasks, in great part because the tightly knit elite network in France made coordination possible. Finally, developments in two small open economies, Denmark and Ireland, diverged in part because the Danish solution built on a private sector association of financial institutions, which collectively supported individual banks with the help of a government guarantee. The differences result from the collective strategies of the financial industry within each setting and the government's responses to their activities.

Given the complexity of financial market regulation, the aim of this book is not to explain all aspects of bailout plans across countries in an exhaustive fashion. As a study of the nature and exercise of power of the financial industry during the recent crisis management, it provides an analytical description of the ways in which the financial industry was able to circumscribe the fate of entire economies and whether and how governments sought to respond to correct potential power imbalances.

42. Brown, *Beyond the Crash*; Steinbrück, *Unterm Strich*; Paulson, *On the Brink*; Darling, *Back from the Brink*; Bair, *Bull by the Horns*; Barofsky, *Bailout*.
43. E.g. Wessel, *In FED We Trust*; Sorkin, *Too Big to Fail.*

Although some variable-oriented readers may have preferred a simple causal theory about successful or failed bank support schemes, the analysis does lead to a series of policy conclusions. First, collective commitments of the financial industry are a crucial mechanism for limiting public expenditures. Second, since collective action is conditioned by factors that may or may not be given during a particular moment of crisis, it is important to deal with systemic questions in a way that requires the industry to organize collectively prior to moments of crisis. Third, there is little use to try and enforce collective action when the organizational foundations are not given. In such cases, the government in question is best advised to impose their preferred solution in order to limit the moral hazard effects of public support schemes. The policy conclusions will be discussed in more detail in the conclusion.

The book is organized into seven chapters. Chapter 2 begins with a brief history of the origins of the banking crisis until the fall of 2008 and provides an overview of nationwide bailout efforts across industrialized countries. Chapter 3 turns to the central issue of the theoretical analysis, which is the power of the financial industry, and proposes a consideration of different aspects of power in particular: structural and productive power. It then develops the argument about collective inaction as an exercise of power. Chapter 4 turns to the normative debate on bailouts, in particular the literature on moral hazard and institutions that are too big to fail. It shows how each strand is rooted in a distinct conception of the financial industry—individual firms versus systemic effects—and discusses how this debate translated into policy practice, most notably through approaches to punishment embedded in rescue packages.

The remaining three chapters present an analytical narrative of the policy evolution in the six case studies, organized into pairs of two. Chapter 5 focuses on capital-marked based finance in the liberal Anglo-Saxon countries: the United States and the United Kingdom. Chapter 6 moves to continental Europe and presents the challenges in bank-based systems such as France and Germany. Chapter 7 examines small-open economies with important financial markets, by studying Ireland and Denmark. Each chapter ends by highlighting the comparative lessons and relating the findings of the case to the previous examples.

The conclusion summarizes the empirical lessons and generalizes the findings in the individual cases. In this way I tie the discussion to the normative questions and finish this book by offering a range of policy implications.

2

Crisis Management across the World

If we don't do this, we may not have an economy on Monday.
—Federal Reserve chairman Ben Bernanke, testimony to Congress,
18 September 2008

The decision to bail out banks is difficult for all governments. At no time was this more evident than the weeks in September and October 2008, when politicians and central bankers in most industrialized countries tried to avoid the collapse of their banking systems after the fall of Lehman Brothers on September 15. The simultaneity of the responses makes bailouts a fascinating study for crisis management in different political and economic contexts. This chapter begins with a brief history of the crisis until its zenith in September 2008, when international financial markets were effectively frozen. It then present an overview of the bailout packages in Europe and the United States, by providing information about the heights and the nature of intervention between the fall of 2008 and the summer of 2009.[1] This overview helps clarify the puzzle and specify the questions that will frame the case comparisons in the following chapters.

An International History of National Economic Crises

Although accounts of the recent financial crisis share common themes, there is presently little agreement on the underlying causes and the main culprits.[2] Initially referred to as the "subprime crisis," it changed names and focus depending on the analyst and is now most often referred to as the global financial crisis.[3] This book concentrates on the banking crisis that

1. This section in particular is based on research undertaken jointly with Emiliano Grossman. See Grossman and Woll, "Saving the Banks."
2. Lo, "Reading About the Financial Crisis."
3. Other names include "the Great Recession," the "Lesser Depression," or various combinations of financial crisis and dates.

started in 2007 rather than the ensuing sovereign debt crisis that hit in particular Europe in late 2009 and 2010.[4]

For many, the early financial crisis was an American phenomenon, and it was common to speak about contagion: the bursting of the US housing market bubble and US-led innovation in financial products led to an explosive mix that triggered the collapse of many financial institutions, which then rippled through other countries. In a momentous conversation on the viability of Lehman Brothers, British chancellor of the exchequer Alistair Darling told US secretary of the treasury Henry Paulson that he did not want "to import [the United States'] cancer."[5] Numerous politicians in European countries went on television assuring their citizens that this was an American crisis, which would not reach the much safer and regulated financial systems in Europe.

By late 2008, it had become evident that exposure to the US subprime market was not the only issue that mattered. Crisis management in one country influenced the others and events abroad affected market sentiment at home, in areas entirely unrelated to the original difficulties. As a consequence, it is helpful to begin by studying the crisis from an international bird's-eye perspective, by tracing the relationship between bubbles, bank failures, policies responses, and market developments. This short transnational history of the financial crisis will help to anchor the country comparisons that follow, which in turn highlight how decidedly national the political responses and the problem structure of the banking crises were in each of the countries. As will be argued later on, banking crises in several countries had very little do to with the original US subprime crisis and need to be studied in their own right, even if international capital markets were central in creating generalized and simultaneous stress and distrust.

Subprime Exposure

Much has been written about the fall in prices on the US housing market, the effect of delinquencies in residential mortgages on mortgage-backed securities and insurers of mortgages and the subsequent unraveling of the market for structured financial products containing such asset-backed securities.[6] After the drop in US house prices in 2006, the subprime mortgage industry crumbled. The first affected were mortgage lenders and insurers of debt payments, the so-called monoline insurers.

---

4. This is a purely analytical choice to focus the inquiry. Clearly, the banking crisis and the sovereign debt crisis are related in a circular manner: banking crises increase sovereign debt and decrease market confidence and sovereign default affect those financial institutions that hold government bonds.

5. Wessel, *In FED We Trust,* 19; Sorkin, *Too Big to Fail,* 348.

6. E.g., Shiller, *The Subprime Solution;* Schwartz, *Subprime Nation;* Acharya et al., *Guaranteed to Fail.*

In early 2007, many subprime lenders announced very significant losses, put themselves up for sale or filed for bankruptcy. Exposure to both the subprime loans and the collateralized securities—asset-backed securities such as mortgage-backed securities and collateralized debt obligations—started being recognized as risky by many financial institutions as early as 2006.

Although the subprime crisis was clearly an American phenomenon, the first bank to collapse as a consequence of such exposure was German. IKB Deutsche Industriebank had invested heavily in the US market and was bailed out by a consortium of German banks and the German government on the weekend of 28–29 July 2007. Less than a month later, it became clear that the Irish subsidiary of the Landesbank Sachsen (Sachsen LB) had also incurred considerable losses in mortgage-backed securities, which led to a merger with the Landesbank Baden-Würtemberg to avert a complete failure of Sachsen LB. In Germany two further regional saving banks, West LB and Bayern LB, encountered similar problems and would receive public support from their regional governments by February 2008.

Frozen Capital Markets and Bubbles Elsewhere

Nervousness had increased markedly during the summer of 2007. When French bank BNP Paribas decided on 9 August to close three investment vehicles that had important stakes in the US subprime market, confidence and interbank lending immediately came to a halt. The European Central Bank, the Federal Reserve, and the Bank of Japan began to inject liquidity into the banking market simultaneously. The most prominent victim of this funding freeze was the British bank Northern Rock. A mortgage bank, Northern Rock had virtually no subprime lending, but relied heavily on short-term funding. In mid-August, it informed its regulators that it was no longer able to roll over its debt.[7] When the Bank of England announced on 13 September 2007 that it would provide emergency liquidity support, depositors queued up outside the banks' branches to withdraw their money. To many observers these images embodied the beginning of the crisis, even though it had reached Germany several months earlier. What is true, however, is that Northern Rock was the first in a long list of bank failures that were triggered by funding problems rather than a simple exposure to the US housing market directly. Eventually, on 22 February 2009, the British government would take Northern Rock into public ownership.

In addition to exposure and funding problems, several countries encountered housing bubbles of their own making. Ireland, Spain, Denmark, and Sweden had all experienced a housing market boom in the 2000s, which

---

7. Shin, "Reflections on Northern Rock."

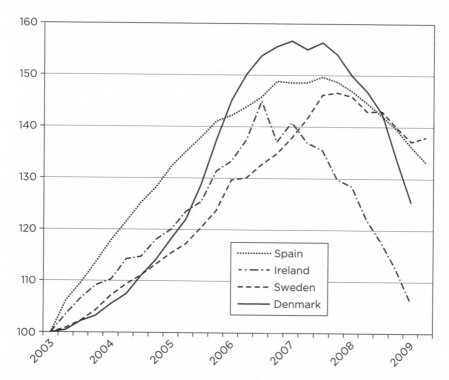

Figure 2.1 Real house prices, 2003–9
Source: OECD, *Economic Surveys: Denmark 2009*, 18.
Note: Prices are indexed to the first quarter of 2003

came to a halt in the second half of the decade. The earliest drop happened in Ireland, with clear signs in 2006 that the boom period was over. Denmark's and Spain's bubbles burst in mid-2007, Swedish house prices dropped by the end of the year, and the United Kingdom followed in 2008.

In some countries, such as Spain, the bursting of the housing market bubbles did not affect the banking sector immediately, although it led to a sharp plunge in the construction sector. In others, such as Ireland and Denmark, the distress quickly amplified. The Irish banking system had lent roughly two-thirds of the gross national product to property developers, in particular Anglo Irish Bank, which had a whopping 75 percent of their loans in construction and property.[8] By early 2008, share prices of banks in Ireland and Denmark dropped due to concerns about exposure to their housing markets. In addition, these banks experienced difficulties

8. Kelly, "Whatever Happened to Ireland?"; Regling and Watson, *A Preliminary Report on the Sources of Ireland's Banking Crisis.*

in raising funds on international markets. Liquidity support by the Danish Central Bank was insufficient to save bankTrelleborg, which was taken over by Sydbank in January 2008. In August 2008, the Danish government would organize a public-private bailout of Roskilde Bank, the eight largest lender in Denmark.

Bailouts Back in the United States

During the early months of 2008, the US government realized that it was dealing with more than just a subprime crisis. Triggered by market distrust, Bear Stearns faced a three-day run by its investors and found itself on the verge of collapse in early March. It had announced the previous year that several of its investment vehicles were experiencing difficulties with mortgage-related securities. Still, its executives were taken by surprise when money market funds withdrew more than $15 billion in cash reserves.[9] One of the major five US investment banks, Bear Stearns was outside the purview of the Federal Deposit Insurance Corporation (FDIC), and the government was very concerned about the repercussions of the imminent collapse. On 14 March 2008, Bear Stearns was taken over by JP Morgan Chase thanks to a government guarantee against future losses between $1 and $30 billion. Bear Stearns was the first bank rescue in the United States outside of the regular FDIC procedure and was severely criticized as having set a precedent for government bailouts of financial institutions that are too big to fail.[10] The criticisms from both sides of the partisan spectrum would haunt the administration and play a decisive role in the unfolding of events in mid-September 2008, when Lehman Brothers was on the brink of collapse. But Bearn Stearns was not going to remain the only rescue.

By the summer of 2008, the principle mortgage finance institutions had entered into great difficulties. On 11 July 2008, Indymac Bank, a subsidiary of Independent National Mortgage Corporation (Indymac), was placed into receivership of the FDIC. The same day, the *New York Times* reported that the government was considering taking over the two government-sponsored enterprises, Fannie Mae and Freddie Mac. Created at government initiative but under private ownership, the housing finance twins owned or guaranteed roughly half of the $12 trillion housing market in 2008. Due to its importance in US housing market finance and its political clout, the market had always considered that the twins benefited from an implicit bailout guarantee.[11] The government made this guarantee explicit with the Housing Market

---

9. Kelly, "Fear, Rumors Touched Off Fatal Run on Bear Stearns"; Financial Crisis Inquiry Commission, *Financial Crisis Inquiry Report*, 289.
10. E.g., Reinhart, "A Year of Living Dangerously."
11. Acharya et al., *Guaranteed to Fail.*

and Recovery Act of 30 July 2008, hoping to reassure investors. Despite this attempt, confidence faltered and the government eventually asked the regulator, the Federal Housing Finance Agency (FHFA), to put Fannie Mae and Freddie Mac into conservatorship on 7 September 2008. This intervention nationalized the two enterprises through a $100 billion acquisition of preferred stock from the US Treasury, and the wiping out of 80 percent of the value of existing stock.

The Crash

By then, market strains had become dire, both abroad and in the United States. Early bailouts had not improved the economic climate in countries such as Germany, the United Kingdom, or Denmark, where several other financial institutions continued to look very fragile. Share prices of Irish banks continued falling and a very disconcerting situation became more and more visible in a country that few considered to be at the heart of the financial industry: Iceland.

Based on excessive borrowing in foreign currencies, the Icelandic banking sector had expanded massively in the mid-2000s.[12] In the first quarter of 2008, the financial system's assets were valued roughly eleven times the GDP of Iceland, with a significant mismatch: the share of assets denominated in foreign currency was much smaller than the share of liabilities denominated in foreign currency.[13] Even though one may argue that Icelandic banks were better capitalized and had a lower exposure to high-risk assets than banks elsewhere, they had simply become "too big to save" by the second half of the years 2000.[14] The Icelandic governments' attempt to counteract these challenges had been too slow to take effect, and it became increasingly clear that Iceland could simply not withstand a liquidity crisis on international wholesale markets, where Icelandic banks obtained about two-thirds of their funding.

By that time, in early fall of 2008, the US administration began to receive catastrophic news about the state of their own banks whose situation seemed to worsen by the day. The weekend following the federal takeover of the housing finance twins, the US Treasury and Federal Reserve worked frantically to save the US investment bank Lehman Brothers from collapsing. Trying to broker another private bailout, Henry Paulson, Tim Geithner, and Ben Bernanke and their teams concentrated their hopes on Bank of America and later the British bank Barclays. Bank of America offered only

---

12. Carey, *Iceland: The Financial and Economic Crisis*; Danielson, "The First Casualty of the Crisis: Iceland."

13. Buiter and Sibert, *The Icelandic Banking Crisis and What to Do About It*, 4; Schwartz, "Iceland's Financial Iceberg."

14. Danielson, "The First Casualty of the Crisis," 11.

half of what Lehman said its assets were worth, effectively requiring the US government or someone else to take $25 billion of Lehman's bad real estate assets. Barclays had similar reservations, so the government gathered the CEOs of the twenty largest investment houses and banks in a conference room to see if they would agree to a "liquidation consortium" to sell off Lehman in pieces. But the difficulties in the financial sector touched every one. All of the CEOs knew that even if Lehman were to be saved, Merrill Lynch, American International Group (AIG), and possibly Morgan Stanley would be next. On Sunday morning, it had become clear that a solution from the US private sector would not come forward. Barclays, in turn, pointed out that the commitment to guarantee all of Lehman's liabilities required a vote from the shareholders, unless the British regulator issued a waiver. In a phone conversation British chancellor of the exchequer Alistair Darling told Henry Paulson that the Financial Services Authority (FSA) would not grant the waiver.[15] The only option left was a publically financed bailout of Lehman Brothers and the administration decided against it.[16] Lehman Brothers filed for bankruptcy on 15 September 2008.

The results of this failure were catastrophic: the Dow Jones plummeted more than 500 points, wiping off $700 billion of value from investment portfolios.[17] Within days, the major investment and commercial banks tumbled. Merrill Lynch had benefited from a government-brokered deal during the same weekend and was taken over by Bank of America.[18] Only one day after, on 16 September 2009, the US government and the Federal Reserve bailed out AIG with a $85 billion loan and received a warrant and equity stake of 79.9 percent. The AIG bailout was secured against AIG's insurance subsidiaries, which were more stable than any collateral Lehman could have offered, the US government argued.[19] Rescuing AIG so shortly after letting Lehman go under raised many eyebrows. A week after the Lehman failure, the two remaining investment banks—Goldman Sachs and Morgan Stanley—asked to be converted into conventional bank holding companies to benefit form additional access to Fed liquidity. The situation of all other banks looked equally alarming. US regulators closed down Washington Mutual, and Wachovia was taken over by Wells Fargo in early October, after initial support and a bid from Citigroup.

15. Paulson, *On the Brink*, 210.

16. The reasons for this decision are still heavily disputed. In their personal accounts and congressional hearings, Henry Paulson, Ben Bernanke, Timothy Geithner, and other observers have cited the belief that markets could absorb the shock, the lack of regulatory instruments, and the unwillingness to create further moral hazard problems. Financial Crisis Inquiry Commission, *Financial Crisis Inquiry Report*; Mitchell, "Saving the Market from Itself"; Paulson, *On the Brink*; Wessel, *In FED We Trust*; see also Blinder, *After the Music Stopped*, 127.

17. Financial Crisis Inquiry Commission, *Financial Crisis Inquiry Report*, 339.

18. Farrell, *Crash of the Titans*.

19. Bernanke, *The Federal Reserve and the Financial Crisis*, 85; Paulson, *On the Brink*, 229.

The fall of Lehman Brothers wrecked havoc abroad. Not only did the Lehman collapse lead to more than eighty insolvency proceedings of its subsidiaries in eighteen countries, its failure also, and more importantly, led to a complete freeze of the interbanking market. Confidence in the solvency of all major financial institutions had all but disappeared. In many countries, cracks appeared quickly in banks that were of concern earlier on, but also ones that had appeared to be healthy. In the United Kingdom, Halifax Bank of Scotland's (HBOS) position had weakened, and the government suspended competition rules to allow Lloyds TSB to take over HBOS on 17 September. Trying to find a similar solution for Bradford and Bingley, the government sold part of its activities to Grupo Santander but had to nationalize the remaining parts on 29 September 2008. Fortis Bank experienced a run on deposits and needed massive liquidity assistance from the governments of the Benelux countries on 26 September, with coordination being a real challenge to the existing multilateral banking resolution scheme.[20] Depfa, an Irish subsidiary of the German bank Hypo Real Estate (HRE), faced severe liquidity pressures on 28 September 2008 and threatened to bring HRE down. Commerzbank, one of the largest German private banks, which had previously taken over Dresdner Bank, was in a similarly dire situation. In France, Natixis, the investment branch of Banque Populaire and Caisse d'Epargne, broke down, losing 95 percent of its stock market value on 29 September. On 30 September, the French, Belgian, and Luxembourgian governments had to cooperate to prop up the bank Dexia. Everywhere one looked, financial institutions fell like houses of cards.

From Failing Banks to Failing Countries: Iceland

For the overinflated Icelandic banking system, the failure of Lehman Brothers was the straw that broke the camel's back. Although Icelandic banks were not directly exposed to Lehman Brothers, financial markets withdrew their assets from banks considered vulnerable. Icelandic banks were no longer able to fund themselves, making Iceland the first country casualty of the financial crisis.

The rapidity of the collapse of Icelandic finance was impressive. When Glitnir requested an emergency loan from the central bank in late September, the government refused and announced that it was planning to take over Glitnir by acquiring a 75 percent stake in its capital on 29 September. Although not carried through, the announcement decreased the Icelandic credit rating and effectively closed the few credit lines that were left for Icelandic

---

20. Kudrna, "Cross-Border Resolution of Failed Banks in the EU."

banks. Landsbanki, which in addition held a large amount of Glitnir shares, was severely hit and suffered a considerable outflow of funds from its Icesave account in the week following the announcement. The British authorities were concerned and required additional cash liquidity reserves to be paid to the Bank of England to protect British depositors. Landsbanki was unable to meet this demand and requested aid from the government. At the same time Kaupthing had similar difficulties and requested a loan as well.

Over the weekend, the parliament passed emergency legislation that would enable the Financial Supervisory Authority to take over ailing banks on Monday, 6 October. The next day, it took control of Landsbanki and Glitnir. On the following day, Wednesday, 8 October, the UK authorities froze the assets relating to Landsbanki using powers under the Anti-Terrorism, Crime, and Security Act of 2001. In addition, the British Financial Supervisory Authority announced that the UK subsidiary of Kaupthing, the last of the three main Iceland banks, no longer met bank registration requirements and placed its assets under administration. This effectively took Kaupthing out of business as well, which was taken over by the financial regulator the same day. Simultaneously, the foreign exchange market in Iceland collapsed.

The extent of the crisis was unprecedented in a developed country. Within less than a week, the banking system had broken down, Iceland had lost its creditworthiness, foreign payments could no longer be made, and the payment system was brought to a standstill. GDP was about to fall 65 percent in euro terms, many companies went bankrupt, and the British and Dutch government demanded compensation for their depositors, equivalent to 100 percent of Icelandic GDP.

In Search for Political Solutions

As banks unraveled and entire economies threatened to fall, governments everywhere began to work frantically on nationwide schemes to stabilize their banking sectors. Although the problems revolved heavily around transborder activities, international cooperation in the initial crisis management was difficult.[21] Central banks, in particular the Federal Reserve and the European Central Bank had coordinated their aid since December 2007 and intervened quickly after the fall of Lehman Brothers, issuing currency swaps and other facilities to the frozen interbanking markets on 18 September 2008, together with the Bank of England, the Swiss National Bank, and the Bank of Japan. However, beyond liquidity provision, joint support for the entire banking systems was impossible to put into place. With time pressing in the second half of September, each government therefore embarked on its own strategy. In almost all major financial centers, governments drew up national rescue scheme or bailout packages designed to prevent the collapse of the national banking sector.

21. Pauly, "The Old and the New Politics of International Financial Stability"; Kudrna, "Cross-Border Resolution of Failed Banks in the EU."

We will examine six of these national solutions in a comparative perspective in the following chapters. Even though the subsequent comparison will concentrate on the national perspectives, this brief overview of the unfolding of the crisis highlights how the evolution and buildup of issues was connected across borders. It also clarifies that the main issues governments faced were not always identical and that it would therefore be misleading to speak only of a US subprime crisis. To be sure financial sector difficulties began with the downfall of the US housing market, but the ways in which this shock was transmitted and reverberated in different countries depended on a multitude of factors. Some banks abroad were directly exposed to the US housing market or the financial products linked to it. Others had business models in which a large part of their short-term funding depended on access to international wholesale markets, which dried up when market confidence evaporated. In addition, several countries had housing bubbles of their own making that national financial institutions were heavily exposed to. In many cases, several of these factors came together to create an explosive mix. The fall of Lehman Brothers was critical in the buildup of events. What the US administration had underestimated was the effect of the fall on market confidence and the shock the failure would represent for interbank lending.

Governments everywhere had learned with great alarm that international coordination would be crucial in the long-term response to the crisis and also in the prevention of future crises. After initial coordination had failed, political leaders huddled in marathon meetings in the first half of October to signal political support to the banking systems and calm financial markets. On the 10 October, the finance ministers of the G7 met in Washington, DC.[22] Negotiations continued under the auspices of the International Monetary Fund (IMF) the following days. On 12 October, member countries of the Eurozone met at a eurogroup summit in Paris, which had been preceded by a Franco-German summit a day earlier. Although the US government had already signed the Troubled Asset Relief Plan (TARP) into law ten days earlier, European governments were still working on their rescue schemes during these days and exchanged information and insights on the most appropriate actions. Most bailout packages were announced in the week that followed. The UK plan had already been unveiled on 8 October, contributing to change the content of the US plan, as Henry Paulson made public on 14 October. The German plan was announced on 17 October and the French on 20 October.[23] For all of these

22. The G7, bringing together finance ministers from France, Germany, Italy, the United Kingdom, Japan, the United States, and Canada, met in April 2008, October 2008, and February 2009 to discuss their responses to the global crisis.

23. In chronological order, the sequence of initial announced bailouts—stand-alone or national—was: Ireland (30 September 2008), United States (1 October 2008), Denmark (5 October 2008), the United Kingdom (13 October 2008), Germany (17 October 2008), Sweden and France (20 October 2008), followed by the Netherlands, Finland, Italy, Greece, Austria, Slovenia, Portugal, Latvia, Hungary, Spain, Poland, Cyprus, Slovakia, Lithuania.

responses, the high-level meetings had provided an opportunity to expose and discuss possible schemes, but most of their concrete design had been elaborated nationally, with few if any consultation of international counterparts.

Bailouts in Practice

Bailout packages refer mostly to government schemes aimed at stabilizing financial institutions. These efforts require making public budgets available and passing legislation, so they are subject to much public scrutiny. Due to their high degree of politicization, they are at the heart of the analysis of this book, since we would expect private stakeholders to have less influence when an issue moves out of technocratic governance and into the public sphere.[24] However, one needs to keep in mind that government schemes exist alongside central bank efforts.

In banking crises, there are two parallel concerns. First, governments need to buy time and stop a panic. To accomplish this, they can provide liquidity and government guarantees. Second, they need to stabilize their banking sector more durably and address the confidence problem that brings interbank lending to a halt. In the recent crisis, this took the form of recapitalization and, in some cases, a transfer of assets.[25]

In the United States, the United Kingdom, the Eurosystem, and most other European countries, central banks are independent from the government and can decide to intervene quickly, most notably by providing liquidity.[26] However, without downplaying the role of central bank efforts, it is notable that the great majority of countries relied not just on liquidity provision but also on government schemes. To grasp what these entail, it is helpful to consider the different instruments and objectives of bank bailout plans.

Central Bank Efforts

Liquidity measures most commonly refer to central bank efforts. Central banks can lower their policy rates and adopt various standard and extraordinary measures to enhance the liquidity of banks, such as changes in the frequency and process of auctions, the volume and maturity of lending facilities, the range of collateral accepted, outright asset purchases, and the expansion of eligible institutions for lending facilities. In addition, central

24. Culpepper, *Quiet Politics and Business Power.*
25. Other instruments include tax incentives for loan-loss write-offs to help banks restructure their balance sheets or more general debt forgiveness. These were not central during the recent financial crisis but are discussed in Calomiris, Klingebiel, and Laeven "Financial Crisis and Resolution Mechanisms."
26. However, decision making in the European Central Bank is arguably more complicated than in other central banks.

banks can lend to banks directly through discount windows, where they charge a special rate, a "repo" rate, normally for overnight lending. Despite its name, the discount window rate is actually higher than the federal funds rate to encourage banks to find credit on the interbanking market and only use the discount window as a last resort. In the Eurozone, the discount window is called Standing Facility and has replaced the discount windows at the national level with the beginning of the Eurosystem in January 1999. The Bank of England's Discount Window Facility was only created in response to the credit crunch in October 2008.[27]

The efforts undertaken by central banks are reflected in the expansion of their balance sheets and were substantial everywhere. In the United States, the Federal Reserve allowed its balance sheet to more than double from $800 billion in September 2008 to 2.25 trillion in the following months. Likewise, the Bank of England contributed to the government's Asset Purchase Facility by creating central bank reserves and buying £200 billion worth of assets. In addition to repo transactions, the efforts of the Bank of England caused its balance sheet to more than double, with a peak at almost three times the size it had in early fall of 2008. The Eurosystem, in contrast, has expanded to a lesser extent, from just under €1.5 trillion to just over €2 trillion by the end of 2008.[28]

The liquidity provided by these efforts has been crucial for financial institutions during the crisis. According to a close observer in the United States, "TARP was not the most significant thing that happened during the fall, it was the Fed, and the FDIC with them, agreeing to step in and guarantee new issuance by the banks." This intervention, even without TARP, he went on speculating, might "have done the trick."[29] Guarantee schemes and liquidity provision through the central bank was of primary importance to the financial industry and tailored much more to their needs than capital injections. In addition to liquidity provision, the US Federal Reserve has the capacity to support individual institutions through specific loans.

Government Instruments

Besides these instruments, governments can help financial institutions to obtain liquidity through a series of indirect measures. They can guarantee deposits or debts and thereby increase the confidence other financial institutions and investors will have in the bank, which crucially shapes the risk premiums it will be charged in money markets. They can also transfer assets

27. This newness is ironic given that discount windows are also referred to as Lombard credit. In this book *Lombard Street*, the UK equivalent of Wall Street at the time, English writer Walter Bagehot analyzes British finance in the nineteenth century and suggests that liquidity support should only be provided to solvent firms, against good collateral and at high rates.

28. Stolz and Wedow, "Extraordinary Measures in Extraordinary Times," 16–17.

29. Interview, 25 May 2012.

or swap them against government bonds, which banks can use as collateral to obtain further liquidity from central banks. Although these measures ultimately affect the access to liquidity, they will be discussed below, according to the type of measure used.

Guarantees are public commitments to repay depositors or other creditors if the financial institution would find itself unable to do so. They are issued in an effort to maintain confidence in the financial system and prevent a run on the banks. The most common form of guarantees are deposit insurance schemes, which have a ceiling on the size of covered deposits. In practice, however, small retail deposits are not the most important liabilities of a financial institution. Large wholesale deposits and interbank lines are more important and more quickly withdrawn when confidence falters. In times of crisis, public guarantees can therefore be extended to cover other liabilities as well as equity.

To begin with, governments can extend the existing deposit insurance to all deposits (retail, commercial, institutional, and interbank ones) and raise or—more often—eliminate the ceiling on covered amounts. Second, the insurance can be extended to bondholders, who are creditors that have made loans to the firm by buying debt securities. Debt securities are typically divided into different risk categories, determined by the order in which creditors will be paid back in case of a bankruptcy. Senior bondholders will be paid back first, holders of subordinated debt only afterward. The risk involved for holders of subordinated debt is reflected in a higher yield. Finally, shareholders have invested funds into a company in exchange for equity. Unlike bondholders, who are creditors, stockholders are owners. They benefit from income through dividends and capital gains, but are also the last in line for repayment in case of liquidation.

A final distinction in public guarantees is whether they are past or future oriented. A guarantee on past deposits and debt aims to avoid a withdrawal of existing assets, while a public guarantee on future debt allows banks to continue having access to additional liquidity. While the former is a defensive measure to shield against a run, the second is more risky because it allows a potentially unhealthy institution to continue operating and even increase its debt.

The payback hierarchy in case of a bankruptcy illustrates the profoundly distortive effect guarantees can have on investment behavior. Bond and shareholders benefit from the types of securities they hold according to the risk involved and chose their strategies accordingly. They can make considerable income from their securities, all the more if they invest in a category that is least likely to be paid back if the company needs to be liquidated. While these gains are private when times are good, the costs arising through the failure of the institution are covered through public money, which effectively eradicates all incentives to monitor risky behavior.

Both liquidity measures and government guarantees are typically employed as emergency measures during the containment phase. In addition, regulators can modify regulatory requirements to allow banks to continue operating despite being undercapitalized or changing the requirements for continuing operations, such as loan classification or loan loss provisioning requirements. As Honohan and Klingebiel point out, forbearance is a matter of degree, which can range from small regulatory exceptions for a short time period to allowing insolvent banks to continue business as usual.[30]

Capital injections or recapitalization entails using public funds in an effort to strengthen a company's capital. The extent to which this implies governmental control over the company depends on the type of stock the government acquires. Common stock comes with voting rights for shareholders, while preferred stock does not carry voting rights. However, preferred stock may have priority over common stock in the payment of dividends and in case of a bankruptcy. Once the government has acquired a controlling interest, it is common to speak about nationalization.

Alternatively, a government can coordinate private capital injections in order to avoid committing public funds. This can take the form of a government-assisted takeover of one financial institution by another. If the government simply acts as a broker for the transaction, such private takeovers are clearly the least intrusive option a government has for stabilizing a failing bank. However, private takeovers depend on the interest and capacity of the potential buyer and are often difficult to engineer. Potential buyers can argue that they can only go ahead if the government provides additional guarantees—for example, on future losses of the company. This is what the US government agreed to do in order to assist the takeover of Bear Stearns through JP Morgan Chase in March 2008.

The government can also try to organize collective and privately financed capital injections. When the conditions at a company have deteriorated to a point where no buyer can be found, a collective recapitalization can help to avoid a collapse and buy time in order to sell the company off in pieces. A collective private bailout was famously orchestrated by the Federal Reserve Bank of New York for the hedge fund LTCM in September 1998.[31] The US government attempted to repeat the exercise for Lehman Brothers in 2008 but was unable to get the main financial firms to engage in a "liquidation consortium," as the head of the New York Fed Timothy Geithner called it.[32]

An important issue for recapitalization schemes is whether they are voluntary or mandatory. Mandatory recapitalization is quite intrusive and implies spending money on companies that might not need to have their capital base strengthened. Voluntary recapitalization, in turn, stigmatizes the companies that agree to it and sends a signal to financial markets that they are

---

30. Honohan and Klingebiel, "The Fiscal Cost Implications of an Accommodating Approach to Banking Crises."
31. Lowenstein, *When Genius Failed.*
32. Wessel, *In FED We Trust,* 17.

in trouble. Under a voluntary scheme, companies will thus hesitate to have recourse to proposed government aid in order not to trigger a chain reaction in which investors withdraw their money.

Asset transfers refer to all public assistance in the relief of assets that have become "troubled" or "toxic." It can cover two related actions. Either the government buys impaired assets directly from financial institutions to prop up their creditworthiness and increase confidence, or it organizes the transfer of impaired assets to a public agency that manages them, sometimes colloquially referred to as "bad banks." These public asset management organizations are responsible for revaluating the market value of low-quality assets and selling them on financial markets. Asset management organizations can be centralized or decentralized. Centralized asset management companies are public entities with the responsibility to dispose of the troubled assets of an entire national banking system, such as in Ireland or Spain in the recent crisis. Decentralized systems consist of either public or private entities created to manage the assets of individual banks or sectors, and have been used in Germany, for example.[33]

The most difficult challenge in asset transfers is determining the worth of the assets in question. Toxic assets refer generally to assets who value has fallen so significantly that they can no longer be sold at a price satisfactory to the holder. This means that there is no longer a functioning market for these assets at the time the government seeks to determine their value. Paying the historic value would clearly lead the government to overpay the asset holder and imposing a fire sale at current market price would destroy the net worth of the company the government is trying to save. One option considered by the US government was therefore to organize auctions to sell off toxic assets. The alternative, transferring assets to a public management organization, has the advantage of being able to sell off assets over a long period of time, at a moment where prices may have risen again. If prices fail to reestablish themselves, however, these management companies can risk turning into the waste buckets of the financial industry, with considerable costs to the public budget, in most cases, or investors.

Constraint Choices

In choosing government intervention, politicians have to manage two contradictory objectives: they have to prevent a market panic, but they also have to be accountable to the general public. Discussing the urgency and extent of the crisis will trigger a panic, but not discussing it will keep citizens from gaining insight about political choices that severely affect public budgets and create considerable societal redistribution. The politics of bailouts

---

33. See Gandrud and Hallerberg, "Bad Banks as a Response to Crisis"; Klingebiel, "The Use of Asset Management Companies in the Resolution of Banking Crises."

therefore are marked by ambiguity and vagueness, not least when it comes to naming government intervention. Despite its name, the US Troubled Asset Relief Program was dedicated most prominently to the recapitalization of financial institutions. Attempts to collect comparative data on different measures vary considerably in their categories, grouping items under liquidity support that could also appear under guarantees or transfer of assets.

Moreover, the appeal of a measure may not reside in the objectives it seeks but also in its feasibility. Governments all over the world relied on guarantees, not least because they are commitments that do not show up in the public budget if they are not called on. This means that guarantees can be issued without the legislative procedures that would be necessary to commit public money. Similarly, liquidity support provided by the central bank is discretionary, as long as it falls within the mandate given to central banks. When the Federal Reserve argued that AIG's insurance collateral could make it eligible for a loan, this provided the US government with a way of saving AIG just a day after having been unable to provide a solution to Lehman Brothers. The interpretation baffled more than one, and Congressman Barney Frank reportedly asked the administration, "Where did you find 85 billion?" to which Ben Bernanke responded by citing the entire balance sheet of the Federal Reserve, "We have 800 billion."[34]

Comparing Bailouts

Although governments embarked on the bank rescues almost simultaneously and arguably had to deal with similar problems,[35] no standard scheme emerges when one compares the responses to crises. To be sure, some transfer of ideas and approaches happened, and many observers noted how the British bailout plan inspired both the American government and the European plans that followed.[36] Yet despite such transfers, bailout packages varied in the amount of money committed, the mix of instruments used, and the degree of burden sharing between public and private stakeholders. The following section presents national responses during the initial crisis management, with particular emphasis on the period from the fall of 2008 to the summer of 2009.

34. Paulson, *On the Brink*, 241.
35. In the EU, only five countries did not propose measures to support their banking sector: Bulgaria, Czech Republic, Estonia, Malta, and Romania. Combined, these five countries account for less than 1 percent of the financial industry in Europe. European Commission, "The Effects of Temporary State Aid Rules Adopted in the Context of the Financial and Economic Crisis," 36.
36. Quaglia, "The 'British Plan' as a Pace-Setter."

Expenditures

The broadest and most comparable data available concern the amounts of aid governments made available to the banking sector. Collected by institutions such as the European Commission, the European Central Bank, the International Monetary Fund, and the Bank for International Settlements, these numbers indicate the extent to which governments agreed to help—"committed" or "approved" expenditures—and which part of this amount was actually extended—"actual" or "effective" expenditures.

Figure 2.2 ranks countries by actual expenditures from the beginning of the crisis to 2010, as a percentage of GDP. One can see that small countries suffered comparably most, with Ireland extending more than two and a half times its national income on saving the banking sector. Denmark, which committed a similarly unsustainable part of their GDP, actually extended only a quarter of its commitment, still two-thirds of its GDP, while most other countries with substantial expenditures spent between 6 percent and 16 percent of GDP.

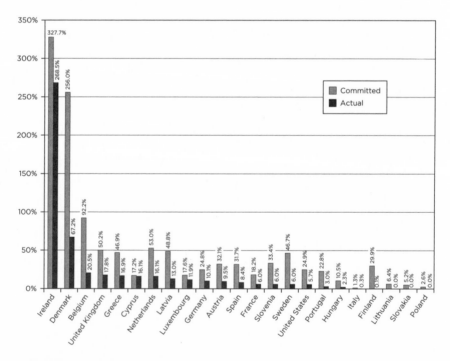

Figure 2.2 Committed and actual expenditures, 2007–10
Source: Bailout expenditures from European Commission competition scoreboard, European Commission, *The Effects of Temporary State Aid Rules Adopted in the Context of the Financial and Economic Crisis,* 2011; Stolz and Wedow, *Extraordinary Measures in Extraordinary Times,* give figures for the United States; percentages are given as percentage of 2010 GDP; all figures include 2010, except for the United States, which runs up to May 2010 only.

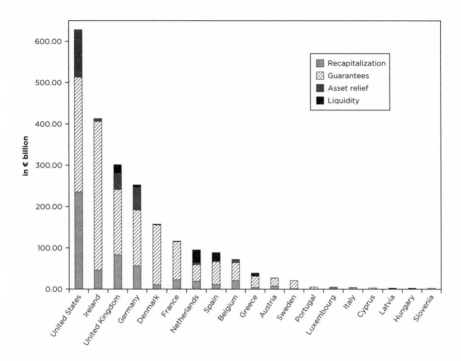

Figure 2.3 Total expenditures, 2008–10 (in € billion)
Source: Author's calculation based on European Commission State Aid Scoreboard: see European Commission, *The Effects of Temporary State Aid Rules;* and Stolz and Wedow, *Extraordinary Measures in Extraordinary Times,* for the United States. Only Germany had expenditures prior to 2008, €0.41 billion in guarantees in 2007, which are included; figures of United States are from 2008–May 2010 only.

Moreover, figure 2.2 shows that the difference between commitments and outlays was considerable in many countries. To be sure, it is difficult to consider these "take-up rates" as a measure of successful or unsuccessful government schemes and/or of effective aid granted. In some cases, take up will be low, because the government plan is inappropriate or highly conditional and thus unattractive for banks; in others it can reflect the fact that the actual health of banks was better than expected or that the program succeeded in coordinating bank rescues without public expenditures via private investment.[37] Still it is important to understand what leads to very striking differences in take-up rates in cases that looked initially similar, such as Ireland and Denmark.

When one considers the total amount of expenditures, the United States leads the ranking with $837 billion (€628 billion) used of its total commitment

37. Panetta et al., "An Assessment of Financial Sector Rescue Programmes, 15–16; European Commission, "DG Competition's Review of Guarantee and Recapitalisation Schemes in the Financial Sector in the Current Crisis," 4.

of over \$3 trillion.[38] As the most important banking markets in Europe, the United Kingdom, Germany, and France figure prominently. Constituting almost 60 percent of the European banking sector when taken together, these three countries also account for 60 percent of the aid granted between October 2008 and December 2010.[39] Two smaller countries, Belgium and the Netherlands, also spent considerable amounts, but unlike the rest of Europe, these two never approved a national scheme to support the financial industry, but intervened through a series of ad hoc measures.[40]

Net Costs

The data so far give an overview of commitments and expenditures. However, these figures do not reflect actual costs to the public budgets. Guarantees may not be called on, loans will be paid back in part or in full, and several instruments generate revenue through fees or interest. In addition, assets the government had acquired (some toxic, others not) can be sold off after a certain period. In some cases, the write-downs on these assets were or are still going to be important, but not always. Even though policymakers never had all the relevant information to know whether their actions would procure the government costs or equity, it is useful to compare which bailout scheme have turned out to be costly, comparatively speaking, and which have actually brought income to the public balance sheet by May 2011 (Table 2.1). Attempts to calculate these net costs are ongoing and often referred to as the "fiscal impact" of bank bailouts.[41]

According to Eurostat's public deficit oversight tables, the most important positive contributions of bank bailouts to public budgets, in absolute figures, were recorded in France, Spain, Denmark, Greece, Sweden, and Belgium.[42] As a percentage of GDP, the most significant deficit reduction was achieved in Denmark, with 0.3 percent of GDP; followed by Greece and Cyprus at 0.2

---

38. Converted at the 2010 exchange rate of 1.33 euros to the dollar. The total commitment of the US bailout is €2.226 trillion or \$3.301 trillion for commitments under TARP and for the government sponsored entities, according to Stolz and Wedow, which is roughly 25 percent of the 2010 GDP, with 5.7 percent of GDP actually spent. Laeven and Valencia estimate the actual expenditures more conservatively at 4.9 percent during the first year of the crisis. Alternative estimates are also available from Pro Publica, which lists outflows in mid-2012 at \$602 billion. Further discussion of the US governments' listed expenditures can be found in the following chapter. Stolz and Wedow, "Extraordinary Measures in Extraordinary Times"; Laeven and Valencia, "Resolution of Banking Crisis," 34.

39. European Commission, "The Effects of Temporary State Aid Rules Adopted in the Context of the Financial and Economic Crisis," 11.

40. Ibid., 36.

41. Laeven and Valencia, "Resolution of Banking Crisis"; Laeven and Valencia, "Systemic Banking Crises Dataset: An Update"; Reinhart and Rogoff, *This Time Is Different.*

42. Both Greece and Spain, but also Portugal, are cases where the banking crisis became visible with considerable delay. Greece spent an additional €30.5 billion (13.2 percent of its GDP) and Portugal €27 billion (15.6 percent of its GDP) in 2011. European Commission, "The Effects of Temporary State Aid Rules Adopted in the Context of the Financial and Economic Crisis." The Spanish banking crisis aggravated in 2012. The actual costs are thus likely to be higher than recorded by May 2011.

TABLE 2.1
Net costs 2008–11

Country	billion €	% of GDP
France	2.40	0.10%
Spain	1.45	0.10%
Denmark	0.72	0.30%
Greece	0.41	0.20%
Sweden	0.35	0.10%
Belgium	0.20	0.10%
Italy	0.13	0.00%
Cyprus	0.03	0.20%
Slovenia	0.03	0.10%
Hungary	0.01	0.01%
Lithuania	−0.03	−0.10%
Luxembourg	−0.04	−0.10%
Latvia	−0.43	−2.30%
Austria	−1.43	−0.50%
Portugal	−2.21	−1.30%
Netherlands	−3.44	−0.60%
United Kingdom	−15.03	−1.00%
Germany	−16.56	−0.70%
Ireland	−35.72	−22.30%
United States	−66.50	0.00%

Source: Eurostat for EU: These figures take into account costs and revenue to public budgets only. Outstanding amounts of assets, actual liabilities, and contingent liabilities are recorded separately. The US net costs are estimated at $50 billion, based on projection of US oversight authorities in late 2011 (SIGTARP, *Quarterly Report to Congress*, 35). The US estimate is conservative and does not include costs incurred through Fannie Mae and Freddie Mac, which could amount to $134 billion according to ProPublica (Kiel, "Behind Administration Spin").

percent; and Belgium, Spain, Slovenia, France, and Sweden at 0.1 percent. At the other end, the bank bailouts in Portugal, the Netherlands, the United Kingdom, Germany, and Ireland are the most costly in Europe in absolute terms, but still much behind the United States.

However, in terms of GDP (cumulated 2008–10), Ireland holds the uncomfortable last place, with a 22.7 percent deficit increase, followed by Latvia (2.3 percent), Portugal (1.3 percent), the United Kingdom (1.0 percent), Germany (0.7 percent), and the Netherlands (0.6 percent). The projected US bailout costs in terms of GDP are below 0.001 percent. As with all estimates, the applied accounting rules crucially affect the outcome. In particular, the creation of a public entity to deal with the unwinding of an ailing financial institution is considered as costs. The public ownership and capital injections into Northern Rock in the United Kingdom or HRE in Germany, for example, are thus not counted as (potential) equity held by the government, which explains the relatively sizable cost figure in both cases.[43]

43. European Commission, *Eurostat Supplementary Table for the Financial Crisis: Background Note*. For an alternative estimation of net costs, see Laeven and Valencia, "Resolution of Banking Crisis."

Instruments

Instruments varied widely. Most countries used guarantees to ward off a panic and potential run on banks. But despite the lead of the United States to propose a focus on the transfer of toxic assets and the UK's example of re-capitalization as the main pillar of intervention, national responses had very different mixes of expenditures. In absolute numbers, the United States, the United Kingdom, Germany, and Ireland spent most on injecting capital into ailing financial institutions (figure 2.3).

As a percentage of their entire effort, however, the picture is quite differ-ent, as figure 2.4 shows. While the United States and the United Kingdom dedicated 37 percent and 27 percent of their government aid to recapi-talization, Germany and France spent around 20 percent (22 percent and 19 percent respectively). Ireland and Denmark, by contrast, use the most sub-stantial part of their support to cover guarantees, 87 percent and 92 percent respectively. Italy stands out as the only country that has used recapitalization measures exclusively. This is indeed quite unusual, since guarantees and li-quidity support through central banks are typically a way for governments to

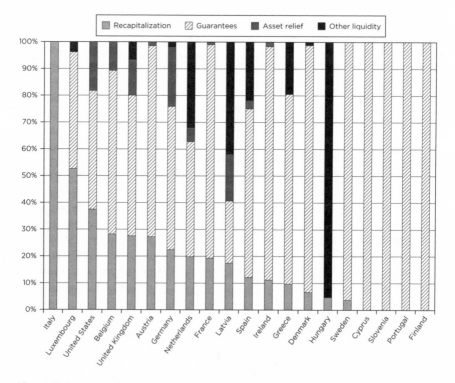

Figure 2.4 Instruments used as percentage of actual expenditures
Source: Author's calculation based on European Commission State Aid Scoreboard, *The Effects of Temporary State Aid Rules*; and Stolz and Wedow, *Extraordinary Measures in Extraordinary Times*, for the United States.

buy time before moving to the more difficult issue of recapitalizing banks.[44] However, Italy, together with Portugal and Luxembourg, offered significantly less support than average, both in absolute terms (figure 2.3) and as a percentage of the size of their banking sectors, by giving well below 1 percent of support.[45] The liberty to choose such an unusual mix of support may thus be a function of an overall small bailout effort.

Finally, it is noteworthy that only a few countries chose to use public funds to transfer troubled assets. After the announcement that the US government would focus its efforts on troubled assets, an announcement that to a great extent failed to materialize, mainly Germany and Austria announced assets transfer mechanisms as part of their early schemes. Ireland and Latvia created similar mechanisms, but much later, in late 2009, early 2010. The British Asset Protection Scheme was announced in January 2009 to ensure assets on the balance sheets of RBS and Lloyds, and this was run by an independent agency that was created in December 2009.

Conditionality

Beyond pure costs, an important element for comparison is the degree of conditionality attached to government support. The conditions attached to bailout schemes varied across countries, but it is difficult to give a complete picture of the variation. A previous study has provided two indicators to tackle this question: one for the strength of lending requirements, and a second one estimating the overall constraint of the support package.[46] For the second indicator, the authors use a proxy: the delay of approval from the European Commission's Directorate General (DG) Competition. Since the European Commission's task is to ensure that aid is given with the least negative effect on competition possible, their approval can be understood as a signal that a government plan is not unduly favorable to its own banking sector, but upholds prices and conditions similar to what would have been granted on the market, if it was still functioning. Although the argument is appealing, one may assume that other institutional factors may play into the negotiation between national authorities and DG Competition that can affect the delay of approval. Moreover, it is difficult to distinguish between lengthy negotiations that revolved around the adequate contribution of the banking sector and negotiations that were due to unequal treatment of national and foreign banks, as appears to have been the case in Ireland, for example.[47] Finally, the approval time does not indicate what the final version looks like, it merely indicates how the initial proposal was judged by the European authorities.

44. In past financial crises, the median time to implement recapitalization programs was twelve months, and contracted to zero months only in the recent financial crisis. Laeven and Valencia, "Resolution of Banking Crisis."

45. European Commission, "The Effects of Temporary State Aid Rules Adopted in the Context of the Financial and Economic Crisis," 39.

46. Weber and Schmitz, "Varieties of Helping Capitalism."

47. Ibid., 653.

TABLE 2.2
(Un)attractiveness of government support for participating institutions

	Indicative entry rate	Conditions for recapitalization	Lending requirement	Approval time
	Minimum remuneration entry rate for hybrid capital (tier 1) injected by the government	LEND = lending commitments; EMPL = maintaining employment; BOARD = board appointment; COMP = executive compensation; DIV = dividend; CAPSTR = capital structure	Points for explicit mention, early inclusion, specificity, additional features	Quick (<7 days), moderate (7–14), long (15–30), very long (>30)
United Kingdom	12.00%	LEND, BOARD, COMP, DIV, CAPSTR	4	quick (2.5)
Greece	10.00%	BOARD, COMP	2	quick (5)
Hungary	10.00%	BOARD, COMP	0	very long (87)
Portugal	9.50%	LEND, COMP, DIV	4	moderate (14)
Finland	9.40%	LEND, CAPSTR	1	quick (2)
Austria	9.30%	LEND, EMPL, COMP, DIV, CAPSTR	2	very long (50)
Germany	9.00%	LEND, COMP, DIV, CAPSTR	2	moderate (14)
Denmark	9.00%	LEND, COMP, DIV	1	quick (2)
France	8.00%	LEND, COMP, CAPSTR	4	quick (7)
Ireland	8.00%	LEND, BOARD, COMP, DIV	4	moderate (10)
Italy	8.00%	LEND, COMP, DIV	3	long (27)
Spain	7.80%	LEND, COMP, DIV	2	moderate (21.5)
United States	5.00%	LEND, COMP, DIV	3	N/A
Sweden	market rate	LEND, COMP	1	quick (2)
Latvia	ad hoc	nationalization of Parex	1	quick (6)
Belgium	ad hoc	BOARD, COMP, CAPSTR	0	N/A
Netherlands	ad hoc	BOARD, COMP, CAPSTR	0	moderate (9)

Source: Entry price for recapitalization from European Commission, *The Effects of Temporary State Aid Rules Adopted in the Context of the Financial and Economic Crisis*, 52; Panetta et al., *An Assessment of Financial Sector Rescue Programmes* for the United States and Department of Finance for Ireland ("Recapitalisation of Allied Irish Bank and Bank of Ireland"). Conditions from Committee of European Banking Supervisors, *Analysis of the National Plans for the Stabilisation of Markets*, Panetta et al. *An Assessment of Financial Sector Rescue Programmes*; and the state aid rulings of DG Competition, lending requirement, and approval time from Weber and Schmitz, "Varieties of Helping Capitalism".
Note: The entry rates given for recapitalization vary according to the specific context of the capital injections, in particular the type of capital covered, the duration, and possible step-up clauses, where remuneration increases over time.

Table 2.2 lists the indicators given by Weber and Schmitz together with a list of conditions formally attached to the recapitalization packages. In addition, it adds new information available now about the pricing of the recapitalization aid, which is a central element in most bailout packages. Pricing is an important factor in making aid attractive or unattractive to banks in difficulty.

In a detailed communication on state aid, the European Commission recommends the adequate pricing of aid to avoid distorting competition and provides a pricing corridor, which suggests that remuneration should take into account the risk profile of the individual institutions and have a rate of return of 7 percent on subordinate debt and 9.3 percent on preferred shares and hybrid debt instruments. Moreover, the price should increase over time to encourage exit from government capital.[48]

The juxtaposition of the different indicators shows that there is not necessarily a relationship between the number of conditions attached to government support and the delay in approval from the European Commission. The similarity of conditions also suggests that we know little about the constraints weighing on participating banks if we do not know how these conditions are reinforced. On the one hand, the approval of state aid in Europe through the European Commission implies a certain degree of harmonization, which means that the formal conditions may appear rather similar. On the other hand, conditions formally attached but with little reinforcement may end up being toothless in practice. In many countries, inquiry reports have highlighted discrepancies between formal conditions and outcomes.[49]

Concerning the remuneration of capital injections, we can see that despite the oversight of the European authorities, variation exists. The United Kingdom, but also Greece and Hungary, are well above the corridor recommended by the European Central Bank (ECB) and the European Commission. In other words, the capital injections are particularly expensive for participating institutions. France, Italy, and Spain are comparatively low, in particular France and Italy, which granted core Tier 1 capital that should be remunerated at the upper level of the corridor.[50] According to the European Commission, the return rate was nonetheless approved as adequate because both schemes entailed important step-up clauses, in other words, increases in the cost of capital granted over time. Nonetheless, comparing different European schemes, the costs for participating banks in the UK scheme are arguably high and in Italy and France quite favorable. This impression is confirmed by interview evidence: one observer characterized the UK plan as harsh, while a representative of the French administration regretted that the government had not tried to extract a higher price from the banks.[51]

---

48. European Commission, *Eurostat Supplementary Table for the Financial Crisis: Background Note.*

49. SIGTARP, *Extent of Federal Agencies' Oversight of AIG Compensation Varied, and Important Challenges Remain;* Cour des Comptes, *Les concours publics aux établissements de crédit: bilan et enseignement à tirer.*

50. The Spanish rate, in contrast, can be explained by the less risky type of capital granted in the Spanish scheme.

51. Interviews, 8 June 2011 and 15 April 2011.

What is particularly striking, however, is the price of the initial capital injections in the US Capital Purchase Plan (CPP) of 13 October 2008. With 5 percent for preferred shares, the United States is far below the 9.3 percent recommended in the European context at the same time. It is true, the 5 percent was annual divided paid for only the first five years, after which it would rise up to 9 percent. Moreover, the second recapitalization (the Capital Assistance Program—CAP) announced by the Obama administration on 10 February 2009 asked for a 9 percent annual dividend for mandatory convertible preferred shares. Still, the initial rate proposed by the Bush administration was extraordinarily low. Vikram Pandit, CEO of Citigroup, brought this to a point, when he exclaimed in the tense meeting the government had convened to announce its recapitalization plan: "This is really cheap capital!"[52] Clearly, the initial US recapitalization plan was tailored to be as attractive as possible in order encourage financial institutions to collectively accept government support.

Public-private Arrangements

A final variation in bailout schemes concerns the extent to which the financial industry is involved in the setup and execution of the bank support scheme. In most countries, the guarantee and liquidity schemes, recapitalization and asset transfer plans are run directly by the national governments, treasuries, or the central banks.

In some countries, special entities have been set up to administer parts of the national schemes. Several of these entities are part of or tightly connected with the public administrations and central bank (Spain, United Kingdom, Ireland, Switzerland, and Germany), although the degree of oversight varied from country to country. In France, Austria, and Denmark, by contrast, the special entities build on private sector participation and contributions.

In France, the Société de Financement de l'Economie Française (SFEF), set up to raise capital on financial markets and provide liquidity to ailing financial institutions, was jointly owned by the six big banks and the governments, which held 66 percent and 34 percent respectively. Seven other financial institutions also signed the SFEF agreement to benefit from the liquidity provided through the state-backed mechanism.[53] The objective of SFEF was to issue securities collectively, backed with a government guarantee, and thus obtain liquidity at a much more favorable rate than would have been possible for individual banks and without government backing.

---

52. Cited in Wessel, *In FED We Trust*, 239.
53. These were mainly housing and consumer credit institutions, often the financial activity branches of large industrial groups: PSA Finance (PSA-Peugeot-Citroën), General Electric, Crédit Immobilier, Laser Cofinoga, RCI Banque (Groupe Renault), S2Pass (Groupe Carrefour) and VFS Finance (Volvo). GMAC had originally signed the SFEF agreement but did not request liquidity support. Cour des Comptes, *Les concours publics aux établissements de crédit: premiers constats, premières recommandations*, 32.

TABLE 2.3
Institutional setup of national schemes

Country	Institution for funding guarantees	Institution for capital injections	Institution for asset purchases
Austria	Special entity: OeCAG	Special entity: OIAG	N/A
Belgium	Government	Government	N/A
Germany	Special entity: SoFFin	Special entity: SoFFin	Special entity: SoFFin
Spain	Government (Treasury)	Special entity: FROB	Treasury: Financial Asset Acquisition Fund
Finland	Special entity under Treasury	N/A	N/A
France	Special entity: SFEF	Special entity: SPPE	N/A
Greece	Government (Treasury) and Central Bank	Government (Treasury)	Government
Ireland	Government	Government	Special government entity: NAMA
Italy	Government (Treasury)	Government	Central Bank
Luxembourg	Government	Government	N/A
Netherlands	Government	Government	ING
Portugal	Central Bank	Government	N/A
Denmark	Danish Contingency Association	Government	Government
Switzerland	N/A	Government	Special entity under Central Bank
United Kingdom	Government Debt Management Office	Special entity under Treasury: UKFI	Central Bank
United States	FDIC	Government (Treasury)	Treasury and Central Bank

Source: Stolz und Wedow, Extraordinary Measures in Extraordinary Times, 63.

In Austria, the Österreichische Clearingbank AG (OeCAG) was set up as a bank with its own license to facilitate interbank lending. It was owned by the major Austrian banks,[54] who contributed €180 million in capital and its operations were backed by a guarantee from the government for up to €4 billion and collateral of up to €5 billion in the form of commercial paper provided by OeCAG. Recapitalization was delegated to Österreichische Industrieholding AG (OIAG), a formerly state-financed holding company for the management of state-owned enterprises, which had turned into a privatization agency and joint-stock company by 2000. OIAG founded a subsidiary in the context of the financial crisis, which acted as a trust company of the government of Austria for the recapitalization of Austrian banks.[55]

54. Raiffeisen Zentralbank Österreich AG, UniCredit Bank Austria AG, Erste Group Bank AG, Hypo-Banken Holding GmbH, Österreichische Volksbanken AG, BAWAG PSK Bank für Arbeit und Wirtschaft, Österreichische Postsparkasse AG, and 3-Banken Beteiligung GmbH.
55. www.fmarktbet.at/cms/start.php.

In the Danish case, liquidity provision was assumed through the Danish Contingency Association, a collective undertaking established by the Danish banking industry for the support of distressed banks in 2007. In exchange for an unlimited government deposit guarantee, participating banks agreed in 2008 to contributed approximately €4.7 billion for a collective guarantee for individual banks and fees paid to the government for the deposit guarantee. Recapitalization was introduced in February 2009 and administered by the Danish Finance Ministry, but the Danish Contingency Association was a central mechanism to share the costs of the extensive guarantees between the government and the private stakeholders.

The overview of these special entities shows that it is possible to find institutional setups that involved the financial industry in the funding and administration of the bailouts. Such institutional mechanism for cooperation between the industry and the government are central features in some countries, but such burden sharing remains somewhat of an exception.[56]

Conclusion

The global financial crisis may have begun in the United States, but it quickly spread and turned into a challenge that was much larger than the initial subprime crisis. Not just the exposure to the US housing market, but also the reliance of many financial institutions on short-term finance in order to roll over their debt, the overextension of local housing markets, and the the uncertain financial condition of foreign branches of domestic institutions came together as an explosive mix for most governments in the fall of 2008. Despite the international nature of the crisis, government responses were decidedly national. Alongside central bank efforts to provide liquidity to struggling financial institutions, governments made public budgets available for bank support schemes, in most countries at staggering proportions.

The six countries that will be studied in greater detail are the highest spenders on bank support schemes in absolute terms: the United States, Ireland, the United Kingdom, Germany, Denmark, and France. All six have been substantially affected by the financial crisis and made important efforts to prop up their banking sectors through national support schemes.

However, they differ on several dimensions that are relevant for the paired comparison in the following chapters, as table 2.4 summarizes. Compared to the United States, the United Kingdom's plan is striking for its stringent

---

56. The term *burden sharing* can also refer to a bank levy through which banks would contribute to their own future bailout or to measures with respect to individual failing institutions, whose unwinding revolved imputing costs to the private stakeholders; see European Commission, "The Effects of Temporary State Aid Rules Adopted in the Context of the Financial and Economic Crisis," 60–62.

TABLE 2.4
Comparison summary

	Initial commitment	Outlays	Net costs	Pricing	Institutional setup
United States	Moderate (25% of GDP)	Low (6% of GDP)	Low (<0.1% of GDP)	Very low	Government
United Kingdom	High (50% of GDP)	Moderate (18% of GDP)	Negative (–1% of GDP)	High	Government
Germany	Moderate (25% of GDP)	Low (10%)	Negative (–0.7% of GDP)	Average	Special government entity
France	Moderate (18% of GDP)	Low (6% GDP)	Positive (0.1% of GDP)	Low	Public-private entity
Ireland	Massive (330% of GDP)	Massive (270% of GDP)	Very negative (22.7% of GDP)	Low	Government
Denmark	Massive (256% of GDP)	High (67% of GDP)	Positive (0.3% of GDP)	Average	Public-private entity

conditions, in particular in the pricing of its recapitalization. However, the British plan risks costing more than the US plan, at least as a percentage of GDP. The French plan appears to have been be more favorable to the financial industry than the German plan but relied in part on a public-private entity for its execution and ended up producing a surplus for the public budget. The Danish plan looked similar to the Irish scheme, at least initially when both countries committed several times their national income to guaranteeing the financial sector. However, the Irish scheme's outlays were equally high and the fiscal impact is likely to be very substantial, while the Danish scheme succeeded in keeping outlays low, in particular through the management of a joint public-private initiative. Explaining these differences requires understanding the interactions between governments and financial institutions during crisis management, more specifically the exercise of power. Providing the tools for such an analysis in the empirical chapters is the objective of the following chapter.

3

The Power of Collective Inaction

Power is the ability to afford not to learn.

—Karl Deutsch, *The Nerves of Government*

Despite many disturbing details about the financial elite's shortcomings, misjudgments, and pure arrogance, financial institutions were bailed out with taxpayer money in all affected countries. In some cases, these decisions brought the entire country to its knees. How could financial institutions be given so much money when everybody agreed that the difficulties were of their own making?

Scholars and popular press alike quickly proposed a simple answer: it is because of the power of the financial industry. This does not get us very far. Arguing that bailouts were granted because the financial industry is powerful, in general, is obvious and has been stated repeatedly throughout history. From Thomas Jefferson to Napoleon Bonaparte, observers have argued that governments should never depend on bankers if they want to control their fate.[1] Scholars like Susan Strange speak of the "destructive powers for evil of money," insisting that its management is "too important to be left to bankers."[2] Have these warning gone unheeded, and we are now paying the price?

Analyzing what constitutes the power of the financial industry and through which mechanisms it operates is crucial for understanding how we got to the policy decisions adopted throughout the industrialized world in 2008 and

1. See Johnson and Kwak, *13 Bankers*, 14–38. The quote attributed to Napoleon is, "When the money of a government depends on banks, they, not the heads of state, control the situation. Money has no homeland and financiers are not patriotic or decent; their only objective is profit."

2. Strange, *Casino Capitalism*, vii. The original text also adds "and economists" since Strange addresses both banking regulation and monetary policy in her book, underlining that in the early postwar years, "money and credit had been so controlled and regulated by governments that its power to disrupt and destroy had been forgotten."

2009. Yet despite the general consensus that finance is powerful, there is little agreement about what this actually means. Have governments have turned into the willing executioner of banks' wishes, against the interests of their citizens? Are the financiers' lobbying activities or their social networks so pervasive that governments caved in to their demands? Or should we look at more structural features, such as the importance of banks and the role of finance in the economy?

Examining the ways in which power operates is necessary to move beyond the tautological statements that infer power from outcome.[3] Power then becomes not the starting point, but the phenomenon that needs to be explained. Only then is it possible to begin and explain the dynamics and variation in government efforts across countries. Yes, the financial industry is powerful, and it is powerful in all market economies. But the relationships banks entertain with their governments are not the same everywhere. Small differences in the nature of their relations can make big differences in the design of bailouts.

Barnett and Duvall have defined power as "the production, in and through social relations, of effects on actors that shape their capacity to control their fate."[4] They highlight a common shortcoming in analyses of power: to concentrate merely on the use of material resources that allow an actor to get others to do what they otherwise would not. As many social theorists have emphasized, power can work in many more subtle ways.[5] And yet the "exercise fallacy"—looking for power as observable action that causes a sequence of events—and the "vehicle fallacy"—reducing power to the instruments through which it operates—are pervasive.[6]

By breaking down the power of the financial industry into different aspects, this chapter argues that pointing to superior resources is misleading. The power of the financial industry is the product of a long-term relationship between finance and the state. In this relationship, being needed is of fundamental importance, not influence peddling, as many assume. This, in turn, puts the ball in the court of the financial industry, which can exert power by remaining inactive in times of crisis. To get at this particular capacity, we need to look at the connections between different types of power. First, we need to reconsider the structural power banks derive from their specific role in the economy. Second, how this structural power plays out is mediated by the ways in which the industry has shaped the terms of the policy debate concerning its own regulation. This discursive power is not a unilateral action to sway the government, however, but part of a dialectical production of meaning, which has been studied under the label "productive power." In combination, the structural and productive power of the industry

3. Gourevitch, "Afterword: Yet More Hard Times?."
4. Barnett and Duvall, "Power in International Politics," 45.
5. Barnett and Duvall, *Power in Global Governance*; Dean, *Governmentality*; Lukes, *Power: A Radical View*; Rose, *Powers of Freedom*.
6. Lukes, "Power and the Battle for Hearts and Minds," 478.

created specific challenges for government intervention. In these particular moments of decision making, governments intervened most intensively not where banks made the most outrageous requests, but where they participated least as a sector collectively. I will discuss this mechanism of exerting power as capacity for collective inaction.

The argument in this book is that the different aspects of power combined to create very specific challenges for crisis management. However, while structural and productive power have been studied in the past and are relatively well understood, they provide only a weak sense of agency—and thus responsibility. The empirical discussion of the book therefore insists most on the last element, the power of collective inaction, to demonstrate how structural and productive power can produce or fail to produce concrete decisions in a moment of extreme pressure.

This chapter discusses the power of the financial industry from a theoretical perspective by presenting first, its structural power, and second, its productive power. It then develops the concept of collective inaction in a third section. A fourth section gives a preview of the arguments laid out in the empirical chapters by outlining how the different aspects of power play out in the individual case studies.

Structural Power

It is very common to deduce power from material resources and the ways in which they were employed in order to obtain an agreement. Although numerous studies exist about lobbying and the use of specific resources of the financial industry, the evidence that this advantage actually shapes precise policy outcomes is scant. The following section argues that the power of A over B does not necessarily rest on activities and influence peddling. The degree to which B needs A is more central. This dependence of B on A is a structural feature and not the result of individual interactions.

It is easy to understand why many studies and popular writings have concentrated on the lobbying activities of the financial industry. It has been the top spender in US politics, for example, leaving behind even the health sector, which went into a frenzy over health care reform in recent years.[7] Moreover, the personal ties between public officials and financial elites are extensive in most countries. Beyond a wealth of anecdotal evidence, studies have shown that the value of firms known to have connections with a public official increases upon his or her nomination, indicating that financial markets expect these ties to be beneficial for the firms. Others have tried to

---

7. Renick Mayer, Beckel, and Levinthal, *Crossing Wall Street.*

establish links between lobbying expenditures and risk taking.[8] But measuring causal influence continues to pose a real challenge.[9] Even when data are available, studies of campaign contributions and lobbying expenditures have been inconclusive with respect to policy decisions.[10] In an extensive study across issues and sectors, Baumgartner et al. find that resources are a poor predictor of choices and outcomes.[11] At best, the link between lobbying activities and policy output is indirect.

The difficulties in studies concentrating on the actual links between financial elites and government reside in the fact that they narrow down power to an interactive concept only. This interactive perspective is expressed most clearly in public choice theory, which postulates that public and private actors engage in a marketlike exchange: votes or money against favorable regulation.[12] It therefore follows that we would need to understand which resources are provided and exchanged to get a sense of the degree of capture of public officials or entire agencies. Given the superior lobbying means of the financial industry, it would thus seem safe to assume that decision makers have been "bought" by the financial industry, a view that largely predominates in US public opinion. Inversely, however, this would imply that in countries where lobbying and campaign financing plays a less significant role, we should expect policies that are less favorable to the financial industry. It turns out that this is not the case. Power in interactions, which has been labeled "instrumental power" in some studies, seems to be conditioned by factors beyond pure resources.[13]

In fact, power does not work only through interaction, it also works through constitutive relationships, as Barnett and Duvall highlight.[14] In these contexts, social relations define who the actors are and what capacities they are endowed with. The nature of the relationship can empower actors differentially. In contrast to the behaviorist tradition, which defines power as "the ability of A to get B to do what B would not otherwise do,"[15] constitutive analysis examines the endowment of capacities that will shape interactions even if A does not become active at all.

Constitutive analyses of the economy have a long tradition, in particular in Marxist thought, which has emphasized how internal relationships among

8. Acemoglu et al., *The Value of Political Connections in the United States*; Igan, Mishra, and Tressel, "A Fistful of Dollars"; Luechinger and Moser, *The Value of the Revolving Door*.

9. Lowery, "Lobbying Influence"; Woll, "Leading the Dance?"

10. See Baumgartner and Leech, *Basic Interests*.

11. Baumgartner et al., *Lobbying and Policy Change*.

12. E.g., Becker, "A Theory of Competition among Pressure Groups for Political Influence"; Stigler, "Theory of Economic Regulation"; Stigler, "Economic Competition and Political Competition."

13. Hacker and Pierson, "Business Power and Social Policy"; Culpepper and Reinke, *The Structural Dependence of Capital on the State*.

14. Barnett and Duvall, "Power in International Politics," 45–46.

15. Dahl, "The Concept of Power."

agents become a structural feature of capitalism that defines the agents and their interests, for example in the capital-labor relationship. The interests of workers are defined through their relationship to capital-owners and vice versa. In business-government relationships, scholars have argued that business enjoys structural power, because governments need to achieve economic growth in a capitalist economy and will therefore be deferential to business demands.[16] The structural dependence of the state on capital, combined with the threat that businesses may leave a country if policy is not carried out in its favor, thus explains the dominance of business over other parts of society.[17]

Contrary to studies of intentional lobbying, structural power perspectives highlight nonintentional domination: even without active interference, business actors can enjoy a policy bias in their favor because of their privileged position in capitalist arrangements and the dependence of the government on their establishment and growth.[18] Thus structural power is understood as the capacity "to change the range of choices open to others without apparently putting pressure directly on them to take one decision or to make one choice rather than another."[19] In Lukes's threefold typology of power, the control over options available to others makes up the two-dimensional view on power, which has developed as a critique of the behavioralist tradition.[20] This perspective emphasizes how actors may use institutional settings to create bias against others, in particular by excluding them from decision making or limiting their choices. Bachrach and Baratz have extended the study of this phenomenon through their focus on nondecisions: issues that are never up for discussion.[21] For Susan Strange, finance was one important domain of structural power that has traditionally been neglected.[22] For her, finance, which controls access to credit, is far more central to growth in recent decades, and "its power to determine outcomes enormous."

But the role of finance is not the same across countries, and differences are very relevant for the type of dependence policymakers will have on financial institutions. Hacker and Pierson focus on capital mobility as a key ingredient of structural power to analyze variation: when firms can leave more easily their power over their governments increases.[23] This can explain structural power differences across and within national settings.

Across countries, the central concern is the difference in financial systems, in particular the difference between capital market–based finance

16. Block, "The Ruling Class Does Not Rule"; Lindblom, "The Market as Prison."

17. Block, "The Ruling Class Does Not Rule"; Cerny, "Globalization and the Erosion of Democracy"; Przeworski and Wallerstein, "Structural Dependence of the State on Capital."

18. Bernhagen and Bräuninger, "Structural Power and Public Policy."

19. Strange, *States and Markets*, 31.

20. Lukes, *Power: A Radical View*.

21. Bachrach and Baratz, "Two Faces of Power"; Bachrach and Baratz, "Decision and Non-Decisions."

22. Strange, *States and Markets*.

23. Hacker and Pierson, "Business Power and Social Policy."

and bank-based finance.[24] This distinction corresponds to the seminal explanation of national diversity of financial systems developed by Alexander Gerschenkron, who argued that large, universal banks were compensatory mechanisms for late development, in contrast to early financial systems, which were fragmented into different market segments and activities.[25] Although many aspects of Gerschenkron's argument have been criticized,[26] the general distinction between financial systems remains, at least at the descriptive level.[27]

In particular the relationship between banks, the government, and other firms is important for understanding the nature of structural dependence. Firms in capital market–based systems rely on financial markets for their funding. In bank-based systems, firms and banks tend to be connected through a dense web of cross-shareholdings, which allows banks to monitor the development of firms and allocate credit. Firms are much more dependent on bank credits and their long-term relationships with these banks have traditionally been central to company networks. Banks and entrepreneurs therefore maintain clublike personal relationships, with close connections to governments in bank-based systems. In capital market systems, banks are intermediaries in an "arms-length system" between the entrepreneur and the financier.[28] Individual banks are thus less important, and we would not expect governments to have an interest in their survival per se, unless their performance threatens financial stability more generally.

Put differently, governments in bank-based systems depend on the banks directly and their ability to give continued access to credit to the so-called real economy, while governments in capital-market systems depend on financial market stability. This implies that governments in capital-market systems will be deferential only to those institutions that can arguably affect financial stability. Unfortunately, this risk, colloquially labeled "too big to fail," has continuously increased over time due to the growing complexity of financial transactions and the size of individual institutions.[29] Still the role of finance in the economy should lead to divergent outcomes across countries: while

24. La Porta et al., "Law and Finance"; Rajan and Zingales, "Financial Systems, Industrial Structure, and Growth"; Zysman, *Governments, Markets, and Growth.*
25. Gerschenkron, *Economic Backwardness in Historical Perspective.*
26. Cf. Forsyth and Verdier, *Origins of National Financial Systems.*
27. Allen and Gale, *Comparing Financial Systems;* Beck, Demirgüç-Kunt, and Levine, "A New Database on the Structure and Development of the Financial Sector"; Beck, Demirgüç-Kunt, and Levine, "Finance, Inequality and the Poor"; Beck, Demirgüç-Kunt, and Levine, "Financial Institutions and Markets across Countries and over Time-data and Analysis"; Demirgüç-Kunt and Levine, *Bank-based and Market-based Financial Systems.* Banking systems are primarily discussed in economic history and economics of finance. An important part of the literature debates the merits of the respective types of finance; in particular for growth see Levine, "Finance and Growth"; another strand debates the reasons for the different developments, e.g., La Porta et al., "Law and Finance"; Malmendier, "Law and Finance 'at the Origin.' "
28. Rajan and Zingales, *Saving Capitalism from the Capitalists.*
29. Stern and Feldman, *Too Big to Fail.*

governments in bank-based systems would need to save the banks in order to save the economy, governments in capital market–based systems need to save financial markets in order to save the economy.

A second structural feature that gives insight into the power of the financial industry is the sheer size of its activities relative to the economy of a country. For small banking countries such as Luxembourg, Switzerland, Ireland, Belgium, Denmark, Iceland, or lately Cyprus, the potential damage of an ailing financial sector is many times more pressing than it is for other countries with developed financial markets.

Despite these variations in intensity, the structural power of finance is high in all market economies, and the so-called "state-finance nexus" is a central feature of modern capitalism.[30] As a consequence, the rigidity of structural power explanations has repeatedly been criticized and led to a certain decline of the approach. A series of studies underlined how institutional capacities, coalitional politics, or ideas were able to counter or mediate the structural power of business.[31] Constructivist political economy, in particular, argued that the interests of elites cannot simply be deduced from their structural positions but need to be interpreted and negotiated. As Blyth puts it, "Structures do not come with an instruction sheet."[32] It is thus insufficient to know what structural advantage the financial industry is endowed with, we also need to know how these positions become interpreted and employed. This leads us to productive power.

Productive Power

Like structural power, productive power is concerned with constitutive social processes that are not controlled by specific actors. While structural power focuses on the production and reproduction of positional capacities, productive power refers to the "constitution of subjects with various social powers through systems of knowledge and discursive practices."[33] As such, productive power is very close to Lukes's three-dimensional view of power as discursively transmitted meaning structures.[34]

Developed in great detail by Foucault and his followers through the analysis of political authority,[35] productive power explains how citizens come to accept

---

30. E.g., Harvey, *The Enigma of Capital.*
31. Block, "The Ruling Class Does Not Rule"; Hacker and Pierson, "Business Power and Social Policy"; Vogel, *Fluctuating Fortunes*; Bell, "The Power of Ideas"; Bell and Hindmoor, "Taming the City?"
32. Blyth, "Structures Do Not Come with an Instruction Sheet."
33. Barnett and Duvall, "Power in International Politics," 55.
34. Lukes, *Power: A Radical View.*
35. Dean, *Governmentality*; Foucault, *Power/Knowledge*; Rose, *Powers of Freedom.*

the rationalities through which they are governed. Productive power relies on discursive practices wielded by administrators and experts, rather than disciplinary power, which achieves conformity through constraints. Put differently, productive power is networked and fluid not hierarchical and stable: "It works though the co-ordination of actors [rather than] their disciplinary normalization."[36] Insisting on the role dispersed actors have in defining and diffusing values, others have labeled this face of power "circulatory power."[37]

The exercise of power through knowledge and discourse, which becomes internalized by individuals and guides their behavior, is captured by the concept "governmentality."[38] Scholars interested in governmentality study political rationalities, how they engender a specific way of problematizing issues, the technologies that are appropriate to employ, and the role of experts that communicate and translate the political rationalities in order to extend networks. In this, the approach is closely linked to actor-network theory, which postulates that those "who are powerful are not those who 'hold' power in principle, but those who practically define and redefine what 'holds' everyone together."[39]

With this insight and the knowledge that financial institutions are in a structurally privileged position, we can turn productive power away from its initial focus on citizens and study also how governments themselves are defined through social relations. Public officials and representatives from the private sector are in closely intertwined networks that have produced and maintain not just the regulatory approach to finance, but also the industry's and the government's self-conception and tasks.

Indeed, many scholars have noted the importance and fluidity of the networks between financial elites and public officials,[40] and many commentators point to revolving doors and friendships between senior officials. However, the most important effect of revolving doors is not that public officials are more likely to grant political favors to former colleagues, as is widely believed. It is the production of worldviews, meanings, and interpretations that develop from shared experiences.

For Baker, the intellectual and cognitive capture resulting from similar training and preexisting policy paradigms is an important element in the power of the financial industry.[41] The production of such paradigms relies on the technical nature of finance, which requires a continuous exchange between regulators and financial elites.[42] Johnson and Kwak argue most forcefully that the influence of the financial industry rests on the successful

36. Merlingen, "From Governance to Governmentality in CSDP," 152.
37. Seybert, Nelson, and Katzenstein, "Two Faces of Power Again."
38. Foucault, *Sécurité, Territoire, Population.*
39. Latour, "The Powers of Association," 273; see also Latour, *Reassembling the Social.*
40. Braun and Raddatz, "Banking on Politics"; Pagliari and Young, "Leveraged Interests"; Seabrooke and Tsingou, "Power Elites and Everyday Politics in International Financial Reform."
41. Baker, "Restraining Regulatory Capture?"
42. Pagliari and Young, "Leveraged Interests"; Seabrooke and Tsingou, "Power Elites and Everyday Politics in International Financial Reform."

diffusion of an entire financial subculture in the United States: "By 1998, it was part of the worldview of the Washington elite that what was good for Wall Street was good for America."[43]

But productive power concerns not just a general mind-set in favor of finance and light-touch regulation. It is manifested in the production and evolution of specific concepts that shape financial regulation, such as liquidity,[44] solvability, moral hazard,[45] or limited liability.[46] Moreover, in the social studies of finance, a series of studies have demonstrated that the technologies and methods employed in finance have performative effects. Rather than simply describing reality and helping to manage it, these technologies create categories and behavior that bring financial markets in conformity with the models—turning them into a self-fulfilling prophecy.[47] It follows that even at the most technical level, seemingly neutral decisions have considerable effects for the organization of the sector and the relationships between agents within it. This means that disputes over meaning are highly political. However, the evolution of meaning in financial regulation is tilted in favor of the financial industry because of the insulation of policy arenas and the high level of expertise necessary to participate in the discussion.

The first issue—insulation—is in part linked to the technical nature of financial stakes, which makes democratic discussion difficult.[48] Especially in areas where there is little interest from the general public, policymakers prefer to work in close personal contact with the industry, which Michael Moran has referred to as the "wink-and-nod" method of governance or "esoteric politics" in his analysis of financial regulation in the United Kingdom.[49] As Pepper Culpepper has argued, business influence is much greater in "quiet politics" where issues are negotiated without much public attention.[50] But even in areas that are under public scrutiny, such as central banking, delegation to independent decision makers has established itself as a norm to shield decisions about the money supply from public pressures.[51] In some cases, financial institutions nonetheless continue to have access, such as in the Federal Open Market Committee of the Federal Reserve Bank, where banks occupy five of the twelve seats. For Jacobs and King, the insulation of decision making in the Federal Reserve Bank relative to discussions on the TARP program explains the "exceptionally

---

43. Johnson and Kwak, *13 Bankers*, 10; see also Hacker and Pierson, *Winner-Take-All Politics*.
44. Orléan, *Le Pouvoir de La Finance*.
45. Baker, "On the Genealogy of Moral Hazard."
46. Djelic and Bothello, *Limited Liability and Moral Hazard Implications*.
47. Callon, Millo, and Muniesa, *Market Devices*; Cetina and Preda, *The Sociology of Financial Markets*; Lépinay, *Codes of Finance*; MacKenzie, *An Engine, Not a Camera*; MacKenzie, Muniesa, and Siu, *Do Economists Make Markets?*
48. See Callon, Lascoumes, and Barthe, *Agir Dans un Monde Incertain Callon*.
49. Moran, *The Politics of Banking*.
50. Culpepper, *Quiet Politics and Business Power*.
51. Cf. Kydland and Prescott, "Rules Rather Than Discretion."

conciliatory approach of the Fed, which contrasts with the actions of the European Central Bank."[52]

Technicality also contributes in its own right to the evolution of expertise in the financial sector. Admati and Hellwig argue most persuasively that financial representatives use the "mystique" of financial issues to press for inadequate policy solutions. "Anyone who questions the mystique and the claims that are made is at risk of being declared incompetent to participate in the discussion," they argue. "The specialists' façade of competence and confidence is too intimidating. Even people who know better fail to speak up."[53] Confirming that bankers tend to treat public officials and scholars as incompetent and simultaneously admitting that those who would be competent have no interest in forging effective regulation, one former financial representative states, "The people talking publicly don't know what they're talking about. The people who do know aren't talking."[54]

According to Admati and Hellwig, this bias in expertise has enabled representatives from the financial industry to create ambiguities and interpret the challenges of banking regulation as a tension between government intervention and economic growth. Governmental constraints through capital requirements, increased oversight, or a reduction of risk, the banks argue, increases the costs of their business operations and prevents them from lending to the real economy. Admati and Hellwig illustrate how the construction of this trade-off is managed by the financial industry, for example in the discussion about higher capital requirements. In the financial industry's rendition of the issue, increasing capital requirements is equivalent to setting aside money that would otherwise flow to the economy.[55] But this interpretation conflates capital, which is nothing other than equity the bank has obtained from shareholders or owners, with reserve requirements. Capital requirements simply specify the proportion of a bank's assets that have to be financed with unborrowed money. It does not imply anything about the use of unborrowed money. Yet banks frequently create an image of being forced to sit on a pile of unusable cash like Scrooge McDuck. Through a combination of confusions and ambiguities, banks have been able to craft a discourse, which leads public officials to defend risky financial institutions as a means to encourage lending and growth. However, this should not be considered a simple manipulation, but a dynamic linked to the fact that financial regulation needs to respond to the vexing problem of fundamental uncertainty.[56]

What is more, this story is not a one-sided interaction. One might be tempted to turn Foucault's analysis from the political construction of docile

52. Jacobs and King, "Concealed Advantage."
53. Admati and Hellwig, *The Bankers' New Clothes*, 2.
54. Interview, 25 May 2012.
55. Admati and Hellwig, *The Bankers' New Clothes*, 2–3.
56. Nelson and Katzenstein, "Uncertainty, Risk, and the Financial Crisis of 2008"; Taleb, *The Black Swan*.

citizens into the bankers' construction of docile governments. But this would omit an important aspect: the government's motivations for letting the financial industry grow and develop the way it did. As several authors have shown, the integration of financial markets was a deliberate strategy, which government's defended both at home and in international settings.[57] As both Krippner and Streeck emphasize, the turn toward financial deregulation in the 1980s and the increased use of public debt borrowed on international financial markets were direct responses to the failure of governments to provide public support and solve distributional issues in the same way they had been able to during the postwar growth period.[58] Although this reorientation followed from a series of often unrelated choices, it had the effect of replacing the public demand management practiced through Keynesianism until the 1970s with "privatized Keynesianism."[59] These policy shifts were not merely negotiated between the political establishment and financial elites, they also involved considerations toward the medium- and lower-income populations.[60]

At the same time, the growth of public debt made many governments increasingly dependent on financial markets and sensible to technologies such as credit rating agencies, which affected the price at which governments could refinance themselves.[61] In the United States, the two trends are linked: the deregulation of financial markets and the ensuing growth of housing market debt created a differential growth in the United States that made it attractive for foreign investors and made public debt an excessively cheap resource.[62] But even where we observe only one of the two phenomena—an increased reliance on private debt or an increased reliance on public debt—we know that government interests have become tied to the well-being of the financial industry, much of it as a result of their concrete search for new policy solutions in the 1980s.

The interconnectedness of interests and the evolution of knowledge regimes demonstrates the flaws of a "capture perspective" in financial regulation.[63] The main story is not about specific goods that are traded to buy off public officials at any particular time, nor is it about banks "winning out" over overzealous regulators. Even if we find some smoking guns pointing into this direction, it is not at the heart of the story. Rather, over time, the financial industry has been able to construct a policy frame that tied their interests with those of the government. It follows that we need to stop studying the power of the financial industry as something that they hold, store, and use. Instead, we should focus on the "intense activity of enrolling, convincing

57. Mügge, *Widen the Market, Narrow the Competition*; Pauly, *Opening Financial Markets.*
58. Krippner, *Capitalizing on Crisis*; Streeck, *Gekaufte Zeit.*
59. Crouch, "Privatised Keynesianism."
60. Seabrooke, *The Social Sources of Financial Power.*
61. Sinclair, *The New Masters of Capital.*
62. Schwartz, *Subprime Nation.*
63. Cf. Young, "Transnational Regulatory Capture?"

and enlisting" people who contribute to perform social relations defined in the interests of the financial industry.[64] Put more concretely, it turns our perspective around: much of the public outcry in reaction to the crisis has tried to point to incompetent regulators sleeping at the wheel prior to 2007. Understanding the coproduction of knowledge and self-conceptions highlights that not incompetence but unwillingness to regulate the financial industry is the real cause of the buildup to the crisis.

For a comparative perspective, it is important to note that the production of these regimes happens in networks that are in many ways nationally circumscribed.[65] Bankers and representatives from international finance face national policymakers with specific national contingencies. In addition, other actors such as scholars, lawyers, or even public commentators participate in the production and diffusion of knowledge. This implies that no participant single-handedly controls the evolution of stakes. As a result, we observe national variation in the introduction and adaptation of financial concepts, which shape the domestic regulatory context, and this dynamic corresponds to the ways in which liberal ideas are adopted and contested across countries.[66] As scholars of banking regulation have demonstrated, national divergence in the regulation of banking and finance still remains despite their global interconnectedness.[67]

To begin with, the historical timing of banking regulation led to rather detailed oversight procedures in some countries compared to rather permissive contexts in others. In the Scandinavian financial crisis of the 1990s, for example, even though Finland, Norway, Sweden, and Denmark had all deregulated their financial markets, the crisis affected Denmark less than the other three countries. Honkapohja argues that Denmark was helped by the fact that it had been deregulated somewhat earlier than its neighbors, that is, before the boom years of the second half of 1980s.[68] This implied that rules for prudential supervision and banking standards were in place and stricter than elsewhere, so that Danish banks were able to continue raising capital on financial markets, even during the difficult years in the 1990s. By 2008, in turn, the Danish financial sector had grown to twice the size of Danish GDP, as the Danish government was less stringent than its Scandinavian neighbors following their experience of the 1990s.

Second, the fragmentation of the financial sector can create regulatory competition over different types of activities. The timing and evolution of different sectors of activity—retail banking, building societies, investment banking—and the corresponding regulatory arrangements can create very

64. Latour, "The Powers of Association," 273.
65. Bell and Hindmoor, *Masters of the Universe but Slaves of the Market*.
66. Fourcade-Gourinchas and Babb, "The Rebirth of the Liberal Creed."
67. E.g., Busch, *Banking Regulation and Globalization*; Story and Walter, *Political Economy of Financial Integration in Europe*.
68. Honkapohja, "The 1990s Financial Crisis in Nordic Countries," 20.

integrated or fragmented and overlapping networks. In addition, financial institutions can find that they have the possibility to choose their respective regulator for different activities, which leads to regulatory arbitrage that weakens governmental control. We therefore need to know the regulatory landscape and competitive structure of the financial industry in order to evaluate the type of business-government relations that can form.

To summarize, a focus on productive power draws our attention to the multiple sites of knowledge production and the networks that support specific interpretations and self-conceptions of both industry representatives and public officials. To be sure, in the poststructural tradition, the approach provides only a thin theory with no concrete causal mechanisms. Still we gain an understanding of how the balance between the financial industry and governments can shift in favor of one or the other. We can identify a high degree of productive power of the financial industry when the regulatory approach enshrines a low level of constraint, high risk-taking, and fragility of financial institutions as a positive contribution to the economy. I will argue in the empirical discussion that this has been the case especially in the United States, the United Kingdom, and Ireland, to a lesser degree in Denmark and Germany, and least so in France.

The Power of Collective Inaction

Now, if the financial crisis resulted from a buildup of structural features and the interactions of multiple actors who produced asymmetries through knowledge regimes that were willingly performed by the majority of participants, it is almost impossible to attribute clear political responsibility. Indeed early studies of the banking crisis reflected the messy nature of the issue either through a faithful rendition of the chronology of events[69] or by adopting a listlike approach of relevant issues.[70]

For a political analysis of decision making, we would want to know who was involved when, where, and how, in order to get a more precise sense of agency. Following Gourevitch, most studies of crisis management in political economy adopt a coalitional perspective and study which stakeholder groups formed and won out over others.[71] In political studies of recent crisis management, however, organized interests are conspicuously absent.[72] To be sure, several authors have called attention to the rise of new stakeholder groups, such as the financial industry and homeowners, which influence

---

69. E.g., Financial Crisis Inquiry Commission, *The Financial Crisis Inquiry Report*; Regling and Watson, *A Preliminary Report on the Sources of Ireland's Banking Crisis*.

70. E.g., Davies, *The Financial Crisis: Who Is to Blame?*

71. Gourevitch, *Politics in Hard Times*.

72. See Bermeo and Pontusson, *Coping with Crisis*, 21–23; Grant and Wilson, *The Consequences of the Global Financial Crisis*.

policymaking in their favor. But their activities appear to be much less coordinated than was previously the case for organized capital or labor organizations or the agricultural sector.

This holds true whether one looks at formal organizations or informal networks. In the postwar period up to the 1980s, business elites were often described as part of an "inner circle" or "power elite."[73] More recent network studies and sociographic analyses have shown that the close connections between corporate elites are slowly dissolving. Mizruchi argues in a detailed study of the American corporate elite that we no longer see public engagement of corporate leaders jointly, as was common during most of the twentieth century.[74] As a result of concomitant developments such as the weakening of labor organization, less direct state intervention, or the change of corporate governance to a shareholder value principle, firms have become short-termist and the corporate elite fragmented. Although they appear to have more power, individually, than they had in previous decades, "they are either unwilling or unable to mount any systematic approach to addressing even the problems of their own community, let alone those of the larger society."[75] The fragmentation of corporate networks is not just an American phenomenon, it is also visible in countries know as coordinated market economies such as Germany.[76] Only some countries display a remarkable stability of elite networks over time—for example, France where interlinked directorates are relatively stable.[77] Still the recent crisis appears to signal that the general trend in the organization of corporate elites is a decline of joint action.

Although counterintuitive, the weakening of collective action of business leaders is in fact a disadvantage for public authorities seeking to negotiate policy reform. In many cases, collective action of business leaders is solicited by policymakers wishing to construct coalitions and to build on private associations able to quietly arrange proposals and resolve internal conflict.[78] When these counterparties can refuse to participate in such negotiations or threaten to leave policy networks, they are exercising power.[79]

This form of power through nonparticipation has so far been understudied, because it implies reversing our usual questions about power and influence. We tend to think about business power as a successful attempt from private actors to obtain privileges from public actors. Bank bailouts are different, because banking crisis are embedded in the setting of structural dependence discussed above. Once a banking crisis turns into a systemic crisis, public authorities need to work with the financial industry to develop a joint

73. Mills, *The Power Elite*, Useem, *The Inner Circle*.
74. Mizruchi, *The Fracturing of the American Corporate Elite*.
75. Ibid., 5.
76. Höpner and Krempel, "The Politics of the German Company Network."
77. François and Lemercier, *Pulsations of French Capitalism*.
78. Martin and Swank, *The Political Construction of Business Interests*; Woll, *Firm Interests*.
79. Kahler, *Networked Politics*, 12–13.

solution for a collective problem: financial stability. The differential power of the industry plays out when it comes to having the industry participate and carry the costs of the bank rescues. This can only be obtained by committing the financial industry collectively. If financiers can manage to be unresponsive, the government needs to organize the bailout based on taxpayer money. Put more simply, when it comes to carrying costs, not to obtaining privileges, collective inaction can create a substantial advantage for the relevant stakeholders. Indeed, for Deutsch, power is defined as "the ability not to learn" from one's mistakes, to continue operating as usual, "insensitive to the present," while the other person is forced to adapt to the new circumstances.[80] Although harder to grasp, inactive power is the mirror image of active power, depending on how the stakes are framed.[81]

Turned upside down, Olson's *Logic of Collective Action* helps us understand the conditions for collective inaction. Olson famously demonstrated that small groups have an advantage over large groups when it comes to organizing collective action.[82] In particular, the provision of public goods suffers from a collective action dilemma: even if everybody has an interest in the good, self-interested individuals will abstain from contributing to it, if their action cannot be enforced, since they can free ride on the efforts made by everybody else. The incentive to benefit without contributing, that is, free riding, can only be diminished in small groups, where the lack of participation of individual members can be monitored and sanctioned. Small groups with intensive preferences can mobilize easily. Large groups, by contrast, will find it difficult to monitor individual participation and have to share benefits among a larger number of members. They are thus less likely to act collectively, even if all members agree on its benefits.

The same fundamental tension operates during banking crises. Even though all banks can recognize financial stability as a public good, propping up a failing competitor carries costs that they would prefer to avoid. When the failure of one financial institution is connected to the stability of the entire industry, banks need to ask themselves if they are able and willing to find a collective solution to stabilize the sector, or whether they prefer to rely on the government. Through the structural dependence between finance and the government, the situation resembles a collective version of a game of "chicken," where two cars drive full speed toward one another. Although neither wants to end up in a car crash, the driver who swerves off first loses. During a banking crisis, neither the financial industry nor the government wants to see the economy collapse. But if the financial industry knows that

80. Deutsch, *The Nerves of Government*, 111.

81. Lukes, "Power and the Battle for Hearts and Minds," 479–80. The threat of inactivity in conjunction with structural power has been acknowledged in other contexts, such as the recent Eurozone crisis, in which Polish politician Radoslaw Sikorski declared, "I fear Germany's power less than her inactivity" (*Financial Times*, 28 November 2011).

82. Olson, *The Logic of Collective Action*.

the government will not let this happen, their best strategy is to be uncoordinated and benefit from a bank bailout scheme financed entirely through the public budget. Because of their structural importance, the capacity to be collectively inactive ultimately determines the degree of domination of a small banking minority over the general public.

A second step is therefore to understand what shapes the financial industries capacity for inaction. When would we expect it to be strongest? To begin with, the mechanisms known to facilitate collective action should work in favor of joint efforts of the financial industry: the size of the group, the homogeneity of members, and the alternatives available to each of them all matter. If the financial industry of a country is constituted by a large number of firms, financial institutions of very different sizes, or types of activities, or ones that can easily shift their activities abroad while others rely on mainly domestic activities, we would expect them to have difficulties agreeing on a joint strategy. Inversely, a small heterogeneous community, where contributions can be shared equally is more likely to make a collective commitment.

Moreover, collective inaction—as an implicit assumption of collective action theory—has been studied in experimental games aiming the test the implications of Olson's theory. As Ostrom pointed out, the logic of collective action is based on a theory of human behavior that conceives of individual action as self-interested rational choices.[83] Individuals do not participate in collective solution because they can gain from being egotistical. She challenged this "zero-contribution" thesis and argued that participation in collective solutions is in many cases motivated by social norms, which do not follow purely individualistic calculations. Reviewing experimental games and scientific evidence, Ostrom discusses how individuals behave when trying to produce public goods and highlights a number of mechanisms.[84] First, faith in the likelihood of cooperation of other participants makes individuals more inclined to contribute to collective solutions. Second, face-to-face communication considerably increases the likelihood of cooperation. Third, learning about the game increases cooperation (rather than decreasing it, as rational choice theory would posit). Fourth, participants are willing to pay in order to punish others that make below average contributions. Correspondingly, we would expect the financial industry to refuse to contribute collectively to a bailout if each of them (1) believes others will not cooperate, (2) cannot exchange amongst each others directly, (3) have never experienced a comparable situation. Finally (4), we would expect individual banks to be willing to accept expenditures in order to have control mechanisms over the behavior of other banks.

To summarize, in a context of structural dependence, collective inaction becomes the mechanism through which power can be exercised in moments

---

83. Ostrom, "Crowding Out Citizenship."
84. Ostrom, "Collective Action and the Evolution of Social Norms," 140.

of crisis. The production of knowledge regimes where financial institutions are individual units whose social contribution rests on profit maximization pave the way to such nonparticipation, because financial institutions increasingly neglect joint political activities in order to concentrate on their own balance sheets. As a rather classical inquiry into collective action, the study of collective inaction across countries necessitates understanding the nature of the financial sector in each country and the ways in which they were included in the negotiation process.

Breaking Down Power to Study Variations across Countries

The aim of this book is to highlight the importance of business-government relationships for bailout arrangements by studying how power is exercised within this relationship. It is not to explain all variations in the bank support schemes across countries. In the empirical discussion, I will argue that the power balance between the financial industry and governments varied quite substantially across countries.

Some governments felt strongly that the financial industry had not only created a mess but also forced public officials into intervention they were rather embarrassed about. Other governments, in turn, quickly emerged as successful crisis managers who had proven that they were able to weather the storm. Likewise, the financial industry in some countries experienced the crisis as the end of an era, which effectively ended the world they had once known. Others lived through it as a thoroughly unpleasant, yet short-lived experience, which did not change their fundamental advantages. Table 3.1 tries to summarize these subjective appreciations at an aggregate level. It is merely a snapshot of general sentiments in 2009, and most countries tried to correct perceived imbalances in the months and years that followed.

In essence, three countries experience the banking crisis not necessarily as a power struggle, but as common challenge. Power, although exercised by both

TABLE 3.1
Experience of crisis management in 2008–9

		Government	
		unsatisfied	satisfied
Financial industry	satisfied	United States Germany	France Denmark
	unsatisfied	Ireland	United Kingdom

government and the financial industry, created a balanced result in France, Denmark, and Ireland. Unfortunately for the Irish, the balance between government and the financial industry was one of shortcomings and overburdened participants. In the United States and Germany, governments found much to their frustration that they could not get the industry to save themselves and were eventually forced to intervene on terms that were rather favorable to the industry, at least initially. In the United Kingdom, the government took a very proactive approach that did not include negotiating extensively with the industry. The imposed solution was experienced as particularly harsh by the financial industry and helped to portray the British government as a role model in the management of the banking crisis in the early years of the crisis.

The perceived balance or asymmetry of power results from the ways in which the financial industry and the government responded in a context of structural constraints. Table 3.2 summarizes the elements of power discussed in the previous sections. The structural power of financial institutions is high everywhere, but particularly high in Ireland and Denmark. Over time, the productive power of the financial industry has created environments particularly advantageous to the industry in Ireland, and to a lesser degree in the United States and the United Kingdom, but also in Germany and Denmark, and to some degree in France.

In this context, we can then turn to the stakeholder responses during crisis management. When the crisis broke in 2007 and 2008, industry participated in a collective solution only in France and Denmark. The comparison with the other cases shows that this is not simply the result of tight social networks, typically cited for the case of France, or corporatist traditions, as often highlighted in Denmark. Ireland, with equally tight links between financial and political elites failed to produce a collective industry solution, as did Germany, despite a strong tradition of corporatist arrangements and coordination.

TABLE 3.2
Power relationship and actions by country

	United States	United Kingdom	France	Germany	Ireland	Denmark
Structural power	High: finance	High: finance	High: banks	High: banks	Very high: size	Very high: size
Productive power	High	High	Medium	High-Medium	Very high	High-Medium
Industry collective action	No	No	Yes	No	No	Yes
Government response	Yield	Impose	Cooperate	Yield	Yield	Cooperate

In the absence of an industry-led solution, governments in the United States, the United Kingdom, Germany, and Ireland had two options: yield to the pressures or impose their own solution. Only the United Kingdom did the latter.

If we return to Barnett and Duvall's definition of power as "the production, in and through social relations, of effects on actors that shape their capacity to control their fate," we can see that under conditions of high structural and productive power, governments have a diminished capacity to control their fate when the financial industry does not organize collectively.[85] And although the response of the UK government was congratulated in most countries, its overall results are mixed. It had the clear advantage of preventing a collapse of the economy and supporting the industry while at the same time imposing severe constraints. The moral hazard consequences of such a support scheme are much less sizeable than the unconditional or generous support elsewhere. Still the UK scheme was rather costly, and it is most likely to have a fiscal impact that is far more significant than in the United States, for example. Despite their determination, the British government's fate was closely tied to the financial industry as well. To grasp this complexity we need to look at the different elements of the power relationship when we study crisis management.

Implications of Power Differences

At the most general level, the analysis in this book makes the following arguments about the ways in which business-government relations affect bailout arrangements.

1. When the banking sector is capable of organizing collectively and contributing to its own rescue, this helps to contain costs and manage banking crises in a manner least painful to the public budget.

However, the inverse is not true: a banking sector refusing or failing to organize collectively can lead to high costs for the public budget, but the government can also get out of the situation rather well. In fact, when the banking sector relies on the government for its own rescue, the final fiscal costs are a gamble: they can be rather low, as will probably be the case in the United States, dramatically high, as was the case in Ireland, or somewhere in the middle, as in Germany and the United Kingdom. Ultimately, the fiscal impact of bank bailouts depends not just on the relationship between the banking sector and the government, but also on the regulatory approach in each country and the size of the banking sector with respect to the economy.

The collective inaction capacity is nonetheless crucial for the bargaining between the government and the financial industry everywhere. In both

---

85. Barnett and Duvall, "Power in International Politics," 45.

Germany and the United States, the government vigorously tried to make the industry commit collectively and lost their battles. In the United Kingdom, the government quickly determined that they could not expect much from the industry and imposed a government-led solution. In Ireland, both the government and the industry were taken aback by the virulence of the crisis, with neither one acting in time to prevent a collapse.

Since power is a relational quality, the governments in all four countries felt the full effect of the structural advantage of the banking sector. How they responded to being overpowered at the height of the crisis was markedly different, though. The United Kingdom acted most decisively with both a rescue package that was costly to financial institutions and reregulation that was very constraining. Although the fiscal costs of the rescue package are not low, the strength of the sector has been severely curtailed and collective moral hazard is rather well managed. The German government adopted similarly constraining proposals for regulation after the initial crisis period, since they were visibly unhappy with how far the financial industry had been able to twist its arm at the height of the crisis. The United States also adopted a more constraining regulatory approach, but it is uncertain how far-reaching the changes will be once they are implemented. This leads us to a second, more normative argument:

2. When a collective commitment from the financial industry is lacking, it is best to act unilaterally and impose a government solution.

Although a government-imposed solution might not be the least costly alternative, it has the advantage of curtailing the moral hazard of government support. Failing to do so necessitates thorough regulatory reform in the immediate aftermath of the bank support to avoid repeating a similar scenario in the future.

Ireland, finally, was brought so close to the brink that it is futile to analyze it in terms of a power struggle between banks and the government only. In the end, both lost, much to the detriment of the Irish population. In terms of collective action capacity, however, it is instructive to see that Ireland relied on interpersonal ties, a small banking elite, and rather favorable and lenient government oversight. The ties between political and banking elites are somewhat comparable to the French elite, and Ireland should serve as a warning to France. Interpersonal ties imply a certain degree of connivance from policymakers. These conditions may favor collective action capacity in times of crisis, but they also hamper regulatory oversight and risk downplaying the need for further regulatory reform. If France fails to enforce external checks and balances on its financial industry and oversight, it may not be able to stand up the next crisis, especially if it is harsher than the last one. Put more theoretically, the foundations of collective action capacity of the financial industry can have positive and negative effects on public welfare:

3. Coupled with a very unbalanced regulatory approach (i.e., high productive power of the financial industry), collective action of the industry may contribute little to increasing financial stability over time or even work against it.

Conclusion

To summarize, the power of the financial industry rests on structural features and became enshrined in collectively produced knowledge regimes over time. Still, both the financial industry and governments retained discretion over crisis management, as the country comparison demonstrates. Studying their responses draws particular attention to the power of collective inaction exercised by the financial industry in four out of six cases.

This collective inaction is all the more remarkable when one considers the fundamental problem that led policymakers to support private institutions through public money: systemic risk. The following chapter will address the policy discussion in favor of or against bank bailouts to clarify the issues that have been identified as justifications behind governmental intervention. Since these issues concern the financial industry as a whole, the rationale for a collective industry commitment appears to be pressing.

4

From Theory to Practice

Capitalism without financial failure is not capitalism at all, but a kind of socialism for the rich.

—James Grant, "The Fed's Subprime Solution"

To bail out or not to bail out? The fundamental question troubling policymakers seems to be this choice between government support for failing financial institutions or the refusal to intervene. An extensive literature in economics theorizes the disadvantages of government support, most importantly by demonstrating that the possibility of future bailouts leads banks to behave in a less cautious manner. Known as "moral hazard," this problem is at the heart of policy debates about bailouts, and proponents prescribe no intervention in order to maintain stability through market discipline.

More recently, an alternative perspective has called attention to the increasing complexity of the industry and the risk of contagion in financial markets. When banks are highly interconnected, the failure of one bank can threaten the solvency of others that depend on its loans or hold its obligations. In addition, financial markets can fear contagion and withdraw funds from otherwise healthy banks. The costs of the failure of large financial institutions will thus be spread far beyond the original bank and might be detrimental for the entire economy. It is posited that it is best to rescue such institutions, which are classified as those that are "too big to fail," because the alternative—propping up the entire economy—is far more costly.

The tension between the two camps—moral hazard versus too big to fail—has dominated the scientific literature and led to a series of proposals about how to deal with failing financial institutions. Interestingly, the theoretical treatment of bank failures is of little insight for understanding the actual politics of crisis responses. Although those defending market orthodoxy have contributed to the political debates in many countries and shaped the timing and evolution of intervention, no country consistently decided to let the

---

Epigraph: Quote from an article critical of the Federal Reserve's response to the financial crisis.

market discipline the banking sector in 2008. Instead all governments have struggled to save their financial institutions, but with varying approaches and instruments.

Dissecting the scientific debate and the arguments of proponents of both camps is nonetheless instructive, because it clarifies two competing conceptions of financial activities and the role of government intervention. Most important, the moral hazard perspective relies on the imaginary of a competitive setting, where market discipline is the most effective tool to shape the behavior of individual firms. The too-big-too-fail perspective, by contrast, considers that firms are never entirely disconnected from one another and thus cannot behave as isolated units. Rather finance is marked by systemic features, and market discipline is incapable of dealing with systemic risk. Regulatory interventions, including bailouts, respond to this need to deal with the industry as a collective entity.

This chapter presents the theoretical discussion about bank bailouts and discusses how it translated into practical consideration. In the following, the first section introduces the theoretical debate in the studies of moral hazard and of institutions that are too big to fail. The second section gives an overview of the challenges to translate these insights into practice. The third section distinguishes ideal types of bailout approaches by considering containment and reregulation policies jointly.

Bailouts in Theory

Moral hazards and institutions that are too big to fail are both undesirable. In a perfect world, they should not exist and from a theoretical perspective, nobody would claim to be in favor of either one of the two predicaments.[1] And yet, these two problems divide experts into two opposing camps, because one's approach to bank bailouts depends on which one is considered to be more problematic. The primary objective for those focusing on moral hazard is reestablishing market discipline in order to ensure financial stability. Those warning that financial institutions have become too big to fail will push for regulation that can prevent or reduce the damage of bank failures for the rest of the financial system. In addition, they will favor pragmatic intervention that is least costly in times of crisis. Although many acknowledge the coexistence of both problems, the resolution of the dilemma will tend to privilege either market discipline or government intervention, so it is helpful to begin by introducing both approaches and then comparing their theoretical underpinnings.

---

1. From a self-interested perspective, the management of such institutions might of course be in favor. Robert Kindler, a vice chairman at Morgan Stanley, famously ordered a license plate, which read "2BG2FAIL." Sorkin, *Too Big to Fail.*

Moral Hazard

Moral hazard refers to the undesirable side effect of insurance: an individual who knows that the costs of his or her actions will be born by somebody else has a greater tendency to engage in risky behavior. Originally developed in the mid-nineteenth century in the insurance literature, the concept carried a normative valence and referred to increasing fraud or conscious misbehavior of the insured.[2] Today it has turned into one of the most basic concepts in economic theory and is often studied in seemingly neutral terms as a problem of information asymmetry between two contracting parties engaged in risk sharing.[3] The insured knows most about the risky action he or she undertakes, and if another party agrees to support this individual, it will always be confronted with "hidden action."[4] Contrary to "adverse selection," which refers to the fact that insurance is most often sought by those that most need it, the causality in "moral hazard" goes in the opposite direction. Risky behavior increases *because* of insurance protection. As a consequence, a simple solution to moral hazard problems is always to reduce insurance coverage to oblige individuals to carry all or a portion of the costs resulting from their own behavior.

The tension at the center of the moral hazard debate is endemic to all relationships where an individual or collective entity, be it public or private, attempts to alleviate the suffering of others. It runs like a red thread through discussions of welfare reform, workers' compensation, liability law, health policy, bankruptcy and business law, and bank regulation. In political debates, those that invoke moral hazard are generally opposed to those that cite collective responsibilities to prevent or cushion damage incurred by others. Because of the negative incentives created through insurance, inverse reasoning would suggest that "less is more," because individuals and their counterparties would then be responsible for monitoring their choices and behavior.[5]

In financial markets, information asymmetries are commonplace. At the outset, the basic activity of financial markets is to channel money from those that save to those that have productive investment opportunities. As a consequence, activities are constantly done with "other people's money," which implies that those who lend need to have mechanisms to ensure how their money is spent and whether it will be paid back. At the most fundamental level, the information asymmetries endemic to such relationships help to explain financial structure and in particular the role of banks and other

---

2. Baker, "On the Genealogy of Moral Hazard"; Rowell and Connelly, "A History of the Term 'Moral Hazard.' "
3. Djelic and Bothello, *Limited Liability and Moral Hazard Implications.*
4. Arrow, "The Economics of Agency," 38.
5. For discussion see Baker, "On the Genealogy of Moral Hazard."

financial intermediaries in evaluating and monitoring risk.[6] Financial intermediaries can thus help to reduce the risk of moral hazard between two contracting individuals. However, as an institution, they can benefit from insurance themselves and thus create another kind of moral hazard problem. This is for example the case in deposit insurance.

Deposit insurance was a government response to the Great Depression, as a mechanism to prevent bank runs. Bank runs arise when a great number of depositors fear that the failure of a financial institution is imminent and seek to save their deposits by withdrawing them. The fear of failure—well founded or not—affects the immediate solvency of banks and turns into a self-fulfilling prophecy. To avoid such behavior, which can amplify and accelerate banking crises, the US government established the Federal Deposit Insurance Corporation (FDIC) in 1934, an agency that insured deposits up to 100,000 dollars. Even in the case of a bank failure, depositors would retrieve their money. In its first thirty years of existence, only six countries adopted similar institutions, but emulation accelerated in the late 1960s and close to a hundred countries had institutions for deposit insurance by the late 2000s.[7]

Although it may be effective in preventing bank panics, deposit insurance creates moral hazard, since the bank can engage in riskier activities knowing that it will receive government support if things turn sour. Moreover, depositors, who are assumed to impose market discipline on banks by choosing where to put their savings, no longer have incentives to monitor the banks' behavior. During the US savings and loans crisis in the late 1980s, it became clear that banks had indeed used deposits in quite opportunistic manners and engaged in regulatory gambling by moving money from one deposit fund to another, which led to a severe critique of deposit insurance.[8]

The dilemma is even more pressing for large financial institutions, because their failure may create damage to the entire economy. Not only is the number of counterparties in such cases much larger, the failure of a big institution can also trigger a crisis of confidence and lead to contagion throughout the banking sector. Governments can chose to extend credit to such institutions when everybody else is no longer willing to do so, in particular by giving their central banks the mandate to act as a lender of last resort in exceptional circumstances. Such government aid, and other forms of government support given to private institutions, thus create extreme moral hazard problems. Even when government bailouts are not explicitly guaranteed, banks can count on them and engage in risky behavior, knowing that they will not have to carry the full costs in case of failure.

6. See Gertler, "Financial Structure and Aggregate Economic Activity."

7. Demirgüç-Kunt and Detragiache, "Does Deposit Insurance Increase Banking System Stability?"; Demirgüç-Kunt, Karacaovali, and Laeven, "Deposit Insurance Around the World."

8. E.g., Kane, *The S&L Insurance Mess.*

When things go wrong, the picture is bleak. A financial institution that has reaped considerable profits through risky behavior, profits that were privately consumed, will be able to transfer the costs of failure to the public safety net, in other words, the taxpayer. Put differently, the fundamental injustice that can result from moral hazard is the privatization of profits but the socialization of costs.

Too Big to Fail

Why then would governments not let the financial institutions carry the costs of their own poor judgments by letting them fail? According to the too-big-to-fail diagnostic, the societal costs from the failure of these institutions would be so disastrous that governments have no choice but to intervene to rescue them. This may apply not only to financial institutions but also to other entities. According to Silber, the federal rescue of the City of New York, heavily indebted in British pounds in 1914, constituted the first event of a too-big-to-fail intervention.[9] With respect to banking, the argument arose in these terms for the first time explicitly in 1984, when the FDIC decided to fully cover not only all losses for the depositors of Continental Illinois, then the seventh largest bank in the United States, but also the bondholders. In the congressional hearing following this intervention, US congressman Stewart McKinney reportedly asked if Continental Illinois was effectively "too big to fail." Todd Conover, at the time controller of the currency, confirmed this analysis and stated that all of the eleven largest banks would have received the same treatment.

Although unintended, this announcement, and the interpretation that was made of it in the *Wall Street Journal*, proved to have considerable wealth effects for the eleven banks and corresponding negative effects for the banks considered "too small to save."[10] The interest rates the largest banks paid on their deposits and borrowings no longer reflected the full risk of bankruptcy, which led to higher profits. In addition, the banks had less incentives to avoid risky operations, which indirectly also affected their returns.

As a result of the Savings and Loans Crisis and the lessons learned from Continental Illinois, the federal government passed the Federal Deposit Insurance Corporate Improvement Act (FDICIA) in 1991. The act considerably strengthened the authority of the FDIC and gave it the authority to intervene early on to limit interbank credit exposure. Most important, it obliged the FDIC to determine the least costly resolution procedure, which had the implicit goal of eliminating the belief that large financial institutions would

---

9. Silber, *When Washington Shut Down Wall Street*. The City of New York was bailed out a second time under Gerald Ford in December 1975.
10. O'Hara and Shaw, "Deposit Insurance and Wealth Effects."

be bailed out. The new act did include an exception in the case of systemic risk, however, which could be invoked by a relatively complex procedure.[11]

Systemic risk refers to potential damage one institution's failure can create for the financial system as a whole, for example, through "spillover effects leading to widespread depositor runs, impairment of public confidence in the broader financial system, or serious disruptions in domestic and international payment and settlement systems."[12] This notion is crucial to understanding what it means to have institutions that are too big to fail. If it were simply a matter of size, government intervention to break up financial institutions would seem to constitute an obvious solution. Former chairman of the Federal Reserve Alan Greenspan summarized this approach in the sentence: "If they are too big to fail, they are too big."[13] Yet the difficulty is not necessarily the actual size of the institution, but the size of the damage induced by its failure to the rest of the economy.

Continental Illinois for instance, even if its story is well known today, would have been nominated by only few observers at the time as a likely candidate for a too-big-to-fail policy.[14] It was not its size itself that was striking, but its interconnectedness and exposure to other financial institutions. As the result of its aggressive growth strategy based on commercial lending, it was heavily exposed to risky investments and sported the highest loans-to-assets ration in the United States in 1981. In July 1982, Continental was fatally struck when Penn Square Bank, from whom Continental had purchased an extraordinary $1 billion in assets, failed. Despite efforts to stabilize itself the following year, Continental did not reestablish its credibility and faced a bank run in May 1984. Fearing contagion throughout the economy, the government chose to intervene, took over Continental's bad loans, acquired 80 percent ownership of the bank, provided it with liquidity, and replaced the bank's management.[15] After the experience of the secondary effects of Penn Square's failure, the FDIC deemed that Continental was too interconnected to fail. Roughly twenty-three hundred banks had funds invested in Continental, almost half of which were well in excess of the insured amount, and sixty-six had invested more than 100 percent of their equity capital.[16]

The banking industry returned to normal in the 1990s, according to some observers as a result of or at least concomitantly with the passage of the

11. A two-thirds majority of the board of governors of the Federal Reserve and the directors of the FDIC has to vote in favor. In addition the secretary of the treasury must approve and document evidence of systemic risk, which is subject to review from the General Accounting Office. Moreover, the banking industry has to pay the costs of such a bailout through an emergency assessment to the FDIC as a proportion of each bank's tangible assets.

12. Moyer and Lamy, "Too Big to Fail," 21.

13. Cited in McKee and Lanman, "More Greenspan Says U.S. Should Consider Breaking Up Large Banks." The quote is also attributed the economist Hyman Minsky.

14. McCollom, *The Continental Affair.*

15. FDIC, *History of the Eighties—Lessons for the Future.*

16. Ibid., 250.

FDICIA.[17] But regulators continued to be worried about the risks of too big to fail. In 2004, Federal Reserve Bank of Minneapolis president and vice president Gary Stern and Ron Feldman published a book arguing that the problem had grown more pressing over time and that the FDICIA would be unable to counteract it because of the systemic risk exception.[18] In particular, they argued that increasing pressure weighs on regulators because of six developments. First, consolidation by the banking industry has created much larger financial institutions than had existed in the past. Second, the number of such institutions has increased. Third, new technology allows even smaller institutions to play important roles in the payments systems and can risk disrupting these. Fourth, with the growth of capital markets, banks rely increasingly on uninsured credit to fund their operations. Fifth, the complexity of financial operations can make their resolution more difficult. Sixth, the expansion of activities that financial institutions can now engage in may require expanding the government safety net to nonbank activities.[19] Put differently, they considered the systemic risks emanating from financial institutions unmanageable within the framework at the time, whether one refers to them as too big, too interconnected, or too complex to fail.[20]

Fault Lines and Policy Prescriptions

To understand the underlying assumptions in each perspective, it is helpful to consider how scholars and experts understand political decision making during financial crises. In this context, what are the interests policymakers pursue when considering whether to bail out financial institutions? According to Stern and Feldman, there are three possible motivations: first, they are worried about the economywide consequences of a failure; second, they concentrate on personal advantage; third, they seek to control the allocation of credit.[21] The authors argue that control over the direction of credit may play a role in countries where the government has a tradition of owning banks and where banks are more central intermediaries, which is not so much the case in the United States. They acknowledge that personal gain might be important for policymakers, who would then overstate the risk of systemic consequences in order to serve their friends, financiers, careers, or out of "preference for a low-stress life," but argue that such calculations are not central, at least in the United States. For them, the concern about systemic risk is the most important motivation. Contrary to personal rewards, they thus suggest that policymakers seek to act in the public interest. Indeed,

17. Mishkin, "How Big a Problem Is Too Big to Fail?" 997.
18. Stern and Feldman, *Too Big to Fail*.
19. Ibid., ch. 6.
20. Herring and Carmassi, "The Corporate Structure of International Financial Conglomerates."
21. Stern and Feldman, *Too Big to Fail*, 43–59.

in many other domains, the government has come to act as the ultimate risk manager in the public interest, even in the antistatist US tradition.[22]

Many analysts do not share this benign view. In fact, scholarship in economics is firmly rooted in a public choice perspective, which considers public and private actors as utility-maximizing self-interested individuals. Bailouts, in such a perspective, are better understood as the result of favoritism or corrupt relationships between the financial institutions and the regulators. This accusation of "cronyism" was central to the analysis of bailouts during the Asian financial crisis and has returned in the recent crisis in a more mitigated version.[23] According to such a perspective, arguments and discourse based on systemic risk are self-serving, and one should discount explanations based on "a perfect storm" or an "impending crisis," considered as pure rhetoric in order to justify intervention.[24]

Ultimately, however, the underlying motivations are not as central to the dilemma as the mechanism that keeps it in place. This, essentially, can be summarized as a commitment problem, as Stern and Feldman lay out.[25] They argue that policymakers are keenly aware of the risks and costs of explicit protection and will commonly make a pledge not to come to the rescue in difficult times, in order to allow the market to discipline financial institutions.[26] Such commitments are future-oriented, since they reduce moral hazard and provides long-term benefits. However, when push comes to shove, governments have to manage the short-term consequences of failure. Whether for private or public interest reasons, the short-term benefits of saving the economy will be greater than the long-term benefits of upholding market discipline, so that creditors are led to discount "no bailout" pledges for institutions that are too big, too interconnected, or too complex to fail. Put simply, even though everybody may agree about the negative long-term consequences of bailouts, the short-term implications of failure are ultimately more pressing and financial institutions know this and behave accordingly. This time inconsistency and credibility problem has received a lot of attention in monetary policy with respect to inflation targeting.[27]

As this discussion shows, most authors acknowledge that both moral hazard and too-big-to-fail problems exist, but they may differ with respect to their underlying assumptions about the functioning of political decision making. More important, however, experts differ in which problem they consider to be more fundamental, which is reflected in the policy proposals put

22. Moss, *When All Else Fails.*
23. Chang, "The Hazard of Moral Hazard."
24. E.g., Congleton, "On the Political Economy of the Financial Crisis and Bailout of 2008–2009"; Reinhart, "A Year of Living Dangerously."
25. Stern and Feldman, *Too Big to Fail,* 11–22.
26. Gerald Ford had famously been quoted to refuse to rescue the City of New York in 1975 with the words "drop dead." He later denied the charges, long after having granted the bailout. Roberts, "Infamous 'Drop Dead' Was Never Said by Ford."
27. Kydland and Prescott, "Rules Rather Than Discretion."

forward to resolve the dilemma. Schematically speaking, one can distinguish three approaches. The extreme orthodox view holds that the too-big-to-fail phenomenon is a direct result of moral hazard created through government intervention and stopping government action will fix the problem. A moderate market-discipline approach seeks instead to fix the incentive structure for interconnected banks in order to eliminate too big to fail through intelligent design of bank regulation. Finally, a pessimistic view holds that the problem can only be solved when one addresses the too-big-to-fail problem through prudential regulation.

The extreme orthodox view is founded in the belief that complete market discipline is the most reliable guarantee of stability. Financial instability is considered to be the direct result of public safety nets, which encourages banks to take on unreasonable risk. A solution to the too-big-to-fail problem would therefore be to revert to a completely private and competitive banking sector, with no regulation and no central bank in charge of issuing currency and acting as a lender of last resort.[28] Referred to as "free banking," the approach has long been considered an economic oddity, but has made it into the political campaigns of US presidential candidate Ron Paul.[29] Although an interesting thought experiment, it is difficult to see how the risk monitoring of individual financial institutions will be able to respond to crises that result from so-called "external shocks," that is, those not created directly by the risky behavior of the banks themselves. As in health insurance, less protection can only increase responsible behavior for difficulties the individual can actually control or avoid.

A more moderate approach acknowledges the positive effects of public safety nets, for example in preventing bank runs and limiting contagion. It nonetheless concentrates on reestablishing market discipline through a series of devices. On the one hand, it attempts to reestablish the credibility of public officials pledging not to bail out banks. Similar to solutions advocated in monetary policy, such an approach includes the appointment of "conservative" regulators and a firm set of rules fixing the conditions for intervention rather than discretionary protection.[30] On the other hand, proposals attempt to organize a possible intervention in a way that make the costs of failure high for those responsible for risk taking but that protect those that would simply be "a victim" of contagion. Others advocate, for example, letting the first bank fail, but intervening to prop up others afterward.[31] Although many of these proposals are sensible, they appear to be overly optimistic. Pure signaling and the threat of cost sharing is not enough to prevent the failure of

28. Leeson, "Review of Gary Stern and Ron Feldman, Too Big to Fail."

29. Hayek, *Denationalization of Money*; White, *The Theory of Monetary Institutions.*

30. See Rogoff, "The Optimal Degree of Commitment to an Intermediate Monetary Target."

31. Mayer, "Should Large Banks Be Allowed to Fail?"; Mishkin and Strahan, "What Will Technology Do to Financial Structure?."

financial institutions, and once a crisis hits it is rather difficult to isolate those responsible (or even "first") from those that are affected as a consequence. One is always smarter with hindsight, but it is striking to read Mishkin's review of Stern and Feldman's analysis, arguing that the problem is overstated and that banking regulation in 2006 is well equipped to deal with institutions that are too big to fail.[32]

The pessimistic approach therefore states that the moral hazard problem cannot be solved if one does not address too big to fail first. This requires increasing, not reducing, public authority, in particular macro prudential regulation and supervision.[33] On the one hand, a governmental approach includes early intervention, strict capital requirements, and the option of shutting down insolvent banks early, when they still have sufficient assets to repay their creditors.[34] On the other hand, banks are required to contribute to their own resolution, either by establishing wind-down plans or by contributing to a safety fund that would finance emergency intervention.[35] The pessimistic view is thus a government-focused approach, which holds that the market cannot solve the tension between moral hazard and too big to fail.

Translating Theory into Practice

The well-structured scholarly debate contributed little to guide policymakers in the fall of 2008. Faced with the imminent collapse of their financial systems, governments all over the industrial world rushed to prop up their banks. To be sure, the intellectual framework did shape policy debates, most importantly in legislative discussions and in the media. Politicians and regulators also agreed that too much and too extensive intervention would send negative signals and tried their utmost to limit government support. But the challenge for governments in the fall of 2008 was not to decide whether or not to bail out their banking sectors, it was determining how and with what instruments. Although many saw the failure of Lehman Brothers as an attempt to teach the market discipline by refusing to intervene, it is better understood as the resignation of the US administration, which felt that it had no more instruments at its disposal that were politically feasible.

For analyzing bailout practices, it is helpful to distinguish three policy phases: (1) During immediate containment, emergency measures are adopted to avoid the spread of or minimize the adverse effects of a banking

32. Mishkin, "How Big a Problem Is Too Big to Fail?"

33. Borio, "Implementing the Macroprudential Approach to Financial Regulation and Supervision"; Brunnermeier et al., *The Fundamental Principles of Financial Regulation*.

34. Benston and Kaufman, "The Intellectual History of the Federal Deposit Insurance Corporation Improvement Act of 1991."

35. E.g., Herring, "Wind-Down Plans as an Alternative to Bailouts"; Moss, "An Ounce of Prevention."

crisis. (2) During efforts to stabilize the financial sector, sometimes referred to as restructuring, policymakers strive to rehabilitate financial institutions by restoring their capital positions and resolving bad assets. (3) Finally, in a structural reform phase, governments review laws and regulation that are said to have led to the crisis and attempt to introduce reforms.[36] During the containment phase, government intervention initially resembles fire fighting. In the second and third phase, the theoretical debates influence policy decisions by providing perspectives on the responsibilities of the financial industry and possible punishment that need to be attached to government support.

Fire fighting

During some of the earliest failures, when there was no generalized sense of crisis yet, it was possible to observe the last flickers of an approach based on market orthodoxy. Germany's Peer Steinbrück was one of the first finance ministers facing a bank failure when the IKB Deutsche Industriebank announced its extensive exposure to the US housing market crisis on 28–29 July 2007. Without a practitioner background in finance, he declares that he assumed market discipline would be the most appropriate response, even if this meant that IKB would go under. Discussing the issue with the head of the German central bank and the financial regulators as well as the main industry representatives, he asked: "Would a painful break with IKB not be better than dragging out the agony?" The response was unanimously negative, he remembers,

> I do not remember a single voice recommending this. On the contrary: there was a consensus that such an insolvency would not only have incalculable consequences and trigger a domino effect in the entire banking sector, it would also severely damage the image of Germany as a financial location if we would be the first to let a bank crash and burn.[37]

Steinbrück remembers being challenged about his change of heart by citizens who argued that a market economy should punish those that had gambled too high. According to him, they only began to appreciate the "highly uncomfortable situation" when he listed the number of institutional and private investors that would have been affected, including possibly a large number of small saving banks or occupational insurance associations.

His British colleague, Alistair Darling agreed early on that banks cannot be allowed to fail like regular companies, because "like dominos, if one fails, it will take others with it."[38] But when the British government realized that Northern Rock risked failing as a result of the liquidity crisis in the summer of 2007,

36. For discussion see Klingebiel and Laeven, "Managing the Real and Fiscal Effects of Banking Crises."

37. Steinbrück, *Unterm Strich*, 198.

38. Darling, *Back from the Brink*, 21.

they were divided about the most appropriate response. Darling and Cullum McCarthy, Britain's chief financial regulator, urged the Bank of England to provide liquidity, but Mervyn King, governor of the Bank of England, advocated a more individualized approach. King, who Darling describes as a "bookish and an academic economist,"[39] had worked as professor of economics at the London School of Economics before joining the Bank of England.[40] Focusing on the risk of moral hazard, King wanted to establish the value of assets Northern Rock owned in order to determine what capital they needed. He was concerned about easy liquidity provision and wanted to apply a penalty interest rate in order to make sure banks would use it only as a last resort.

For the UK government, a quicker solution seemed necessary, all the more when depositors began a run on Northern Rock after they had learned that the Bank of England would provide it with liquidity support on Friday 14 September. To stop a panic, the government announced that it would guarantee all the deposits of retail customers and institutional investors. During a meeting with Henry Paulson, which had coincidentally been scheduled that same weekend, the US secretary of the treasury insisted that the Bank of England did not seem to measure the extent of the crisis, quipping: "Your guy Mervyn has a high pain threshold. I hope you have, too."[41]

Of course, decision makers everywhere were aware of the risks of government intervention. Any aid extended to one bank might have to be repeated for other banks, and this would clearly exceed the capacity of public budgets everywhere. And yet, a hands-off approach was ill equipped to deal with the enormous costs generated daily as financial institutions began to stumble. Mergers of failing institutions with healthy ones became increasingly difficult to arrange, not only because the troubled institutions contained considerable risk that was impossible to measure precisely, but also because healthy firms were more and more difficult to find. As Kevin Warsh, member of the Federal Reserve's board of governors put it: "We were running out of buyers before we were running out of sellers."[42]

By the fall of 2008, it had become clear that the private sector would be unable to stem the wave of failures. In addition, many of these mergers required additional government guarantees, such as a backstop on the losses of Bear Stearns provided by the US government to JP Morgan Chase in March 2008. British prime minister Gordon Brown summarized the sentiment at the height of the crisis:

> Reading the latest grim data about the state of British banks, I knew that doing nothing was not an option. We were days away from a complete

39. Ibid., 14.
40. Previously, King had also been a visiting professor at Harvard University and MIT, where he shared an office with the future governor of the Federal Reserve, Ben Bernanke, at the time an assistant professor.
41. Darling, *Back from the Brink*, 29.
42. Cited in Wessel, *In FED We Trust*, 17.

banking collapse. . . . Economic orthodoxy was proving irrelevant; the market seemed intent not on self-correction, but on self-destruction.[43]

In an interview, a French official declared, annoyed by a question about the motivation for the government's choices:

> Everything went so fast during these days. We desperately needed to buy time. Then the British government announced it would recapitalize their banks. We came to a consensus that this was the best approach. We had no time to sit down. Prices dropped every day. The situation was extremely serious; we were in meetings day and night. These are not rational decisions, like scholars tend to assume.[44]

Discussions were similar in the United States, where the legislative passage of the proposed TARP billed pitted Republicans pleading for market orthodoxy against Democrats who largely supported the proposal of the administration. When Senator Richard Shelby tried to insist on the economic doctrine advocated by the profession in a key meeting in the Oval Office, President George Bush interrupted him, "No, this is a situation where we need to act. We do not have the time to have hearings with a bunch of economists."[45] The "whether or not" question had given way to "how?"

Crime and Punishment

Bailout decisions are made with great urgency, but a crucial issue cutting across the choice of instruments is whether or not the financial industry should be punished for its past choices. Should a government simply throw a lifeline to the drowning financial sector, or does it need to reprimand those responsible in an effort to keep the situation from repeating itself? The normativity carried by the debate about moral hazard may not lead government to let the industry fail, but it returns through the backdoor: by determining the degree of punishment that should accompany a bailout. But before discussing punishment, we need to return to the crime that financial institutions are accused of in the context of a bailout.

In well-functioning markets, poor judgment and risky behavior leads to the failure of a company. Punishment through market discipline is thus quite simple and intuitive: banks are closed or taken over by another bank, which means that management is fired and equity holders lose much of their investment. All those responsible for making decisions thus have strong incentives to monitor their behavior and environment. Preventing failure through a bailout not only eliminates these incentives, it also uses public money to stabilize the banks, and thus creates massive redistribution within society.

43. Brown, *Beyond the Crash*, xvii–xix.
44. Interview, 12 April 2010.
45. Cited in Paulson, *On the Brink*, 298.

Moreover, the redistribution benefits the rich and is carried equally by the rest of society, including the poor, which has led Stiglitz to decry the US bail-outs as the "robbery of the American people."[46]

Such a perspective considers banks as individual players that should be accountable for their (poor) rational decisions. One line of defense against these accusations points out that financial institutions did not have all the sufficient information about their decisions, because bundled investment products and faulty ratings made risky products appear as safe investments. Since everybody used these products and made considerable profit, a bank might have put its competitiveness on the line by investing into equally highly rated, but less profitable products. Former CEO of Citigroup, Chuck Prince, famously summarized this pressure by stating, "As long as the music is play-ing, you've got to get up and dance."[47] Another, more urgent line of defense cited by many financial institutions is that they did not put into danger the solvency of their institutions, but that they are simply facing a liquidity crisis. While solvency is the responsibility of an individual institution, liquidity is a market phenomenon on which they are dependent. Financial institutions can fail because they no longer have access to liquidity, but it is not "their fault" in the same way solvency is.

Solvency refers to the capacity of an institution to meet its long-term fixed expenses, that is, pay its debts. A financial institution whose assets have de-preciated in value to a point where they are no longer sufficient to meet the liabilities is considered insolvent. Liquidity, by contrast, merely refers to the capacity to monetarize one's assets. During a liquidity crisis, financial institu-tions are unable to sell assets to meet their short-term debt as it falls due. A credit crunch on money markets can thus transform previously liquid into illiquid assets and lead to cash flow insolvency. Individual institutions may have highly valuable assets but would nonetheless fail if they do not gain ac-cess to additional liquidity. Because liquidity is a characteristic of the market, not (just) the balance sheet of the bank, it is perceived as more legitimate for governments to intervene to allow the market to function as in normal times, to prevent the failures of financial firms that would result from a li-quidity crunch. But even in this case, open-ended liquidity provision will lead banks to rely on it and to stop preparing for changes in liquidity. As Farhi and Tirole argue, a bank's choice to expose itself to liquidity risks is part of its strategy and changes with the likelihood of public liquidity provision.[48] In all cases, one can thus argue that government aid should come with some costs in order to avoid distorting the incentive structure.

---

46. Stiglitz, *Freefall.*

47. Henry Paulson remembers Prince acknowledging that he could not escape these pres-sures despite knowing about the risks, "Basically he asked 'Isn't there something you can do to not make us take these risks?'" Paulson, *On the Brink,* 70.

48. Farhi and Tirole, "Collective Moral Hazard, Maturity Mismatch, and Systemic Bailouts."

Not all bailout approaches share this perspective. According to some, attempting to fix an incentive structure in times that are clearly not "normal" will do more harm than good. If the main objective is to prevent a collapse of the economy and to do so without taking the entire financial sector into government control, then aid has to be designed in way that makes it acceptable to the affected financial institutions. Mandatory recapitalization, for example, that will be forced even on healthy financial institutions can deteriorate their situation if it is too costly. A European central banker remembers that initial discussions always revolved around combining aid with "punishment," but the situation got too dire too quickly: "I am convinced the concept of moral hazard is useless in times of crisis."[49] If you pull somebody out of the water, is it useful to slap them once they come into the boat in order to dissuade them to risk falling in again?

There are different ways of making bailouts carry costs for those saved. To begin with, the government support provided has a price tag, which can be fixed low or high. Companies have to pay an interest on liquidity support, will have to pay dividends in order to buy back the securities held by governments after capital injections, and typically pay a fee for being covered by a public guarantees.

In addition, governments can attach conditions to their aid. Participation in recapitalization schemes, for example, has sometimes been tied to the requirement to maintain lending, to corporate governance changes including board participation, to changes in the remuneration policy and executive compensation, to maintenance of employment levels, or to an assessment of the bank's dividend policy.[50] An important matter of degree is always whether the conditionality of aid is accepted as a code of conduct or with precise surveillance mechanisms.

The pricing of aid and its conditionality is a way of inserting costs at the time of the bailout. Another way of making the banking industry pay is not to insist on high costs of the aid itself, but to use the aid to advance on and justify reregulation in its aftermath. This reregulation can entail structural reforms of the functioning of the banking sector: for example, by raising capital requirements, limiting leveraging, or establishing liquidity requirements. It can also address the resolution mechanisms of financial institutions, in particular those that are too big to fail.[51] In addition, a government can establish that the likelihood of a future bailout is not zero and make financial institutions contribute to a fund that will be used for their rescue in the future, similar to an insurance fund.

The different approaches to punishment reflect different believes about functioning markets. Those concentrating on immediate costs and on fixing

49. Interview, 10 December 2012.

50. Committee of European Banking Supervisors, *Analysis of the National Plans for the Stabilisation of Markets.*

51. French et al., *The Squam Lake Report.*

TABLE 4.1
Approaches to bank accountability

| | | Reregulation | |
		No	Yes
Conditions and constraints	No	Free bailout	Rescue now, pay later
	Yes	Discourage	Discourage and punish

the incentive structure tend to believe that markets can function properly if left alone. The culprit is the government for disturbing market discipline, and the only way to fix it is to do so by upholding market mechanisms through the imposition of costs. Moreover, they would urge a "no more bailouts" policy, where governments have to make sure they are credible in announcing that this will not happen again in the future. On the opposite side, market pessimists would argue that the market will never function orderly in all circumstances and no amount of fixing the incentive structure will do the trick. They would therefore advocate preparing for the next meltdown, in particular, in order to make sure the ultimate costs are not carried by the general public.

If we cross attitudes toward the financial sector at the time of the bailout and in the period of potential reregulation, we can see four different possibilities. If governments attach no or only few conditions to their bank support schemes, they may have decided to address bank responsibility through reregulation and future commitments. Other bailout designs may favor high levels of conditions to discourage financial institutions from taking the support offered in order to make sure only the most desperate one will actually seek out help. This approach can be combined with stringent reregulation, a double punishment approach. If neither conditions nor reregulation follows from rescue packages, we can consider the bailout to be a free lunch for the banking industry, where they got off the hook and are not held accountable.

It is thus possible to characterize variation in bailouts by the way in which containment policies are linked to reregulation. Considering bailouts and reregulation jointly helps us envision different approaches to banking sector policies that reflect the theoretical distinction arising from economic thinking: while some governments emphasize fixing the incentive structure weighing on banks in order to prevent future bailouts, others focus on preparing for the next bailout by putting into place ex ante burden-sharing arrangements.

Conclusion

Moral hazard is the most fundamental concept in the theory of bailouts, but it is curiously sidelined when governments face imminent bank failures.

The interconnection of financial institutions prevents reasoning in terms of individual behavior and incentive structures. The theoretical debates are nonetheless reflected in bailout approaches to punishment. Market optimists insist on fixing incentive structures while market pessimists insist on reregulation. Depending on the emphasis on conditionality or reregulation, we can distinguish four different approaches to bank rescues. In addition to the ways in which financial institutions contributed financially toward the bailout of their industry, we need to consider how and when they were held responsible for the malfunctioning of their activities, in other words, whether they had to meet tough conditions in accepting government aid and whether they were subjected to regulatory constraints in the period following the bailout. For a long-term evaluation of business power, these issues need to be reviewed jointly.

The scientific debate has made clear that there are two competing conceptions of the functioning of financial markets, which necessarily leads to contradictory policy recommendations. While the moral hazard perspectives consider financial markets as competitive markets where market discipline is the most effective way to encourage low risk taking of individual firms, too-big-to-fail perspectives highlight the systemic nature of finance and thus adopt a more holistic approach to financial markets. According to the later perspective individual choices affect not just the firm that makes them, but also others in a way that is impossible to predict entirely. These externalities cannot easily be integrated into individual behavior and have to be dealt with as an industrywide issue. The fundamental distinction is thus whether the financial industry is a collection of individual firms or a whole that is greater than its parts. In the crisis management of 2008, we will see that most industries argued the former, while policymakers were urgently aware that it is actually the later.

In the empirical chapters that follow, we will study collective strategies. For the central argument of this book, the comparison between the United States and the United Kingdom provides the weakest evidence, since the industry in neither country ended up developing a collective response. Because of the size and the importance of the two financial sectors, we will nonetheless begin by comparing these two bailout schemes in order to study how governments react in the absence of collective industry mobilization. In fact, governments have two options: they can try to accommodate the industry with favorable conditions for a government-led bailout or impose a more stringent policy response on an unwilling industry. The French-German and the Danish-Irish comparisons then highlight that the financial industry does sometimes propose a collective response. The goal of these two empirical chapters is to discuss under which conditions this is possible.

The United States and the United Kingdom

This is really cheap capital!

—Vikram Pandit, CEO Citigroup, when confronted
with TARP recapitalization details

Wall Street and the City of London are arguably the two most important global financial centers and both the United States and the United Kingdom pride themselves on being liberal markets where government policy supports capital market finance. To those concerned about the undue power of the traditional banking elite, the capital market systems in the two Anglo-Saxon countries were considered the ideal to strive for, since competition supposedly replaced the importance of insider networks.[1]

Historically, the financial markets in both countries developed early and without direct government support or ownership. As a result, the banking sector was traditionally fragmented into different types of retail functions as well as geographically. Although sectorwide associations for the banking industry exist, relationships between the senior management of the banks and the regulators are important for business-government relationships in both countries. In addition to their large capital markets, both the United States and the United Kingdom have independent central banks with discretion over monetary policy. In times of crises, the central banks can choose to intervene quickly. The United Kingdom had thus a policy lever different from its neighbors in the Eurozone. As mentioned above, both countries used this option in a comparable manner, letting their respective money supply grow more than twice its size in the fall of 2008.[2]

With respect to government intervention, approaches to prop up the financial sector appear somewhat similar in both countries at a first glance.

Epigraph: In a meeting with the US administration, on 13 October 2008, Pandit added, "I just did the numbers on the back of an envelope: this is very inexpensive capital!" Cited in Wessel, *In FED We Trust*, 239.

1. E.g. Rajan and Zingales, *Saving Capitalism from the Capitalists*.
2. Stolz and Wedow, "Extraordinary Measures in Extraordinary Times," 16–17.

Governments intervened quite forcefully and did not shy away from breaking up and even nationalizing ailing institutions, although the language used to explain intervention was somewhat different.[3] However, when one regards the terms of the comprehensive bank support schemes in both countries, one can see that the US bailout package was much more favorable to the interest of the financial sector than the one in the United Kingdom, both in terms of pricing and in terms of conditions and design. In addition, while the US recapitalization was imposed on all banks, the United Kingdom one was voluntary, thus stigmatizing those banks that benefited from it.

This difference in approach can be explained by the structure of the banking industry, their status, and their capacity for collective action and inaction. In particular, the United States has a large investment banking industry, which fell outside of the purview of the more traditional banking regulation. In this particular segment, which really constitutes the heart of modern finance, the financial sector had heavyweight institutions that the US government sought to accommodate when designing its intervention. The UK government, by contrast, abandoned its attempts to let the industry speak for its collective interests and simply imposed the solution they had developed. This government-led solution was particularly hard for the weakest institutions

As the discussions of structural and productive power have highlighted, it is helpful to review the structure of the financial sector and its exposure to the crisis in both countries before discussing the respective bank support schemes. We will then turn to the way in which the financial industry coordinated amongst itself and interacted with the government. A final section assesses the bailout schemes comparatively.

Financial Systems in the United States and the United Kingdom

The US banking industry was traditionally quite fragmented, both regionally and across segments. Private banks were chartered by the states and interstate banking only developed in the 1980s and 1990s. Insurance was state-regulated as well and banking regulation was organized according to industry segments. To overcome the fragmentation, banks increasingly developed holding companies in the second half of the twentieth century that allowed them to combine activities in separate markets, in particular after the Riegle-Neal Interstate Banking Act of 1994. Associating retail banking with investment banking in securities markets was prohibited by the Glass

---

3. UK chancellor of the exchequer Alistair Darling remarks of the US intervention to save Freddie Mac and Fannie Mae: "It was not called 'nationalization' but rather 'conservatorship.' . . . Whatever it was called, 5 trillion USD of American housing debt now belonged to the US taxpayer." Darling, *Back from the Brink*, 117.

Steagall Act of 1933, which also established the FDIC, a public agency which issues a public guarantee on deposits and is responsible for unwinding banks that are failing. Liquidating a bank was thus well organized and quite common during times of economic downturn, in particular during the savings and loans crisis of the late 1980s.

The prohibition of universal banking through the Glass Steagall Act was repealed by the Gramm-Leach-Bliley Act of 1999, which allowed the creation of holding companies across industry segments. This act, together with others such as the Commodities Futures Modernization Act of 2000, marked an increasing trend toward the deregulation of financial markets in the decade prior to the crisis. The financial sector had become an ever-growing part of the economy, producing highly sophisticated instruments, very rapid transactions, and a vast geographical extension of activities.[4] As a result, the profits made from financial activities have increased dramatically and overtaken profits made in service or manufacturing sectors in the mid-1990s, a trend referred to as the financialization of the US economy.[5]

In this context, a very large market for asset-backed securities emerged, in particular ones that insured and bundled mortgages. The US housing market had experienced a remarkable rise starting in the 1990s, when the Federal Reserve was holding its policy interest rates at usually low levels. Encouraged by regulation to support home ownership, even for low-income families (which had to rely on so-called "subprime" mortgages), and by the implicit guarantee of mortgages insured by the government-sponsored Federal National Mortgage Association ("Fannie Mae") and the Federal Home Loan Mortgage Corporation ("Freddie Mac"), asset-backed securities became an attractive investment and quickly became part of most banks portfolios. Together, Fannie Mae and Freddie Mac held about 60 percent of mortgage-backed securities. In June 2008, their combined debt and obligations totaled $6.6 trillion, exceeding the total publicly held debt of the US government by $1.3 trillion.[6]

The UK financial industry's development is in many ways comparable. Traditionally a highly segmented market, British banks used to specialized in different parts of the banking business (clearing banks, building societies, etc.). However, banking regulation was far lighter throughout most of the twentieth century, in great part due to the remarkable stability of the sector: banks active in the 1970s had operated in almost unchanged fashion for more than half a century. Even the depression of the 1930s had little effect on British banks. As a consequence, the Bank of England developed a light supervisory regime, resting on the mutual understanding between bank management and the Bank of England's supervisory board.[7]

---

4. Lavelle, *Money and Banks in the American Political System.*
5. E.g., Krippner, "The Financialization of the American Economy."
6. Congleton, "On the Political Economy of the Financial Crisis and Bailout of 2008–2009," 300–302; Gorton, *Slapped by the Invisible Hand.*
7. Lütz, "Convergence within National Diversity: The Regulatory State in Finance"; Busch, *Banking Regulation and Globalization,* 113.

The traditional British model changed with the massive influx of foreign capital in the 1960s and 1970s. In order to compete with new financial centers such as New York, the Thatcher government decided to deregulate financial markets and break up the "old boys network" of the City of London, most notably by changing the rules of the London Stock Exchange on 27 October 1986, soon dubbed "Big Bang Day."[8] At the same time, banking regulation tightened and became statutory: the Banking Act of 1979 obliged financial institutions to be licensed in order to accept deposits, and the Banking Act of 1987 increased regulatory oversight. In the 1990s, the failure of Bank of Credit and Commerce International (BCCI) and the near collapse of Barings Banks put into doubt the oversight by the Bank of England and its regulatory capacity and created the momentum for a fundamental revision of the regulatory structure under the Labor government elected in 1997, in particular at the initiative of Gordon Brown, then chancellor of the exchequer.

The reform began in May 1997 with the creation of a centralized structure overseeing banks, financial services, and insurance, the Financial Services Authority (FSA). Losing its regulatory authority, the Bank of England gained a semiautonomous role in the setting of monetary policy. Moreover, a standing committee was created for coordination between the FSA, the Bank of England, and the Treasury, who are also referred to as the tripartite authorities.[9] Prior to the financial turmoil, the UK banking system was thus characterized by a segmented banking structure and centralized oversight. Traditionally light touch, the oversight had become increasingly statutory in banking, in particular in response to the bank failures of the 1990s. Financial market regulation, by contrast, continued to be minimal, to encourage the development of the City of London as a global financial center.[10] As in the United States, financial market activities had become a massive portion of financial activities, overshadowing traditional banking.

In both countries, finance was at the center of the economic growth model. Financial institutions, of which in particular the largest ones were highly mobile, had significant structural power in both. In addition, regulatory changes had created an even more favorable environment for the industry, which was able to enshrine light oversight as the central maxim. Only banks covered by the FDIC were subject to well-structured government intervention, including their liquidation if the regulator deemed it necessary. However, the FDIC had been under attack in the deregulatory years of the 1990s, seeing its staff reduced from 12,000 in 1995 to 4,500 in 2006.[11] Overall, it is thus fair to say that both the structural and the productive power of finance were high in the two liberal market economies.

8. Moran, *The Politics of the Financial Services Revolution*; Augar, *The Death of Gentlemanly Capitalism*.

9. Busch, *Banking Regulation and Globalization*, 156–60.

10. Sukhdev, Moran, and Williams, "The Financial Crisis, Financial Regulation and Financial Change in Britain."

11. Bair, *Bull by the Horns*, 16.

Exposure to the Crisis

At the center of the financial meltdown, the United States began to experience its first difficulties in late 2006 when the house price index peaked and then began falling. Unsurprisingly, the construction sector contracted, but the US public also learned with breathtaking speed how much the financial sector had become intertwined with housing.[12] With the drop in the value of US homes after 2006, delinquencies on residential mortgages sharply rose. It became clear that securities backed by mortgages were not as risk-free as they had been made out to be, despite various ways of bundling them. Moreover, the insurers of mortgages and mortgage-backed securities had maintained insufficient levels of reserves and were ill prepared for the amount of delinquencies they were asked to cover. With the additional risk of defaulting insurers, the value of asset-backed securities fell rapidly.[13]

Several insurers of mortgage-backed securities had to file for bankruptcy by the spring and summer of 2007: New Century Financial Corporation in April, Countrywide Financial Corporation in July, and American Home Mortgage Investment Corporation in August. In June 2007, Bear Stearns announced that two hedge funds it sponsored were experiencing considerable difficulties associated with their holdings of mortgage related securities. The Federal Reserve began actions to stabilize the economy as a whole, in particular through reduction in the federal funds interest rates and lending facilities, since major financial corporations experienced difficulties obtaining credit as private investors increasingly shied away from risk.

The symbolic beginning of the financial crisis in the United Kingdom was the 14 September 2007, when depositors queued outside Northern Rock to withdraw their holdings after the bank had approached the Bank of England for a loan facility. This first run on a bank in 150 years eventually forced the British government to take Northern Rock into public ownership on 22 February 2008, after two unsuccessful takeover bids from private investors.[14] The nationalization expropriated shareholders, offering compensation only at a level fixed as appropriate by the government.[15]

In the United States, only a few days after the nationalization of Northern Rock, the first major institution also started crumbling. Bear Stearns faced a run by money market funds, and it became clear that it would not survive. One of the big five Wall Street investment banks, Bear Stearns was a nondepository institution and thus outside of the purview of the FDIC and the usual instruments the government could rely on for unwinding banks. The Treasury and

---

12. Shiller, *The Subprime Solution.*

13. Congleton, "On the Political Economy of the Financial Crisis and Bailout of 2008–2009," 300–302; Gorton, *Slapped by the Invisible Hand.*

14. House of Commons, *The Run on the Rock.*

15. "Northern Rock to Be Nationalized," *BBC News Online,* 17 February 2008. Available at http://news.bbc.co.uk/2/hi/7249575.stm.

the Federal Reserve therefore sought to broker a deal with JP Morgan Chase, but the private market rescue was only possible with backing from the US government. JP Morgan took over Bear Stearns on 14 March 2008 for a severely reduced price and with a "backstop" guarantee from the US government on future losses after the first 1 billion and up to $30 billion. This backstop was made possible through a purchase of $30 billion of Bear Stearns securities by the Federal Reserve, by means of a special discount loan.[16] Since the loan was without recourse, all losses on those securities would accrue to the Fed, which thereby established the precedent of a bailout guarantee for failing investment banks.[17]

By the summer, another set of non-FDIC covered institutions faced collapse. The government-sponsored enterprises, Fannie Mae and Freddie Mac were not longer able to stand up to the difficulties of the US housing market. The government made their backing explicit with the Housing Market and Recovery Act of 30 July 2008, hoping to reassure investors. Despite this attempt, confidence faltered and the government eventually asked the regulator, the Federal Housing Finance Agency (FHFA), to put Fannie Mae and Freddie Mac into conservatorship. This intervention nationalized the two enterprises through a $100 billion acquisition of preferred stock from the US Treasury, and the wiping out of 80 percent of the value of existing stock. But only one week later, the government had to deal with the imminent collapse of Lehman Brothers, Merrill Lynch, and immediately after, American International Group (AIG).

The situation in the United Kingdom was no less dire. Despite efforts of the Bank of England to maintain liquidity, most notably through a scheme introduced in April 2008, the functioning of the UK banking system deteriorated and credit dried up, affecting both financial institutions and the real economy, as well as home owners. As the crisis unfolded, it became clear how badly British banks were affected. At the height of the credit crunch in September 2008, HBOS's position had weakened to a point that a public takeover seemed likely. In the end, the government brokered a deal with Lloyds TSB, who took over HBOS on 17 September. Bradford and Bingley became the next prominent victim and the second British bank nationalized by the government on 29 September 2008 after its deposit and branch network had been sold to the Grupo Santander for £612 million.

In October 2008, the Bank of England estimated "that capital losses for the six largest UK banks were above £100 billion, threatening the solvency of individual institutions and the collapse of the entire banking system."[18] Indeed, the government realized that a comprehensive solution had to be found to avoid having to resort to individual ad hoc measures for other banks

---

16. Reinhart, "A Year of Living Dangerously," 76–79.
17. See Cohan, *House of Cards*, for a detailed account of the fall of Bear Stearns.
18. Quaglia, "The 'British Plan' as a Pace-Setter," 1068.

in difficulties. Time was pressing as markets deteriorated, despite central bank efforts. On 6 October 2008, the FTSE100 recorded its biggest one-day fall ever, larger in terms of points than in the wake of 9/11 or the stock market crash of 1987.[19]

Simultaneously, the UK government was drawn into the Icelandic financial crisis. Two of the failing Icelandic banks—Landsbanki and Kaupthing—had UK-based business and a large UK depositor base. To protect the assets of UK depositors, the government issued a freezing order on 8 October, relying on antiterrorism rules, which greatly angered the Icelandic government.[20]

By September 2008, both the US and the UK governments had realized that their capacities to prop up individual institutions were insufficient. To be sure, the central banks of both countries supported the governments' intervention through additional liquidity schemes and in the United States even through loan facilities that could benefit individual institutions such as Bear Stearns and AIG.[21] Still something more substantial seemed to have become necessary to strengthen market confidence. On 17 September, Federal Reserve chairman Ben Bernanke insisted in a conversation with Henry Paulson,

> We can't keep doing this. Both because we at the Fed don't have the necessary resources and for reasons of democratic legitimacy, it's important that the Congress come in and take control of the situation.[22]

At that time, both the US and the UK governments decided to put forward a comprehensive national bailout plan to prevent the financial sectors from going under.

National Bank Support Schemes

The US Bailout Plan

Initial meetings on the most appropriate scheme the government could draw up to prevent a banking crisis had started in mid-April 2008, a month after the rescue of Bear Stearns. Henry Paulson and Ben Bernanke discussed a ten-page memo with the title " 'Break the Glass' Bank Recapitalization Plan" drawn up by Philip Swagel and Neel Kashkari from the Treasury. The memo

---

19. "Stocks Slide Despite Reassurances," *BBC News Online*, 6 October 2008. Available at http://news.bbc.co.uk/2/hi/business/7655288.stm.
20. "Icelandic Anger at UK Terror Move," BBC News Online, 24 October 2008. Available at http://news.bbc.co.uk/2/hi/uk_news/politics/7688560.stm.
21. The nine new facilities created by the Federal Reserve in order to intervene during the banking crisis in 2008 are discussed in Jacobs and King, "Concealed Advantage: The Federal Reserve's Financial Intervention after 2007."
22. Cited in Cassidy, "Anatomy of a Meltdown."

proposed that the Bush administration ask Congress for $500 billion to buy off toxic assets from financial institutions, in particular subprime mortgages. Alternatives included a government guarantee for these assets, a refinancing plan from the FHFA, the buying off of safer mortgage-backed securities as in the case of Bear Stearns, and an "Alternative D," the recapitalization of banks through public equity, detailed on less than half a page. The two Treasury officials behind the plan optimistically assumed that the first toxic assets auction could be organized within a month of the signing of the bill. Simultaneously, officials at the New York Fed developed a plan for a privately financed but publicly backed asset management company that would buy troubled assets from banks and sell them on the market. Both initiatives failed to gather the support of the administration, essentially because the crisis did not appear bad enough in the spring of 2008 to ask for such substantial amounts of public funds.[23]

By mid-September 2008, the tides had turned. Returning to the initial "Break the Glass" exercise, the Bush administration proposed what it now termed the Troubled Asset Relief Program (TARP). Ben Bernanke and Henry Paulson defended the need to intervene in the starkest terms possible. Henry Paulson defended the asset relief strategy as the only viable option, while members of Congress inquired about buying equity stakes instead.[24] Given the substantial financial commitments asked of Congress, the plan was heavily disputed and garnered much public attention. The initial three-page memo submitted by the Treasury Department turned into a forty-page document in the Senate, under the chairmanship of Senator Chris Dodd, and more than one hundred pages in the House, under Congressman Barney Frank.[25] During the negotiations in the second half of September, the crisis continued to worsen by the day, but public opinion grew quite hostile to the initiative. Considering TARP as a $700 billion gift to Wall Street, a substantial part of the US public wanted to see financial institutions pay the price of their risky investments, rather than being bailout out with taxpayer money.

When Congress finally voted on TARP on 29 September 2008, the House of Representatives rejected the proposal in a 228–205 vote. After intense negotiations and an additional three hundred pages, a revised version was voted in the Senate on 1 October and passed the House on 3 October 2008, with a vote of 263–171. President George W. Bush signed the Emergency Economic Stabilization Act of 2008 into law only hours after the vote, creating a $700 billion program for the purchase of troubled assets managed by a newly created Office of Financial Stability in the US Treasury, headed by Neel Kashkari. The fund's money was authorized for spending in two tranches. An initial $250 billion were approved upon the start of the program and could be increased to $350 billion if the president could certify to Congress that

23. Wessel, *In FED We Trust*, 176–78.
24. Paulson, *On the Brink*, 260.
25. Ibid., 305.

this was necessary, which happened on 15 January 2009. Several oversight mechanisms were put into place to monitor the execution of the government program, in particular a Financial Stability Oversight Board, a Congressional Oversight Panel, and a more administrative Special Inspector General for the TARP (SIGTARP), in addition to oversight provided by the Government Accountability Office and the Congressional Budget Office.

The announcement of this massive effort in early October did little to calm market concerns. With disheartening news from Europe, the Dow Jones continued to plummet by the day. By 6 October, the worldwide drop in stock markets had wiped off $2 trillion in value.[26] Given this urgent need to intervene quickly, the asset auctions initially envisioned looked less and less promising. When the British government unveiled their bank rescue scheme built around capital injections, the Bush administration began to reconsider the instruments proposed under TARP and decided to focus on capital injections, a possibility that had been written into the legislation. On 14 October 2008, the Bush administration announced that it would buy senior preferred stock from the nine major US financial institutions. Other US financial institutions with significant operations in the United States could apply to participate. At the same time, the FDIC issued a guarantee on bank debt and fully insured noninterest bearing deposits, and the Federal Reserve opened a new commercial paper facility to provide liquidity in short-term funding markets.[27]

In order to send a strong signal, the US government decided to make the TARP capital program mandatory for the major investment banks. To avoid making the government plan to difficult to accept, it decided to set the interest payment at 5 percent.[28] To encourage rapid repayment, the interest rate would go up to 9 percent after the first five years. Conditions and fees on other TARP programs varied according to the type of aid. Moreover, participants agreed to control executive compensation, accept clawbacks on compensation obtained on the basis of inaccurate earning statements, prohibit golden parachutes to senior executives, and limit tax deduction on executive compensation to $500,000.[29] The constraint on executive compensation was a real concern for the CEOs of the companies that initially participated, as accounts of the negotiations highlight[30]

Starting as a capital purchase program, TARP is thus fundamentally a misnomer and became the umbrella for a variety of tools to stabilize the economy during the crisis. Over time TARP expanded into four separate sets

26. Ibid., 335.
27. For further information on the FDIC's Temporary Liquidity Guarantee Program, see www.fdic.gov/regulations/resources/TLGP/index.html. For further information on the Commercial Paper Funding Facility of the Federal Reserve Bank, see www.federalreserve.gov/monetarypolicy/cpff.htm.
28. SIGTARP, *Quarterly Report to Congress*, June 21, 2009.
29. US Department of the Treasury, *Treasury Announces TARP Capital Purchase Program.*
30. Paulson, *On the Brink*, 365.

of programs, ranging from (1) support for financial institutions, (2) asset support programs, and (3) automobile sector aid to (4) support for homeowners.[31] With an initial budget of $700 billion, TARP is one of the major tools of the US Treasury but exists alongside other means of intervention, most notably by the Federal Reserve and other federal agencies.[32] In the most expansive list, SIGTARP includes more than fifty initiatives and programs created by federal agencies between 2007 and mid-2009, committing potentially as much as $23 trillion.[33]

The Federal Reserve Bank, the most central of these agencies, implemented a wide range of programs to stimulate liquidity, but also provided aid to specific institutions, in particular Bear Stearns and AIG.[34] The FDIC provided deposit insurance and most notably a temporary debt guarantee program announced together with TARP. FHFA, charged with regulation of Fannie Mae and Freddie Mac, carried an important part of the costs associated with the bailout of these two institutions. Finally, the US Treasury had instruments beyond TARP, in particular under the Housing and Economic Recovery Act of 2008, which it used for the housing finance twins, but also to support for homeowners and mutual funds. In a rare effort to give a cumulative picture of these different initiatives, SIGTARP estimates the expenditures by June 2009 to have been $1.4 trillion for the Federal Reserve, $600 billion for TARP and $300 billion for non-TARP measures mainly by the Treasury Department, $300 billion by the FDIC, and $300 billion by other agencies such as the FHFA.[35]

The British Bailout Plan

The United Kingdom was among the first European countries to announce its bank support scheme on 8 October, less than forty-eight hours after the historic stock market drop. The British plan had begun to take shape in late September, in a series of meetings between by the Prime Minister's Office, the Treasury, the FSA, and the Bank of England, and later with the CEOs of the largest banks. As coordination with the EU proved unsuccessful and UK stock markets continued to plummet, Prime Minister Gordon Brown and Chancellor of the Exchequer Alistair Darling decided to announce a £500 billion bailout package upon returning from the Ecofin Council on 8 October.

The initial British plan had three pillars: (1) recapitalization through a Bank Recapitalization Fund, for £50 billion; (2) a Credit Guarantee Scheme,

31. Ibid.; Sorkin, *Too Big to Fail*, 528–29.
32. SIGTARP, *Quarterly Report to Congress*, January 26, 2012. The Treasury extended TARP on 9 December 2009, through 3 October 2010. This meant that Treasury could make new obligations after that date but may continue to expend money that had been obligated prior.
33. See Congressional Oversight Panel, *Final Report of the Congressional Oversight Panel*, 34.
34. SIGTARP, *Quarterly Report to Congress*, June 21, 2009, 137.
35. Jacobs and King, "Concealed Advantage."

a government loan guarantee for new debt issued between British banks for up to £250 billion; (3) liquidity provision through short-term loans made available through the Special Liquidity Scheme opened in April and operated by the Bank of England, now extended to a maximum amount of £200 billion. While the first pillar sought to address the solvency problems several British banks were facing, the other two were designed to alleviate the liquidity problems, by addressing the confidence crisis and jumpstart bank lending.

The Bank Recapitalization Fund allowed the government to buy ordinary and preferred shares in banks that decide to take the rescue package. The plan was open to all UK incorporated banks and building societies. Although banks such as HSBC Group, Standard Chartered, or Barclays declared their support for the plan, they announced that they would not seek government aid. Only the Royal Bank of Scotland and Lloyds TSB together with HBOS applied for government funding, initially for £20 billion and £17 billion respectively. The Credit Guarantee Scheme provided a public guarantee on new debt issuance with a maturity of up to thirty-six months. To qualify for the guarantee, eligible English incorporated companies had to raise their capital by an amount considered appropriate by the government.[36] Finally, the Special Liquidity Scheme of the Bank of England allows banks to swap high quality mortgage-backed and other securities for more liquid Treasury Bills in return for a fee.

Unlike the US recapitalization program, the UK bank support plan was voluntary. The price of capital injections was much less favorable than in the United States and banks benefiting from the rescue package had to accept restrictions on executive pay, changes in corporate governance, and reduced dividends to existing shareholders. They furthermore committed to offer reasonable credit to homeowners and small businesses. To monitor continued lending, the government set up a Lending Panel in November 2008, which ensured data collection through the Bank of England.

However, more important, the purchase of ordinary shares gave the government considerable control over the banks and led several observers to speak of partial nationalization in some cases. Following a series of adjustments and transactions, the capital injections eventually led the British government to acquire 83 percent of the Royal Bank of Scotland (but only 68 percent of the voting rights) and 41 percent of Lloyds.[37] Following the nationalizations of Northern Rock, Bradford and Bingley, and the use of the Bank Recapitalization Plan, the government found itself obliged to establish

36. SIGTARP, *Quarterly Report to Congress*, June 21, 2009, 138. SIGTARP stopped including such a cumulative estimation in its quarterly reports to Congress after July 2009. Reports are available on the SIGTARP's website: www.sigtarp.gov/pages/reportsaudits.aspx.

37. UK Debt Management Office, *The Commissioners of Her Majesty's Treasury Rules of the 2008 Credit Guarantee Scheme*.

United Kingdom Financial Investments (UKFI) in November 2008 as a vehicle for managing public ownership in the banking system.[38]

The October 2008 bailout package was produced under pressure to respond to the crisis, but the government also worked to draw the lessons from previous shortcomings and to adjust statutory arrangements. Despite these changes and continued intervention to support individual institutions, confidence in the banking system remained weak, which led to a continued shortage of credit. The government therefore augmented or adjusted the bailout package over the course of 2009. On 19 January 2009, Alistair Darling announced a series of new measures that extended or complemented the initial government plan.[39] To begin with, the government restructured its shareholdings in RBS and Lloyds and extended the window for the Credit Guarantee Scheme from April to December 2009. Most important, however, it introduced the Asset Protection Scheme, which aimed to insure assets on the banks balance sheets in order to increase bank's capital and ability to lend without further capital injections. The Asset Protection Scheme was particularly designed for the needs of RBS and Lloyds, but only RBS ended up participating in the scheme.[40] The government's maximum liability under this scheme was fixed at £200 billion. For the management of the Asset Protection Scheme, the Treasury set up a dependent agency, the Asset Protection Agency, launched on 7 December 2009.[41] In addition, the government launched the Asset-Backed Securities Guarantee Scheme to guarantee newly issued AAA-rated mortgage backed securities and thus stabilize housing market finance, with an initial volume of £50 billion.

On the legislative side, the Banking Act of 2008 that had provided for the nationalization of Northern Rock was replaced by a more ambitious Banking Act in February 2009. Under the new rules, the FSA and the Bank of England obtained powers to determine the viability of British financial institutions and to exercise stabilization measures, including the sale of all or parts of the business to a private sector purchaser or a transfer to a "bridge bank" to organize the orderly dismantling. Moreover, the Treasury retains the right to take a bank into public ownership.[42] The Banking Act of 2009 thus granted considerable powers to the tripartite authorities to intervene in the business of private financial institutions, in particular by forcing the resolution of a bank deemed to pose a risk for national financial stability. The legislation sought to prevent situations in which the government might be forced to

---

38. National Audit Office, *Maintaining the Financial Stability of UK Banks: Update on the Support Schemes.*

39. www.ukfi.co.uk.

40. National Audit Office, *Maintaining the Financial Stability across the United Kingdom's Banking System*, 21–22.

41. Lloyds decided instead to raise additional capital from shareholders and pay a fee of £2.5 billion to exit the scheme. National Audit Office, *The Asset Protection Scheme.*

42. See http://www.hm-treasury.gov.uk/apa.htm.

bailout banks when it was already too late, and it influenced similar legislation in other countries, for example, the *Restrukturierungsgesetz* in Germany agreed on in December 2010.

Collective Action by the Financial Industry

Because they were embedded in liberal market economies, the US and the UK governments had little tradition of negotiating with the banks collectively. Dealing with large financial institutions therefore led both governments to impose their solutions in a rather authoritative manner, but the two chose markedly different strategies: while the United States tried to engage the largest financial institutions collectively by proposing very favorable conditions, the United Kingdom gave banks the choice not to accept public recapitalization and made support rather unattractive. In both cases, the frustrating experiences led to stringent reregulation, in an attempt of the government to regain control over the financial industry in the future.

The United States

The United States had a functioning system for the management of struggling financial institutions through the FDIC but found itself overwhelmed by the difficulties of large holding companies and other institutions that did not fall under the purview of the FDIC. With respect to these systemically important institutions, the government sought to engineer collective solutions, first, by trying to create a liquidation consortium when individual takeovers failed, and second by making recapitalization mandatory in order to avoid stigmatizing the banks with difficulties. The first attempt largely failed and the second was only possible because the initial recapitalization was designed on quite favorable terms. Ultimately, the US financial industry succeeded in signaling that it was unable and unwilling to act collectively, making the government carry the burden of the stabilization. To prevent being caught in such an uncomfortable situation again in the future, the US government began to develop more stringent regulation, most importantly through the Dodd-Frank Act, which has the ambition to formally prohibit the use of public funds for future bank bailouts. It is helpful to review these different steps to understand the power balance of business-government relations in US finance.

The Shortcomings of Routine Resolution

Because the banking sector in the United States has traditionally been composed of a great number of small banks, managing the liquidation of an insolvent deposit-taking institution is nothing extraordinary. During the

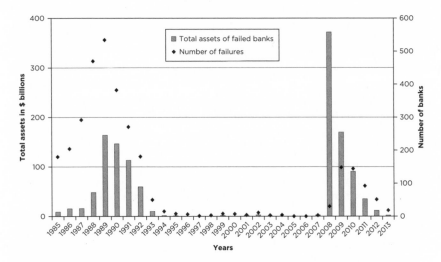

Figure 5.1 FDIC resolution of banks
Source: Based on data provided on FDIC website, www.fdic.gov/bank/individual/failed; figures for 2013 are up to September 2013.

savings and loan crisis in the late 1980s, the FDIC managed the closure or takeover of more than twenty-five hundred banks, a much greater number than during the recent financial crisis.[43] The institutionalized nature of this regulatory process leaves little room for tailoring unconventional solutions. Insured institutions have to follow capital requirements monitored by the FDIC, which can issue warnings when a bank becomes undercapitalized. When the number drops below a threshold of 6 percent, the FDIC can force the bank to take corrective action, change its management, and ultimately, declare the bank insolvent and take it into receivership. Typically, in such cases, the FDIC either organizes a takeover by another healthy bank and may auction off some of the remaining assets, or it can pay the deposits out of its fund and liquidate the receivership estate of the failed bank. The FDIC's fund is constituted by an insurance premium banks pay in order to be covered. As figure 5.1 shows, such resolution was tested massively during the savings and loan crisis and functioned well even in the recent crisis, where some institutions were disproportionately large, in particular Washington Mutual in 2008.[44]

Designed to prevent a run on banks, this insurance and resolution system applies to deposit-taking institutions. With the development of financial

43. Subsequent legislative reforms also concerned the institutional structure of bank supervision in 2012, most notably the abolition of the FSA, whose activities were split between the new Prudential Regulation Authority of the Bank of England and a Financial Conduct Authority.
44. For a complete timeline, see Moss, "An Ounce of Prevention."

intermediation, in particular after the Gramm-Leach-Bliley Act of 1999, however, financial institutions could develop into holding companies, which were not necessarily required to provide a resolution plan. Moreover, these large financial institutions were able to engage in banklike activities like extending credit through shadow-banking arrangements, without taking regular deposits and thus falling under the purview of the FDIC. As a consequence, the government found itself dealing with investment banks or stock brokerages, like Bear Stearns, which faced a run that was entirely unrelated to deposit withdrawal, but instead concerned derivatives obligations, commercial paper, or uninsured deposits. For these uninsured financial institutions, the government had to tailor individual solutions often directly developed by the administration, in association with Federal Reserve and the respective regulators.

As in the FDIC procedure, the government always looked for a private buyer first and attempted in several instances to arrange for a liquidation buyout from the industry. To be sure, it did not have a dedicated fund, which led it to the much-criticized assumption of some of the risks of the takeover of Bear Stearns through JP Morgan Chase. However, the government acted quite quickly and authoritatively, as the case of Fannie Mae and Freddie Mac illustrated. Once the government had established that the two housing finance institutions were on the edge of collapsing, it simply summoned their CEOs and presented them with the solution proposed by the FHFA, Treasury, and the Federal Reserve Bank. The regulator announced that it would put the two entities into conservatorship and assume the power of the board, in exchange for capital injections and the purchase of debt. The management was asked to resign and had no room to negotiate the solution devised by the government. Likewise, Dick Fuld, the CEO of Lehman Brothers did not participate in the discussions concerning Lehman's rescue and was actively shut out of negotiations.[45]

Put differently, once the government was sure that an institution was no longer viable, it stopped negotiating and was quite strict in applying market discipline: a takeover or liquidation. Unlike the ties that may exist in crony capitalism with a "Minister's nephew" syndrome, even family relations could not reverse the situation. For Lehman Brothers, it did not help that George Walker IV, a member of the executive committee of the investment bank, was a great-cousin of US president George W. Bush. After the Lehman executive's management had learned that the government would not bail them out, they urged Walker to make a last, desperate call to the president. Walker reluctantly agreed, but the call went unanswered.[46]

---

45. Washington Mutual, at the time the sixth largest bank in the US, was put into receivership with assets valued at over $300 billion.
46. Sorkin, *Too Big to Fail.*

What was more difficult was establishing exactly when an institution's financial situation had deteriorated sufficiently for the government to declare it as unviable. By September 2008, most major financial institutions were experiencing considerable liquidity issues, which meant that they could no longer monetarize an important portion of their assets. Since the business model of these banks relied heavily on short-term finance, firms needed to be able to roll over their debt constantly. Establishing a simple indicator based on the bank's capital ratio would have been misleading according to most observers, in particular from the banking sector.

> When Lehman and Bear Sterns went bankrupt, they had plenty of capital. But they couldn't issue! They couldn't raise money and there was a run on the bank by counterparties. Lehman raised equity six months before they failed. I would argue that they could have raised an unlimited amount of equity, it wouldn't have solved it. They needed help with issuing debt, to keep rolling over their debt.[47]

Similarly, Jamie Dimon, CEO of JP Morgan stated that he did not know what "solvency" means. With reference to Lehman Brothers, JP Morgan's chief risk officer Barry Zubrow declared, "From a pure accounting standpoint, it was solvent," although "it obviously was financing its assets on a very leveraged basis with a lot of short-term financing."[48] When a short-term liquidity crisis can turn into a long-term liquidity crisis, liquidity becomes tantamount to solvency.[49]

Beyond the most extreme cases, banks kept arguing that they did not have a solvency issue, but simply the need for more liquidity. Unfortunately, liquidity provision in a context of almost completely frozen markets became a bottomless pit. The government therefore devised TARP to send a strong signal to markets in order to stabilize confidence. Despite the size of the program, TARP was rather marginal for the actual situation of the financial institutions, notes one policy expert: "The equity injected to the banks relative to the problems the banks had was not that large. It was an issue of signaling."[50]

However, by injecting public funds into private companies, the government engaged in a rescue measure that was quite similar to stabilization under the FDIC, without trying to appear as such. In fact, the government declared—as was crucial for this signaling measure—that all the institutions that had been recapitalized were healthy. The intervention therefore varied

47. Interview, 25 May 2012.
48. Cited in Financial Crisis Inquiry Commission, *The Financial Crisis Inquiry Report*, 325.
49. I thank Mark Blyth for discussion of this point.
50. Interview, 22 February 2012.

significantly from the principles fixed for bank support ever since the New Deal:

> When you walk into a bank that you think is sick, very first thing you got to do is fire the management. If you don't, you will never find out what's going on in the bank. [Second], you do a hard valuation of the banks' assets. [Third], you restructure the balance sheet by wiping out the stockholders and by requiring the bondholders to accept stock in exchange for their bonds. . . . In TARP we did none of these things. We did not fire the management of these banks. We did not try to find out the real values of the assets and the liabilities. [And in several cases,] stockholders were only dilluted to a minor degree and nothing was asked of the bondholders.[51]

Similarly, Elizabeth Warren, a bankruptcy expert and chair of the Congressional Oversight Panel for TARP, lamented with reference to AIG and Citigroup: "The very notion that anyone would infuse money into a financially troubled entity without demanding changes in management is preposterous."[52]

To summarize, the regime for bank failures varied considerably between deposit-taking institutions and large financial companies. As banks became larger and relied on increasingly complex business models, the US government was unable to deal with them in the same way it would with traditional banking institutions. It did try to uphold market discipline and intervened authoritatively in the cases that were most dire. But it had difficulties coming up with a comprehensive approach that would apply to all financial institutions, in particular the nine major ones. To tackle these difficulties, the government tried repeatedly to engage the sector collectively.

Engineering Collective Engagement

The US financial sector has several associations such as the American Bankers' Association, the securities industry association SIFMA, and several community banking associations. However, their membership can be very diverse and heterogeneous, despite the fact that financial services have become rather concentrated in the hands of the largest financial institutions. These, in turn, lobby directly, most often through their CEOs who tend to be on first name basis with the most senior public officials. Numerous authors have noted the personal ties between individual financial institutions and the government, in particular, Secretary of the Treasury Henry Paulson

---

51. Ibid.
52. Cited in Doran, "US Watchdog Calls for Bank Executives to Be Sacked"; see also Congressional Oversight Panel, *Assessing Treasury's Strategy: Six Month of TARP.*

who had been CEO of Goldman Sachs, but also Timothy Geithner who had a close relationship with Bob Rubin of Citigroup.[53] Whether these ties led to favoritism or whether they created tensions, because other CEOs continued to consider Henry Paulson as one of their peers rather than a representative of the government, is of secondary importance for this analysis.[54] What is certain is that the major US financial institutions relied more on their individual relationships with the public authorities than on collective initiatives to find a way out of the crisis.[55]

In an early attempt, the US Treasury sought to get these banks to support the industry through a collective solution in response to the first liquidity crisis in the summer of 2007. At the time, investors were particularly concerned about structured investment vehicles, which banks had used to move some of their activities off their balance sheets. As uncertainty grew about the value of these investment vehicles, the sponsoring banks risked liquidity problems. The Treasury therefore insisted that major banks pool their resources to buy out the assets of these investment vehicles in order to help to go through the liquidity crunch. In October 2007, several major US banks announced such a Master Liquidity Enhancement Conduit that would buy several hundred billion dollars' of troubled investment vehicles from several banks. Funded entirely by private banks, the solution would have provided an alternative to the public liquidity provision through the Fed's facilities. Unfortunately, it was quietly dropped by the end of the year. Johnson and Kwak suggest that the failure of the private conduit was due to a lack of conviction of banks, but may also have to do with the divergence in the situation of individual banks, in particular the fact that a substantial amount of the support would have benefited Citigroup.[56]

At the height of the crisis, the most important attempt to engineer a collective solution was the government's effort to put together a liquidation consortium from the industry for Lehman Brothers. In 1998, the Federal Reserve Bank of New York had succeeded in getting the industry to provide such a plan for LTCM, by merely "providing the cookies" to get the major financial institutions into a room and develop a solution.[57] In September 2008, the New York Fed, together with the Treasury, pushed for a similar solution for Lehman Brothers during a weekend negotiation with the private sector. At the time, the major financial institutions agreed to finance about $30 billion of Lehman's illiquid assets in order to make a merger more attractive to a potential buyer.

53. E.g., Johnson and Kwak, *13 Bankers.*
54. McDonald, *A Colossal Failure of Common Sense*, 306–7.
55. The most telling evidence of the incessant individual contacts during the crisis are the telephone logs of Henry Paulson, Ben Bernanke, and Timothy Geithner, which have in part been published, e.g. Sorkin, *Too Big to Fail.*
56. Johnson and Kwak, *13 Bankers*, 158.
57. Interview, central bank representative, 2 December 2011.

However, the potential buyer, the British bank Barclays, was asked to provide a guarantee of Lehman's trading operations between the signing of the merger and its closing. Unlike in the case of Bear Stearns, the US government refused to take on this guarantee itself, since it would be "unsecured and not limited in amount, and would put the US taxpayers at risk for the entirety of Lehman's trading obligations."[58] The UK government, in turn, vetoed the transaction. The British government and in particular Alistair Darling thought that it would be foolish to rescue a US bank that was in trouble, "when the US authorities wouldn't and when other US banks were running for a mile."[59] Without government backing, the private sector consortium was thus insufficient to provide a credible solution for Lehman Brothers. And the major banks were indeed unwilling to take on the remaining risk themselves.

The recapitalization plan under TARP was the final instance in which the government sought a collective commitment from the industry. After realizing that TARP would be unable to provide a quick and workable solution to the crisis through a troubled asset auction, the US Treasury followed the British example and decided to recapitalize its major institutions.[60] In order to avoid stigmatizing those that accepted capital injections, the US administration made the recapitalization plan mandatory, using a combination of negotiation, threats, and peer pressure to get an agreement from all of them to accept the capital injections of $250 billion on 13 October 2008.[61]

The recapitalization meant that weak institutions obtained fresh capital under very attractive conditions, because they were essentially treated as if they were still healthy. Stable institutions, in turn, had to accept the heavy intervention and some complained bitterly, in particular Wells Fargo.[62] To keep these complaints manageable, the administration offered an interest rate of 5 percent, which was below the market rate, and much lower than the 10 percent interest Warren Buffett had asked for investment made in Goldman Sachs at almost the same time.[63] In addition, the administration assured the institutions that it would not seek to control decisions or vote in the board of directors. According to Philip Swagel of the US Treasury, the objective of these favorable conditions was to make banks a sweet deal "they could not refuse."[64]

58. Baxter, *Too Big to Fail*, 4.

59. Darling, *Back from the Brink*, 124; see also Financial Crisis Inquiry Commission, *The Financial Crisis Inquiry Report*, 336.

60. Paulson, *On the Brink*, 337.

61. Sorkin, *Too Big to Fail*, 522–31; Bair, *Bull by the Horns*, 1–7. The participants of the recapitalization scheme were Citigroup ($25 billion), JP Morgan ($25 billion), Wells Fargo ($25 billion), Bank of America ($15 billion), Goldman Sachs ($10 billion), Morgan Stanley ($10 billion), Merrill Lynch ($10 billion), BNY Mellon ($3 billion), State Street ($2 billion). Financial Crisis Inquiry Commission, *The Financial Crisis Inquiry Report*, 374.

62. Interview with a US government representative, 23 February 2012.

63. Johnson and Kwak, *13 Bankers*, 154.

64. Cited in ibid.

Getting a collective agreement from a sector that had proven unwilling at least twice before to link their fortunes through a joint rescue plan thus succeeded only when the government made a concerted effort to accommodate the industry. The collective solution also went no further than this initial recapitalization scheme, which several banks repaid as quickly as possible.[65] According to a foreign bank representative, allowing for quick payback diminishes sector solidarity considerably, because healthier banks can still try to escape the stigma of government intervention.[66] Moreover, the most substantial support for large institutions was not a collective solution or the recapitalization under TARP, but the individually negotiated aid they were able to obtain through the Federal Reserve facilities, in particular through individually tailored solutions such as the Maiden Lane I (for Bear Stearns) and II and III (for AIG).[67]

Reregulation

The government's frustration with the financial industry grew even stronger when it became clear that financial institutions also took their individual obligations rather lightly. The most telling symbol of this laxness was a series of executive compensation scandals. The high salaries and bonus payments in the financial industry had been central in the political debate surrounding the bailouts but gained even more public attention in the context of the AIG bailout. Only days after the government support, it become public that AIG executives and employees participated in expensive outings, hunting events, and spa treatments, for several hundred thousand dollars, at the time effectively supported by taxpayer money. Despite the outrage and the apologies issues at the time, AIG announced in March 2009 that it would pay $1.2 billion in bonuses for the entire company. President Barack Obama and representatives from both parties heavily criticized the decision and asked AIG to renounce the bonus payments. In a meeting with the CEOs of the major financial institutions in the White House in early April, Obama underlined the public outcry against this behavior, stressing: "My administration is the only thing between you and the pitchforks."[68] As a consequence of the scandals, compensation oversight legislation was modified several times. In June, Kenneth Feinberg was appointed as special master of executive compensation under TARP, commonly referred to as "compensation tsar."[69]

Even within the banking sector, the support given to the largest institutions was perceived as dishonest favoritism. Unlike the initial capital purchase

---

65. Interview, 23 February 2012.

66. Interview, 10 May 2012.

67. Jacobs and King, "Concealed Advantage"; Nelson and Katzenstein, "Uncertainty, Risk, and the Financial Crisis of 2008."

68. Javers, "Inside Obama's Bank CEOs Meeting."

69. Solomon, "White House Set to Appoint a Pay Czar."

plan, banks applying for aid under TARP had to prove that they were healthy in order to receive their money and had to go through a series of tests.

> Goldman Sachs was on the verge of collapse . . . and they got TARP money. Small banks throughout the country had their applications rejected because they weren't healthy. . . . Imagine how this played in the mind of 8000 small bankers all across this country and every one they had lunch with.[70]

In the months that followed, Congress and the administration sought to correct the unbalanced relationship they had experienced with the financial sector, in particular through the Dodd-Frank Wall Street Reform and Consumer Protection Act passed on 21 July 2010. The act attempted to address the regulatory loopholes large financial institutions had benefited from during the crisis, in particular by integrating oversight over the entire sector. All financial institutions were made subject to FDIC oversight and had to provide a resolution plan with details about how the institutions wished to dissolve their different assets in case they needed to be unwound. This meant that the FDIC, in cooperation with the Fed and Treasury, obtained similar authority over holding companies and gained power to deal with them through the sale of assets or bridge banks, even in cases that were not "black or white bankruptcies."[71] By putting into place an orderly liquidation authority funded by the financial institutions themselves, the Dodd-Frank Act aims to prevent any taxpayer-funded bailout in the future.

Although the real impact of Dodd-Frank remains to be seen and will depend on the implementation of the provisions, the desire to become more authoritative vis-à-vis large financial institutions becomes quite clear from the design of the reform. For the administration and Congress, the main lesson from the financial crisis in 2008 and 2009 was that they had only very limited means to pressure the financial industry into behavior that appeared urgently necessary for the survival of the entire sector and the economy as a whole.

The United Kingdom

As in the United States, in the United Kingdom the largest financial institutions also maintained privileged individual relationships with the public authorities rather than engaging in collective commitments, despite the government's attempts to get the CEOs of the largest institutions around a table to broker adequate solutions. When the government realized the lack of interest of the industry to engage collectively, however, it went ahead and

---

70. Interview, 22 February 2012.
71. Interview, 23 February 2012.

imposed a solution that was much less favorable, in part even against the will of the financial industry.

Direct Contacts

As everywhere, the senior management of the financial industry maintained close contacts with politicians and the administration, even with the Labor government, which was not a natural ally for the industry. The governor of the Bank of England, traditionally at the center of business-government contacts, had moved away from maintaining a close relationship with the representatives of individual institutions. According to Chancellor of the Exchequer Alistair Darling, Mervyn King, the governor of the central bank, was quite opposed to systemwide solutions such as liquidity provision, which would introduce moral hazard. Instead King supported a penalty interest rate that would have applied to any help given and insisted on establishing the value of assets the banks owned.[72] The hesitation of the central bank governor created tensions between the Treasury and the FSA, who pressed for quick intervention, and the Bank of England. Despite several meetings organized by the governor with the major banks, the CEOs felt that the central bank did not understand their concerns and that the governor "only gave them a lecture on moral hazard." Darling felt that the relationship had deteriorated, possibly because the Bank of England considered that oversight should be in the hands of the FSA after the regulatory reform of the 1997. He regretted that King did not maintain closer contacts with the CEOs, not because "the bankers were right, far from it," but because "we needed a far tighter grip on what they were up to."[73]

At the height of the crisis, contacts with the banks were organized by the Treasury and partially through the economic advisors and the policymaking team of the prime minister's office. In April 2008, Gordon Brown met with British bank leaders several times to discuss the Special Liquidity Scheme the government and the Bank of England announced on April 21.[74] The CEOs of the largest banks also sought to speak with the public officials individually, even if the frequency of contacts in the United Kingdom seems much lower than in the United States.[75] As the government advanced on a comprehensive bank support plan, however, it started organizing collective meetings.

72. Darling, *Back from the Brink*, 21–23.
73. Ibid., 70.
74. Brown, *Beyond the Crash*, 31.
75. Compare the frequency of phone calls made to senior bank management by Henry Paulson to the description of individual meetings by Alistair Darling. Paulson, *On the Brink*; Darling, *Back from the Brink*, 59–63. In the UK, much of the "sounding out" of the banking sector appears to have been in the hands of Treasury staff such as Permanent Secretary of the Treasury Nick Macpherson, Financial Services Secretary Paul Myners, as well as Tom Scholar, chief of staff of the prime minister, and Minister for Business, Enterprise and Regulatory Reform Shriti Vadera, a close confidant of Gordon Brown.

Government Action, Industry Reluctance

The United Kingdom's experience was marked by the early experience with Northern Rock. The first discussions about intervention in case of bank failures had included an exercise carried out in 2006 by the Bank of England and FSA, but the time was not ripe to create new legislation for fear of a panic. This changed with the images of depositors queuing to withdraw their funds from Northern Rock, and the government decided to intervene quickly, not shying away from nationalizing the bank, despite the negative connotations of such heavy-handed intervention, in particular for a Labor government that did not want to be labeled as retrograde. According to several observers, the determination of the government was linked to the effect a possible failure of Northern Rock, and later of Bradford and Bingley, would have on retail business: "Both banks were not associated with investment and speculation. They were not Lehman's. They might have failed for similar reasons, but they affected normal people. They were banks that had an every-day connotation."[76]

As elsewhere, the UK government tried to see whether a private takeover was a viable option for a failing bank, but the possibility did not materialize. Rather than searching for a single bank able to take over a struggling competitor, the Treasury decided to explore a collective solution from the financial industry for Bradford and Bingley in late September 2008. Gathering the CEOs of the major British banks in a meeting room at the Treasury, Darling remembers "here was a chance for them to step up to the plate and help their own industry and country." Although the financial industry felt very wary about nationalization and the signal it would send to financial markets, they were "not enthusiastic" about a collective commitment. The meeting lasted barely more than an hour: "No one wanted anything to do with it."[77]

Over the course of 2008, the administration had become increasingly concerned about the stability of British banks and watched their sometimes desperate attempts to raise capital on the markets. Apart from HSBC and Standard Chartered, it appeared that all major British banks needed additional capital and the government began to focus on recapitalizing the industry in order to provide a systemic solution to the deteriorating market conditions. As the plan took shape in late September 2008, the heads of the Bank of England, the FSA, and the Treasury consulted with banks. The industry, in turn, argued that they had a simple liquidity issue and were vividly opposed to government capitalization. One chairman insisted that taking capital from the state would constitute "expropriation, nothing less than a return to the 1970s—or worse, the 1940."[78] For Gordon Brown, the financial

76. Interviews, 8 June 2011.
77. Darling, *Back from the Brink*, 134–35.
78. Ibid., 151.

industry was in a state of denial: "We could no longer trust some of the banks to judge their own interests, or those of the public."[79]

The government decided to go ahead without the banks' collective input, asking Standard Chartered to cooperate confidentially on running a test of how recapitalization would work out in practice.[80] Mervyn King insisted that recapitalization should be made mandatory in order to avoid stigmatizing those that accepted. Instead of forcing the banks to accept government capital, however, they were given a choice. They would have to raise capital to a level assessed individually by the FSA, but they could chose to do so on the markets or through government aid. In addition, the government would increase the Special Liquidity Scheme of the Bank of England from April 2008 and offer a credit guarantee to facilitate interbank lending.

When the Treasury announced the details of the plans in a final meeting with the major British banks, they were outraged. The banks were incredibly unhappy, arguing that they did not need nor want government capital and feared the market signal this would send. When they realized the government would not negotiate, they attempted to at least half the £50 billion made available for recapitalization. Tom McKillop, chairman of RBS insisted that the plan was unnecessary, since all he needed "was overnight finance."[81] Gordon Brown took it on himself to call Stephen Green, the CEO of HSBC directly, to assure that he would support the plan, since HSBC (along with Standard Chartered) was clearly not affected. Both CEOs assured him that they would not use the occasion to set themselves apart from their more vulnerable competitors. Still, US secretary of the treasury Henry Paulson recounts that he met Mervyn Davies, chairman of Standard Chartered Bank, who "proudly told me that Standard Chartered would not participate in the UK plan. It did not need government capital."[82] As a voluntary rescue scheme, the UK plan had the effect of stigmatizing the participating institutions, even if HSBC and Standard Chartered raised more capital and did not speak out against the government support.

The government support was unattractive from many angles: not only did it send a negative signal about the state of British banking, it also came with lending conditions and suggested changes in remuneration policy. Most important, however, it gave the government very important stakes in the companies that needed the money.

Unfavorable Conditions

After the plan was made public, three banks applied for recapitalization: RBS, despite its denial a day earlier, HBOS, and Lloyds, the latter two in the middle of merging into a single entity. The tripartite administration and the

79. Brown, *Beyond the Crash*, 52.
80. Ibid., 51.
81. Ibid., 58.
82. Paulson, *On the Brink*, 344.

three banks agreed one by one on the precise numbers and conditions. As a result, the UK government ended up recapitalizing RBS, Lloyds, and HBOS with £37 billion, taking an initial 57 percent stake in RBS, 58 percent in HBOS, and 32 percent in Lloyds. The considerable state ownership ensuing from the bank support plan also affected corporate governance. The management of RBS resigned, and the chairman of HBOS agreed that he would not work for the merged entity with Lloyds. Fred Goodwin, RBS's resigning CEO, said of the government talks, "This is not a negotiation, it is a drive-by shooting."[83]

Contrary to the US strategy, the UK plan was not very favorable to the financial industry in general, and particularly harsh for participating banks. Markets had already singled out the banks that were considered most fragile— RBS and HBOS/Lloyds for which funding markets were effectively closed—so the government did not see the need to pretend that they were healthy. The pricing of the recapitalization was considered as an important way to avoid the excessive use of the scheme, making sure that only those that could no longer rely on the market rate would use the government support.[84]

Lending conditions were only moderately affective in ensuring continued access to credit for small- and medium-sized companies.[85] But the government's insistence to cut down on remuneration and other advantages proved difficult to challenge. When the substantial retirement payments to Fred Goodwin became public in 2009, a virulent debate ensued to determine whether his contract should be honored, given that RBS was already under substantial public control. The debate led among other things to the annulment of Fred Goodwin's knighthood, but also brought political momentum for a 50 percent tax on bank bonuses of over £25,000 introduced in late 2009. The bonus and retirement debate even drowned out discussions of the new Asset Protection Scheme proposed in January 2009.[86]

The authoritative government action in the United Kingdom is in stark contrast to what one generally expects from liberal market economies. According to a German regulator, the British were never as liberal as they wanted to be made out, but this has now become very visible in banking regulation: "Adair Turner, the head of the FSA, just went on record with a nice speech suggesting that every bank should be required to have a 20 percent capital ration. There, done, dry up industry! The British now say: 'Let's show the world what hardcore regulation looks like.'"[87]

On the industry side, the crisis and the lost battles of negotiation with the government left a bitter aftertaste. A French observer commented, "The crisis

83. Cited in Anonymous, "Hubris to Nemesis: How Sir Fred Goodwin Became the 'World's Worst Banker.'"

84. Interview, 8 June 2011.

85. Anonymous, "Good Sport: Banks Are Getting By, a Pity about the Customers."

86. Interview, 8 June 2011.

87. Interview, 24 March 2011.

was a terrible blow to the British Bankers' Association, because they ended up being nationalized. . . . The entire liberal reasoning was ripped apart. . . . We never see them taking a stance at international meetings anymore."[88]

With the exception of the few banks that passed the crisis unscathed, the British financial industry had lost not only its economic but also its political standing.

Comparative Assessment

Before discussing the industry-government relations in more detail, it is helpful to compare the performance of the two bailout schemes, in terms of costs, conditions, and criticisms that have been voiced.

Although TARP was an umbrella for a myriad of interventions to stabilize the economy, the expenditures to support financial institutions were by far the most significant part of the expenditures, followed by the bailout of the two automakers.[89] By June 2009, Treasury had committed $474.8 billion, later adjusted to $470.1 billion by the end of December 2011. Of that amount $413.8 billion had actually been spent and $51 billion remained committed.[90] By 2012, 928 companies have benefited from TARP money, including the automakers GM Motors and Chrysler.[91] As of 31 December 2011, 302 TARP recipients had paid back all or a part of their shares for a total of $277.9 billion. Treasury announced that it had written off and lost $12 billion in total; $121 billion in TARP funds remained outstanding in 2012.[92]

The different government agencies responsible for TARP oversight apply slightly different assumptions when estimating the final costs of TARP. While the Office of Management and Budget and the Congressional Budget Office initially estimated the costs of TARP to be around $350 billion in 2009, they now believe it will be somewhere around $50 billion only. The precise final costs fluctuate due to changes in the market price for AIG and GM stock still held by the Treasury and the final amount that will be spent on the housing program. According to Treasury, the largest losses from TARP are expected in housing assistance, as well as AIG and the automobile industry.[93]

Concerning individual programs, the oversight panel felt that homeowner programs made up too small a portion of TARP intervention.[94] The Obama administration initially predicted the homeowner programs would help to keep 4 million families in their homes. Only 600,000 homeowners

88. Interview, 3 May 2011.

89. SIGTARP, *Quarterly Report to Congress,* June 21, 2009, 39.

90. An additional $5 billion had served as an asset guarantee, which was never called on and expired by 3 October 2010.

91. A complete list of recipients is assembled by the nonprofit organization ProPublica: http://projects.propublica.org/bailout/list.

92. SIGTARP, *Quarterly Report to Congress,* January 26, 2012, 33.

93. Ibid., 35.

94. Congressional Oversight Panel, *Final Report of the Congressional Oversight Panel.*

received aid under the program by the spring of 2011.[95] According to several observers, the homeowner program is not very effective because it did not include a mechanism to ensure banks would comply, in particular by accepting write-downs of unpaid loans.[96]

In the United Kingdom, the Special Liquidity Scheme of the Bank of England closed as initially announced on 30 January 2009.[97] However, the Bank of England presented a Discount Window Facility as an immediate and permanent successor. This facility allows for the exchange of a wide range of collateral for up to one year.[98] Since its creation the scheme has been used by thirty-two banks and building societies. Treasury bills with a face value of approximately £185 billion have been lent against collateral of securities of approximately £287 billion in total nominal value. During the remaining life of the scheme, until the maturity of all loans have been reached, the Bank of England can continue to call for margin should the value of the collateral fall relative to the value of the Treasury bills lent.[99]

The Credit Guarantee Scheme closed to new issuance at the end of February 2010. By December 2010, outstanding issuance stood at £115 billion and the government had obtained £2.53 billion in fees for the guarantees.[100] The Asset-Backed Securities Guarantee Scheme window was open until the end of December 2009, but was never actually used.

The recapitalization of Lloyds and RBS turned out to be the most risky part of the British support plan, as the value of shareholding is inherently volatile. After the initial outlay of £37 billion (£20 billion for RBS and £17 billion for Lloyds), the government undertook a series of transactions that raised the capital injections into RBS to £46 billion, to which one can add £8 billion of contingent share purchases, and to Lloyds to £21 by December 2010, totaling an outlay of £75 billion. At that time, the depreciation of the value of stocks was estimated at £12.5 billion if the government were to sell them at market price.[101] As with the equity held in AIG and GM in the United States, the final cost of the British plan depends to a great extent on the final value of the government equity in RBS and Lloyds.

As additional expenditures, the National Accounting Office lists deposit insurance for bank customers. During the financial crisis the Treasury lent £37 billion to the Financial Services Compensation Scheme (FSCS), a fund set up in 2000 to covers deposits of up to £50,000, which was mainly used for the customers of Bradford and Bingley. Furthermore, government support included other loans and guarantees to wholly owned banks, that is,

95. Reuters, "Congressional Oversight Panel."
96. Interview, 22 February 2012, see also Barofsky, *Bailout,* 226–27.
97. Bank of England, *Market Notice: Special Liquidity Scheme.*
98. See www.bankofengland.co.uk/markets/money/dwf/index.htm.
99. Bank of England, *Market Notice: Special Liquidity Scheme.*
100. National Audit Office, *Maintaining the Financial Stability of UK Banks.*
101. Ibid., 14.

Northern Rock and Bradford and Bingley, which amounted to £50 billion in 2009 and £47 billion in 2010.

Using several hypotheses to estimate the final costs, the Treasury estimated the net cost to the taxpayer to lie around £20 to £50 billion in 2009.[102] In 2010, the National Accounting Office reported that default on assets guaranteed is becoming increasingly unlikely, which would mean that there will be no overall net loss on the guarantee schemes, namely, the Special Liquidity Scheme, the Capital Guarantee Scheme, and the Asset Protection Scheme.[103] The most important costs will thus arise from the depreciation of capital invested in wholly or partially owned financial institutions. In a newer estimation, the Treasury suggested that the final fiscal outlays are more likely to be around £2 billion.[104]

In the Eurostat country comparison published in April 2011, capital injections are considered as government expenditures not equity, so the nationalized banks therefore weigh heavily on the estimated public deficit.[105] With the European estimates, the United Kingdom ranks third after Ireland and Germany in absolute terms, with a net cost of €15 billion, and fourth in terms of GDP, with a loss of -0.9 percentage points of GPD.

Considered in the context of economic collapse, both TARP and the British plan worked rather well in calming markets and stabilizing the economy. The Congressional Oversight Panel acknowledged the effectiveness of the TARP but cautioned that it is difficult to untangle its precise impact from other stimulus initiatives.[106] The British plan was generally hailed as an exemplary way of intervening to stabilize markets and became a template for bank support on both sides of the Atlantic.[107]

Politically, the United Kingdom appeared quicker and more decisive. Alistair Darling was himself puzzled by the difference between the two systems:

> The US president, although frequently described as the most powerful man in the world, cannot automatically get what he wants at home. He has to horse-trade. In contrast, when I wrote a check to buy 50 billion pounds of bank shares in the UK, I did not even have to get specific parliamentary authority to do so.[108]

The US administration was slowed down by the procedural requirements of its political systems, but also by the fact that crisis management happened

102. National Audit Office, *Maintaining the Financial Stability across the United Kingdom's Banking System,* 7.

103. National Audit Office, *Maintaining the Financial Stability of UK Banks,* 6.

104. HM Treasury, *Budget 2010,* 74.

105. European Commission, *Eurostat Supplementary Table for the Financial Crisis,* 3–4.

106. Calmes, "Audit Finds TARP Program Effective."

107. Quaglia, "The 'British Plan' as a Pace-Setter."

108. Darling, *Back from the Brink,* 190.

in part in the transition period between the outgoing Bush government and the incoming Obama administration in late fall of 2008.[109]

When comparing the US and the UK bailout plans, most observers argue that the United States has been rather favorable to the financial industry, while the UK plan is described as particularly stringent. In addition to the cheap price tag attached to recapitalization, none of the CEOs of the major US financial institutions were fired, while the UK government insisted on replacing the CEOs of the institutions in which it injected money. Only Culpepper and Reinke propose an opposing assessment, with a similar focus on power relations as the one in this book.[110] According to them, the mandatory nature of the US recapitalization was a key success for US public authorities, which the UK authorities failed to achieve because HSBC and Standard Chartered could more effectively threaten to leave than Wells Fargo or JP Morgan. Put differently, the healthy British were structurally less dependent on the government than the healthy US banks, which led to the particular design—the voluntary nature and the steep fees for participating institutions—of the British plan. This also had an effect on the costs of the rescue packages, Culpepper and Reinke argue, since the British authorities imposed punitive measures on the weakest institutions only. In the end, the government was forced to take the weakest institutions over, which meant the punitive measures remained at its own charge and were not supplemented by contributions from healthier institutions.

Although the authors are right about the power differential among healthy banks in the two countries, their analysis on the costs of the US bailout focuses too narrowly on only the recapitalization program of TARP. Most important, however, they do not consider the long-term moral hazard effects of the US design, where support came with very few strings attached. In the United Kingdom, healthier banks may have gotten away more easily, but they now face a regulatory regime that is very stringent. They have also learned that government support comes with such substantial conditions and changes in corporate control that we would expect few executives to consider a failure scenario as a viable option.

Conclusion

Contrary to what one would expect from liberal market economies with large capital markets, the US and the UK government were quite distinct in their attitudes toward the financial industry and the design of their bank support scheme. While the United States eventually imposed a mandatory capitalization of the major financial institutions, it did so at very favorable

109. Interview, 2 March 2012.
110. Culpepper and Reinke, "The Structural Dependence of Capital on the State."

conditions. The United Kingdom in turn imposed high prices and very stringent conditions on government aid and imposed sector solidarity only by encouraging healthy institutions to raise their capital by a token amount on the markets. The banks that did ask for government support, in turn, had to deal with numerous constraints linked to the substantial government ownership. In both countries, financial institutions also benefited from central bank intervention, in particular massive liquidity provision, but UK banks continuously complained that this aid could have been greater and more tailored to their needs.

The comparison underlines how little the liberal market traditions and the importance of the two financial centers in the overall economy shapes government crisis management. It also reveals how different the US management was with respect to different parts of its financial industry. While the US government dealt with smaller institutions in ways that were routinized and authoritative, it was much more deferential to the major financial institutions, in particular compared to the British way of dealing with equally large institutions. In the United States, the desire to intervene as little as possible in commercial activities led the government to attempt repeatedly to engineer a collective private sector solution. The final bank support plan was shaped by the failures of these attempts. In the United Kingdom, by contrast, the government had visibly no faith in the industry's capacity to save itself and quickly abandoned collective solutions. The final support plan was very much a government-imposed plan, quite different from the preferences of the British banks.

The paths chosen by the US and the UK governments are thus markedly different. In both countries, the financial industry has no tradition of organizing and speaking collectively on competitive issues. Instead of acknowledging this incapacity for collective action, the US government sought to engineer an industry consortium of the largest financial institutions in the midst of the crisis, while the UK government decided to go ahead without the support of the banking sector. Comparing these different paths with the routes chosen in the other two country pairs will help illuminate the implications of these choices for the power balance between public authorities and the financial industry.

6

France and Germany

Unfortunately, bank bailouts are not a lucrative business.
—Hannes Rehm, chairman of the management committee of FMSA

Did things happen differently in continental Europe, where stakeholders have a tradition of economic coordination? Certainly, many aspects in the political and economic organization of the financial systems of France and Germany are comparable. To begin with, both continental European countries are often cited as a prime example of the universal-banking model, in which financial institutions combine retail and investment banking, as well as insurance activities. Both have a high degree of bank intermediation, in particular compared to the United States and the United Kingdom. Moreover, both have a long tradition of government intervention, even though the German state remained arguably somewhat more at arm's length in finance than in France.[1] Still, in both cases, state ownership was common until the 1990s, at least in parts of the financial industry, until liberalization and internationalization began to transform both models.

The main difference between the two countries is the concentration of the sector: while the French industry is dominated by a handful of large banks, the German industry is decentralized and fragmented. In the following, I will argue that the structure of the financial sector and the political organization that follows from it crucially shaped the crisis responses. More than the socio-economic traditions in the two coordinated market economies, the structure of the sector conditioned the collective action capacity of the banking industry and led to divergent outcomes. While the French industry was willing and able to negotiate a common crisis response with an unusual public-private arrangement to increase liquidity during the fall of 2008, the German industry failed to move beyond initial attempts to provide a common industry

1. Busch, *Banking Regulation and Globalization*, 75.

solution. Deutsche Bank in particular even publicly marked their distance from the national scheme.

In the following chapter I review the French and German financial systems and discuss their exposure to the financial crisis. I then lay out the French bank bailout and the German bailout, before turning to the details of the collective action of the banking industry. A comparative assessment discusses the features of the two plans and compares their advantages and disadvantages. The conclusion returns to the central argument about the power of the financial industry in both cases.

The French and German Financial Systems

The French banking industry is one of the most concentrated banking systems in Europe, dominated—before the crisis—by two commercial banks, BNP Paribas and Société Générale, and four mutual banks, which are majority owned by their depositors: Crédit Agricole, Banque Populaire, Caisse d'Epargne, and Crédit Mutuel. These six financial institutions provided about 80 percent of French bank lending. Decentralized between the regional and the federal level, the German financial industry is among the least concentrated in Europe, and characterized by a three pillars: (1) large private banks, most importantly Deutsche Bank, Commerzbank, and previously Dresdner Bank (2) private cooperative banks, the *Volks- und Raiffeisenbanken*, and (3) public saving banks, the Sparkassen and the regional *Landesbanken* (LB). In Germany, public saving banks, which had been protected through a public guarantee against bankruptcy until 2005, specialized in retail banking and loans to Germany's small- and medium-sized companies, considered as the backbone of the German political economy. In both countries, the relationship between banks and nonfinancial firms used to be very tight, particularly through interlocking shareholding and directorates.[2]

In recent decades, the internationalization of financial markets put pressure on the three-pillar decentralized universal bank-based financial system in Germany.[3] Commercial banks sought to develop their investment banking activities and pushed for increasingly liberal security markets, while the federal government set out to centralize regulatory control over these financial activities.[4] With the breakdown of the special regime for the public savings banks through the EU,[5] the Landesbanken in particular rushed into investment activities in foreign markets. Over the course of the 1990s and 2000s,

---

2. Höpner and Krempel, "The Politics of the German Company Network"; François and Lemercier, *Pulsations of French Capitalism*.

3. Busch, *Banking Regulation and Globalization*; Deeg, "Change from Within"; Krahnen and Schmidt, *The German Financial System*.

4. Lütz, "From Managed to Market Capitalism?"

5. Grossman, "Europeanization as an Interactive Process."

the German financial system opened up to increasing securitization and capital-market finance, partially liberalized its three pillar regime, centralized regulatory authority, and internationalized its banking activities, especially in corporate lending and investment banking. An important part of this internationalization happened through takeovers or mergers with foreign firms, both by banks with private shareholders such as Deutsche Bank, Dresdner, and Commerzbank, and by public banks, such as WestLB.[6] As a consequence, the German company network has disentangled and relationship banking with German firms is being replaced by a more market-oriented exchange.[7]

The French system has also evolved considerably in recent decades, moving toward a quite liberal financial sector.[8] Internationalization and trading activities gained increasing importance in the 2000s and nonbank financial institutions began to enter the French market, even if traditional banks held about 70 percent of financial institution assets at the beginning of the crisis.[9] The importance of bank finance for French companies declined dramatically over the course of liberalization, and French banks compensated by developing investment banking.[10] Still, 72 percent of company financing in France was bank based in 2009, and only 28 percent came from capital markets.[11] Despite recent developments, France still has a high degree of bank intermediation. Moreover, retail banking remained the comparative strength of French banks, which some argue sheltered France from exposure to the subprime crisis.[12]

With hindsight, we can see that the French system as a whole has been somewhat less exposed to the financial crisis than the German system. This is in part due to the different internationalization strategies and the strength of French retail banking, with margins that allowed French banks to cushion some of their losses on financial markets. It is also due to precrisis regulation, which was quite stringent in France and somewhat more permissive in Germany, for example, with respect to accounting rules and allowing special purpose entities.[13]

In terms of structural power, both countries are thus quite similar, with an important role for bank intermediation, but also an impressive growth of capital market activities. The increasing reliance on finance and the will to become major financial centers in continental Europe testifies to the

---

6. Hardie and Howarth, "Die Krise but Not La Crise?"

7. Deeg, "Industry and Finance in Germany Since Unification"; Höpner and Krempel, "The Politics of the German Company Network."

8. O'Sullivan, "Acting Out Institutional Change."

9. Hardie and Howarth, "Die Krise but Not La Crise?" 1018.

10. Morin, "A Transformation in the French Model."

11. Cour des Comptes, *Les Concours Publics Aux Établissements de Crédit: Premiers Constats, Premières Recommandations*, 24.

12. Ibid., 15; Hardie and Howarth, "Die Krise but Not La Crise?" 1018.

13. Thiemann, "Accounting for Risk"; Interviews, 20 April 2011, 24 January 2012.

productive power of the industry. However, the regulatory approach was somewhat more interventionist than in the two liberal market economies and offered fewer opportunities for investment in financial innovation. Oversight of the main activities of the financial industry was well institutionalized, in particular in France where retail banking was a core activity, unlike Germany where financial institutions had diversified through subsidiaries abroad that followed different regulatory standards. Compared to the United States and the United Kingdom, the productive power of the financial industry appears to be lower in continental Europe, particularly in France.

Exposure to the Crisis

Still, both countries were highly concerned when the financial crisis reached Europe: Germany with one of the first bank failures, and France when BNP Paribas's decision to close two investment vehicles triggered the first freeze on international capital markets in the summer of 2007. The first fissure in the German banking sector came in July 2007, when IKB Deutsche Industriebank announced that it had suffered important losses in the US housing market and needed to be rescued. Despite this early experience, the extent of exposure of German banks to the unfolding of the crisis in 2008 came as a shock. With the significant growth of trading activities, both for the large private banks and for the Landesbanken in the mid-2000s, the US-subprime crisis hit German banks hard. Traditionally perceived as rather conservative investors, they had registered almost a quarter of Europe's write-downs by the end of September 2008. About two-thirds of these have been in public or quasi-public sector banks.[14] Between the summers of 2007 and 2008, WestLB and BayernLB received guarantees and recapitalization aid from the federal and regional governments. SachsenLB was merged with the Landesbank Baden-Würtemberg to avert a complete failure of the bank, which also let to the resignation of the finance minister and the prime minister of Saxony.

But the large private banks also suffered. Dresdner Bank, a wholly owned subsidiary of the insurance company Allianz, was sold to Commerzbank, which announced its bid in late August 2008. The severity of the difficulties became evident in the month that followed, in particular for the commercial property lender Hypo Real Estate (HRE) and for Commerzbank. HRE had considerable exposure to international housing market difficulties and a particularly heavy debt burden through its German-Irish subsidiary Depfa.[15] Fearing a chain reaction in case HRE would go bankrupt, the federal government and private banks agreed on a bailout credit line on the last weekend in September 2008, which was revised in early October. Commerzbank

14. International Monetary Fund, *Germany: 2008 Article IV Consultation*, 12.
15. Brost, Schieritz, and Storn, "Hypo Real Estate."

held out until December 2008, but eventually it also asked for substantial government aid.

In France, the two commercial banks managed to absorb their initial difficulties: Société Générale experienced a single day trading loss of €4.9 billion due to fraudulent activities of a junior trader in January 2009, and BNP officials announced that they were the first French bank affected by the subprime crisis. Still, the two banks most critically affected banks were Natixis—the investment branch of Banque Populaire and Caisse d'Epargne—and Dexia. Exposed to both the subprime crisis and the Madoff fraud at €450 million, the value of Natixis's stock dropped by 95 percent in the fall of 2008. The heavy effect on both of its main shareholders eventually led to the resignation of the CEOs of Banque Populaire and Caisse d'Epargne in March 2009. In a deal brokered by the French president Nicolas Sarkozy, the two banks merged and François Perol, a former banker, *inspecteur des finances*, and the economic advisor to the president, became chairman of the board of directors of the new bank BPCE.[16] The Franco-Belgian public finance bank Dexia also came into trouble in September 2008 due to liquidity difficulties when other banks refused to continue lending because of potential problems with its US subsidiary Financial Security Assurance. Dexia was quickly forced to apply for state aid and was bailed out by a uniquely coordinated action between the Belgian, the French, and the Luxembourg governments, after net losses in 2008 of €3.3 billion. But troubles continued. In the second quarter of 2011 alone, Dexia announced a €4 billion loss and saw its share price drop by 22 percent. Negotiations with the three governments resumed, which agreed to buy parts of Dexia's operations and to fund a bad bank for its troubled assets in late 2011.

It would have been presumptuous to say anything definite about the variation in exposure of the French and German financial industries in the fall of 2008. Without the certainty of hindsight, both industries appeared shaken by the crisis and early fissures signaled the need for more comprehensive intervention in both cases. A French official underlines how parallel concerns were in both countries: "Bank intermediation in Europe is around 80 percent. In the US and the UK it is about 20 percent. This means that their main objective is to keep the economy going. Ours is to save the banks."[17]

National Bank Support Schemes

Parallel to their individual measures, both the French and German governments began to develop national schemes once the failure of Lehman Brothers rippled through financial markets worldwide.

16. Jabko and Massoc, "French Capitalism under Stress."
17. Interview, 12 April 2010; see also Goldstein and Véron, *Too Big to Fail.*

The French Bank Rescue Plan

Announced one day after the EU summit on emergency measures in the Eurozone on 12 October 2008, the French plan was put into place by law on 16 October 2008 through the *Loi de finances rectificative pour le financement de l'économie*. It consists of two ad hoc institutions: the Société de Financement de l'Economie Française (SFEF), set up to raise capital on financial markets and provide liquidity to ailing financial institutions, and the Société de Prise de Participation de l'Etat (SPPE), through which the government would buy equities from the French banks and thus help to recapitalize them. The government agreed to guarantee bank bonds issued by the SFEF up to €360 billion for a maximum maturity of five years.[18] At the same time, the SPPE would invest €10.5 billion in the recapitalization of French banks by January 2009.

In the European landscape, the SFEF is a rather unique arrangement, as it is jointly owned by the six big banks and the government, which hold 66 percent and 34 percent respectively. Seven other financial institutions also signed the SFEF agreement to benefit from the liquidity provided through the state-backed mechanism.[19] Interestingly, HSBC France did not sign the agreement, but was a shareholder of the SFEF. Because of the systemic risk they represented, the six main French banks were the beneficiaries of the SFEF and the SPPE. To avoid stigmatizing any one particular bank, all six agreed to be recapitalized simultaneously through the SPPE. Put differently, the government struck a deal with the six main institutions, which effectively constrained them to accept capital and increase domestic lending. However, the capital injected by the state initially took the form of supersubordinated debt securities. Despite their subordinated status, these securities were supposedly less risky than equity shares and allow great payback flexibility to banks.

In return for this government support, the banks committed to maintain domestic lending at a growth rate of 3–4 percent, despite the difficult economic context. Recapitalization was furthermore tied to curbs on dividend payments, a ban on executive bonuses for 2008, and increased trade financing. Concerning executive pay, the banks agreed to follow a code of conduct drafted jointly by the main French business organization, the Mouvement des entreprises de France (MEDEF), and the association of the largest listed French companies, the Association française des enterprises privées (AFEP).

---

18. This amount also included the guarantees granted to Dexia.

19. These were mainly housing and consumer credit institutions, often the financial activity branches of large industrial groups: PSA Finance (PSA-Peugeot-Citroën), General Electric, Crédit Immobilier, Laser Cofinoga, RCI Banque (Groupe Renault), S2Pass (Groupe Carrefour) and VFS Finance (Volvo). GMAC had originally signed the SFEF agreement but did not request liquidity support. Cour des Comptes, *Les concours publics aux établissements de crédit: premiers constats, premières recommandations*, 32.

The severest conditions imposed by the French government were tied to the rescue of Dexia. In exchange for its participation in the guarantee scheme and the recapitalization via the SPPE, the French, Belgian, and Luxembourgian governments demanded a change of the management, the presence of a government representative on the board of directors, and a restructuring plan, all of which was needed for all state aid approved by the European Commission. Similarly, the French state completely restructured Banque Populaire and Caisse d'Epargne in order to deal with the difficulties of Natixis and demanded that a state representative be included on the supervisory board of the newly formed BPCE bank. According to Christine Lagarde, then minister of the economy, the difference in government control over the French banks receiving government support is tied to the nature of the aid. The SPPE was put into place as a measure necessary to maintain liquidity and the financing of the French economy. The French government therefore did not want to tie recapitalization to government control over the banks, in contrast to Dexia, which it rescued to avoid bankruptcy. For BPCE, she insisted that the reasoning was again different: state control was only temporary and meant to accompany the merger of Banque Populaire and Caisse d'Epargne and to help develop their business project.[20]

Over time, the SPPE recapitalization evolved: in 2009, the government agreed to expand recapitalization to an additional €10.25 billion.[21] Whereas all six banks had participated in the first tranche by issuing supersubordinated debt securities to the SPPE, the rational for participating in the second tranche was less evident for banks that were not in obvious financial difficulties. Crédit Agricole and Crédit Mutuel therefore decided not to participate in the second phase of SPPE intervention. The other banks chose to issue preferred shares. BNP Paribas even demanded that the initial €2.5 billion of its supersubordinated securities held by the SPPE be replaced with preferred shares in March 2009. Prior to each support through the SPPE, the general secretary of the French banking supervision authority wrote a letter to the European Commission to assure them that the banks were viable and that the support aimed to maintain the financing of the economy, not rescue an ailing bank, with the exception of Dexia, where the equity bought through the SPPE was an explicit rescue measure.

The two ad hoc institutions were created for a limited amount of time and ended their programs according to schedule. The SFEF stopped issuing securities in late 2009 and remained in place merely to manage the reimbursement of existing securities that had not reached their maturity. The

20. Cited in ibid., 122.
21. The first phase of bank equity acquisition began at €10.5 billion in December 2008. The second one, initially announced in January 2009 as an addition €13 billion, was put into place in July 2009 for €10.25 billion. The total amount of bank support managed by the SPPE thus rose to €20.75 billion.

SPPE recapitalization support was available until the end of August 2009. Aid to Dexia continued well beyond the national scheme. In addition to a series of individual measures, the French, Belgian, and Luxembourg governments agreed jointly in October 2011 to set up a bad bank that would manage Dexia's troubled assets to avoid reinjecting more capital into Dexia.[22]

The German Bank Rescue Plan

Like the French government, the German government realized by late September 2008 that individual bank bailouts would be insufficient to avert a crisis. To avoid a run on the banks and strengthen confidence, Chancellor Angela Merkel declared on 5 October that the government would guarantee all individual saving deposits. The same day, the German government, the central bank, and representatives of the German financial industry met to devise a comprehensive support plan for the German banking system. After discussions within the Eurogroup and the G7, and an accelerated legislative process, which lasted for only a week, the initiative resulted in the German Financial Market Stabilization Act (*Finanzmarktstabilisierungsgesetz*) of 17 October, aimed at restoring confidence and facilitating lending.

The law set up a fund administered by a new Federal Agency for Financial Market Stabilization (FMSA), established as a dependent agency at the Bundesbank, but supervised by the Finance Ministry. FMSA's fund, the Sonderfonds Finanzmarktstabilisierung (SoFFin), provided support to ailing banks. Unlike France, the United Kingdom, or the United States, where separate institutions were in charge of different instruments, SoFFin could provide funding guarantees, capital injections, and manage asset purchases in order to deal with risky assets. A maximum of €100 billion financing was allocated for the stabilization package. Of these, €70 billion were set aside for recapitalization and risk assumption, with an additional €10 billion available upon legislative approval, if necessary. Part of these €80 billion is a risk assumption facility, where SoFFin can buy up to €5 billion of toxic assets from each eligible institution.[23] Concerning guarantees, the fund was allowed to assume guarantees up to an amount of €400 billion: on the basis of an assumed default rate of 5 percent, it had been equipped with €20 billion in case any default would occur.[24]

The most striking feature of the German bank support plan was its voluntary basis and its openness to any financial institution, not just systemically relevant banks. Banks, insurance companies, or pension funds could choose

---

22. Martens and Brunsden, "Dexia to Set Up 'Bad Bank' With Guarantees from France, Belgium."

23. This provision was never actually used. Instead, toxic assets were handled through an additional legal provision in July 2009, which allowed for the creation of "bad banks" (see below).

24. Deutsche Bundesbank, *Cornerstones of the Financial Market Stabilization Act.*

various stabilization measures, and the government remained very hesitant to acquire control in the banks it supported. Recapitalization was undertaken in the form of "silent" or nonparticipatory shareholding. Still German financial institutions were reluctant and largely requested state guarantees rather than recapitalization. Commerzbank was the first big bank to apply for government participation for an initial €18.2 billion. As in most other countries, recapitalization and asset support came in exchange for a commitment to maintain lending and present a restructuring plan, as well as restrictions on dividend payment and executive pay. Financial institutions receiving capital injections had to limit the salaries of their executive board members at €500,000 and follow compensation guidelines by SoFFin.

As economic conditions continued worsening, the German authorities revised the initial bank support plan. In particular the deterioration of HRE's situation led to repeated extensions of the initial rescue package, initially mainly in the form of guarantees. Given the amount of support granted to HRE, around €100 billion at the end of 2008, the German government and the other stakeholders replaced the supervisory board and began to participate in the capital of HRE. In April 2009, the Financial Market Stabilization Extension Act (*Gesetz zur weiteren Stabilisierung des Finanzmarktes*) provided for the possibility to nationalize banks, including the possibility to expropriate shareholders that refused to relinquish their holdings.[25] On 5 October 2009, HRE became the first bank in the history of the Federal Republic of Germany to be nationalized since 1949.[26] In parallel, the Financial Market Stabilization Continuation Act (*Gesetz zur Fortentwicklung der Finanzmarktstabilisierung*) of July 2009 enabled the FMSA to create bank-specific transfer institutions (so called "bad banks") for the liquidation of toxic assets for an expected amount of up to €200 billion.[27] HRE and West LB applied for such liquidation institutions, which led to the creation of FMS Wertmanagement (FMS-WM)[28] responsible for the assets of HRE and Erste Abwicklungsanstalt (EAA)[29] for WestLB, both managed by the FMSA.

By late 2009, the German government, initially hesitant to intervene, sought ways to ensure that liquidity problems and insolvency would be detected earlier and that banks could not force the government into repeated and costly bailout measures. In November 2010, the government passed a law on restructuration and orderly dismantling of credit institutions (*Restrukturierungsgesetz*), which gives the government and the financial regulator BaFin (Bundesanstalt für Finanzdienstleistungsaufsicht) new

---

25. This measure targeted in particular the US investor J. C. Flowers, who had refused to sell his HRE shares to the federal government.

26. See Brost, Schieritz, and Storn, "Hypo Real Estate: Die Mutter aller Pleiten."

27. The two legislations are also known under the tongue breaker name "Finanzmarkt-stabilisierungsergänzungsgesetz" and "Finanzmarktstabilisierungsfortentwicklungsgesetz."

28. www.fms-wm.de.

29. www.aa1.de.

possibilities for the control and supervision of banks in difficulties and modifies the bankruptcy procedure. If oversight authorities detect severe problems, they can force the financial institution to transfer the "healthy" parts of its assets into a public "bridge bank" and liquidate its risky assets, at the costs of the bondholders.[30] Additional costs of such restructuring are carried by a new obligatory bank levy to avoid imposing costs on the taxpayer.

The *Restrukturierungsgesetz* also transformed the responsibility of the FMSA and SoFFin. FMSA was given the responsibility to manage two funds, SoFFin and a newly recreated restructuring fund. Originally set up until the end of 2009, SoFFin's life was first extended until the end of 2010. After that date, it was no longer charged with giving new credit, capital, or guarantees to financial institutions. Still the FMSA remains in place in order to manage the restructuring fund and the new bank tax levied on financial institutions. However, in 2012 the German government decided to reopen SoFFin through an additional financial market stabilization law, which allowed for the same initial coverage in case systemic institutions may need public support.

Collective Action by the Financial Industry

France

The pillars of the French bailout plan, the SFEF and the SPPE, would not have taken shape in the same way without the collective action of the industry. However, even in the homogenous French banking sector collective action is not given and started to crumble as the crisis lost in urgency. In the following, we will review the details of the public-private cooperation in creating the SFEF and the SPPE before discussing the tensions and risks of collective action in French finance.

A Collectively Negotiated Plan

The SFEF was created jointly by the major French banks and the government, in order to issue collective bonds, backed by a public guarantee, for the French financial industry. The government contributed 34 percent to the capital of the SFEF, but the starting capital was rather small (€50 million). The potential to issue up to €265 billion was possible mainly because

---

30. In contrast to the "bad banks," the liquidation institutions charged with the selling off of toxic assets managed by the FMSA, these bridge banks are thus considered as "good banks" because they preserve the most valuable assets of a financial institution. Interview with a German regulator, Frankfurt, 23 March 2011.

participating banks had to put down collateral, which was pooled by the SFEF. The operation of the SFEF was thus comparable to a privately owned and run company, but with a public guarantee.

The government did have an important role in the administration of the SFEF, however. For one, the government had a veto right concerning all decisions affecting the interest of the state. In addition, it participated in the executive board with representatives of the seven stakeholder banks by appointing Michel Camdessus, a former governor of the French Central Bank and former director of the IMF, who also became the president of the board; Jean Bassère, at the time head of the Inspection générale de finance; and Françoise Malrieu, as independent administrator. In late 2009, Malrieu would replace Michel Camdessus as president of the SFEF. In addition, the French Central Bank played a role in the oversight of the collateral of the banks.

Apart from these mechanisms, the SFEF was run like a private company with personnel and contributions from its member banks. It had a small staff of three to four people with an executive director, Thierry Coste, who had previously been the CEO of Crédit Agricole Asset Management.[31] Crédit Foncier, a subsidiary of the Groupe Caisse d'Epargne, managed the back and the middle office. In addition, the SFEF worked with outside experts on issues such as audit and legal advice, and was also subject to all other public oversight mechanisms.[32]

The arrangement had advantages for both the banks and the government. For the banks, most important, the SFEF gave access to liquidity at a time in which markets were frozen and access to market liquidity was impossible for individual banks. In addition, pooling collateral through the SFEF made the fee for the public guarantee cheaper than elsewhere.[33] Moreover, the collective issuing allowed the French sector to produce a great volume and thus a better price on financial markets, compared to other countries. As expressed by a German public official, "With hindsight, we admire [the French] solution, since they were able to offer a much better price thanks to the centralization and the volume this allowed them to create. In Germany, the risk profile of the state-backed bank bonds was the same, but the price was much higher."[34]

To some degree, the success of the SFEF came as a surprise. One participant remembers, "We issued more than we thought we would. Initially, we were aiming for €10–15 billion, but we ended up issuing over 70 billion."[35]

---

31. Thierry Coste was replaced by Henry Raymond after the SFEF had stopped issuing bonds in late 2009.
32. Cf., Banque de France, *De la crise financière à la crise économique*, 57–58.
33. Ibid., 57–58.
34. Interview, 22 January 2012.
35. Interview, 20 April 2011.

The issuing was so advantageous that the Treasury branch responsible for issuing government bonds requested close coordination with SFEF, fearing that its bonds would create competition with French government bonds.[36] But the government accepted this risk, because it also obtained a major advantage in organizing a collective private but government-backed liquidity instrument: unless called on, the public guarantees would not show up as public deficit.

For the French government, which was concerned about meeting the Maastricht criteria and maintaining a high rating on international financial markets, the calculation of its debt by Eurostat was crucial. Including the SFEF exposure would have increased the ration of the deficit to GDP by 5–6 percentage points. The French Treasury had complicated discussions about this issue with Eurostat in Brussels, but in the end, the insistence of the French minister Christine Lagarde paid off and the guarantee for SFEF's €70 billion was excluded from public accounting.[37] The criticism of German politicians did little to change this decision.[38]

An observer summarizes the SFEF experience as a remarkable feat: "Banks, which typically pass their time thinking about competition with the others, sat down and developed a powerful funding mechanism and agreed on the allocation of credit within less than 15 days."[39]

Despite the mutual benefits of the arrangements, banks were eager to leave the SFEF and raise their own liquidity as soon as market conditions allowed. First, this would mean that they no longer needed to pay the public guarantee, and second, it allowed them to get their collateral back, which freed up a significant amount of assets. Baudouin Prot, at the time president of the French banking association Fédération bancaire française (FBF), thus declared at a Senate hearing that the SFEF would cease its issuing in October 2009, three month before schedule.[40]

The second ad hoc institution of the French bank support scheme, the SPPE was 100 percent state owned and designed to inject capital into the French banking sector. Nonetheless French banks simultaneously accepted this capital and jointly agreed on the conditions attached to this support.

With the experience of two bank failures in which the government intervened heavily to avert bankruptcy—Natixis and Dexia—the SPPE was promoted as an instrument to help stabilize the financing of the economy, not a bailout measure per se. The French government insisted that all banks accepted the capital so that they could continue supplying credit to the real economy, not because any one of them needed a bailout. This argument

36. Interviews, 3 May 2011, 6 June 2011.
37. Interview, 15 April 2011; Bronnec and Fargues, *Bercy au cœur du pouvoir*, 213–14.
38. Bonse and Vogel, "Bankenrettung: Eurostat weist Vorwürfe zurück."
39. Interview. 3 May 2011.
40. Deneuville, "Les banques françaises prêtes à se financer toutes seules à compter d'octobre."

was somewhat disingenuous, remembers a public official, in particular concerning one bank, which remains unnamed. Without a collective solution, this bank might have been considered insolvent, in which case the European Commission would have requested that aid be tied to a restructuring plan. "In the end, the fact that the French plan supported healthy banks in order to sustain the financing of the economy helped to avoid a restructuring plan for [possibly one of the] French banks."[41]

Because the SPPE worked as a collective arrangement supporting "the economy" rather than any one bank in particular, it was considered as quite different from the recapitalization of Dexia and the restructuring the government undertook when it merged Banque Populaire and Caisse d'Epargne into the new BPCE group. As a consequence, the government wanted to avoid taking any form of control in the banks recapitalized through the SPPE and opted to buy supersubordinate securities rather than ordinary stock. As bonds, these securities were less risky than stock, but the government also did not reap as much profit as it would have made with other types of equity. "If the government had taken stock, it would have made more money. But it was important to [be] different from Dexia, to avoid appearing as the crutch of a dead man."[42]

Likewise, the French banks all agreed that they were not interested in a mechanism for toxic asset relief, because they had few illiquid assets and were thus able to carry them for longer than some of their competitors abroad.[43] In addition, the French government had a negative experience with a bad bank ("consortium de réalisation") set up for Crédit Lyonnais after its bankruptcy in 1993. At its closure in 2006, the losses were estimated at €16 billion.[44] For the collective plan, asset transfer was thus excluded by all participants.

In exchange for the support through both the SPPE and the SFEF, the government asked for two main conditions: maintaining lending and limiting executive compensation.[45] The lending requirement was fixed at 3–4 percent credit expansion. A senior bank executive suggests that the figure was determined directly by the banks. He remembers a telephone conversation with a colleague, who had been summoned to the Ministry of Finance the next morning: "We absolutely must give them a forecast: what level of credit can we commit to for 2009? . . . I called my colleagues, business partners, we all looked at our data, we called around. . . . In three hours, we had arrived at 3–4 percent."[46]

41. Interview, 15 April 2011.
42. Interview, 3 May 2011.
43. Ibid.
44. Follorou, "La fermeture du consortium de réalisation marque la fin du feuilleton des dérives du Crédit Lyonnais."
45. Interview, 2 April 2013.
46. Cited in Jabko and Massoc, "French Capitalism under Stress," 13.

Similarly, restrictions on executive compensation relied much on cooperation from the industry itself. While the initial agreement was rather precise with respect to executive compensation, it was vague concerning the bonuses for traders and had no sanctioning mechanisms. The Cour de Comptes repeatedly criticized the loopholes of the framework, which relied on a code of conduct developed by the business associations AFEP and MEDEF and on compensation committees put into place by each financial institution, with great flexibility concerning appointments.[47]

In sum, the French bank support plan was designed in very close cooperation with the banking sector, which succeeded in coordinating among its different members in order to devise collective solutions for both liquidity and recapitalization. How can we explain such seeming consensus and at what price did it come about?

Sector Solidarity—Origins and Tensions

Of course, crisis times can facilitate cooperation, but interactions among the French banking elites were always close. Even in normal times, the CEOs of the major banks get together once a month and discuss various topics, which is helped by the fact that all of their headquarters are in the same city: Paris. In the fall of 2008, conference calls with the CEOs were organized by the banking association FBF every other day at 8:00 a.m.[48] However, most of the government contacts happened between the individual bank executives and the public decision makers directly.[49] The back and forth between the banks, their association, and the government are easily manageable, since there is only a small number of banks involved. The finance minister did not need to negotiate with the FBF, she could simply talk with the CEO directly.

Owing to common education and work experiences, not only the ties among banks, but also the links with the government are unusually close in France.

All the heads of the French banks have worked in public administration, including HSBC France. Of course they are competitors in normal times, but they share a common language, a common experience, which means that in times of crisis, they have been extremely united.[50]

Indeed, when one looks at the profile of the senior executives, it becomes easy to understand how a British subsidiary, HSBC France, could decide to be a stakeholder in SFEF, without even seeking to benefit from its issuing.

---

47. Cour des Comptes, *Les concours publics aux établissements de crédit: premiers constats, premières recommandations*; Cour des Comptes, *Les concours publics aux établissements de crédit: bilan et énseignement à tirer.*
48. Interview, 3 May 2011.
49. Interview, 2 April 2013.
50. Interview, 3 May 2011.

Prior to being acquired by HSBC in 2000, HSBC France had been a French bank, Crédit Commercial de France, and was run by Charles-Henri Filippi, a former ENA student with experience in public administration who joined CCF in 1987. The solidarity of French banking thus extends to HSBC France, in times of crisis management as much as in a recent scandal on check fee collusion.[51] Jabko and Massoc have labeled the almost cartellike structure of French banking an "informal consortium."[52]

Despite these links, establishing a collective solution is not easy when individual interests diverge too much. It is thus important to note that the financial situation of the banks was somewhat equivalent during the crisis. Out of the five banks, four had significant difficulties obtaining liquidity, even if their situation was not as catastrophic as elsewhere. As one observer notes, "The four banks had roughly the same interest, the four biggest in fact. And the fifth, which was also the smallest, was really in perfect health, but it got its arm twisted."[53]

Differences in the situation of the four biggest banks may have played at the margin, but they were not important enough to change their position toward a collective rescue scheme. In the spring of 2009, Société Générale decided to sell its asset management division, which held €11.2 billion potentially toxic assets, most notably CDOs, which the management appears to have been to a great extent uninformed about.[54] BNP Paribas was seemingly better off after closing the investment vehicles that had been exposed to the US housing market, but its chairman, Michel Pébéreau, was nonetheless centrally involved in designing the French plan.[55] All the French banks liked the support arrangements, with the exception of Crédit Mutuel, which considered that it did not need it. "But they ended up going along with it, out of solidarity with the French financial sector."[56]

The divisions within the French industry become more visible over time. In particular the second recapitalization through SPPE divided the banks. BNP Paribas insisted that the second tranche be committed earlier than originally planned. By obtaining fresh capital, they were able to acquire the Belgian bank Fortis, only one day after the SPPE injection. As Jabko and Massoc note, recapitalization served to help the group's expansion.[57] The other banks were not only dismayed at the government's response to BNPs individual timing needs, they also did not all agree that a second round of capital injections were at all necessary. Both Crédit Mutuel and Crédit Agricole therefore decided not to participate in the recapitalization scheme the second time

51. Autorité de la concurrence, "Collusion in the banking sector."
52. Jabko and Massoc, "French Capitalism under Stress."
53. Interview, 15 April 2011.
54. Anonymous, "Le nouveau fiasco à 5 milliards de la Société Générale."
55. Jabko and Massoc, "French Capitalism under Stress," 16.
56. Interview, 20 April 2011.
57. Jabko and Massoc, "French Capitalism under Stress," 16.

around. The exit of the two banks signaled that SPPE no longer served the simple financing of the economy. It had also become clear that some banks had used the capital to expand rather than just weather the crisis.

With hindsight, some public officials wonder whether the conditions for aid were not too favorable, as the Court of Audit had stated, but underline that the objective at the time was to be as risk adverse as possible. "We were actually quite nice with the banks [and] we could have certainly made more money. Had we taken ordinary stock in BNP rather than preferred shares, for example, we would have made five times more than what we ended up earning."[58]

But given the fact that the government got out of the bank rescue with positive figures, such issues appear minor and did not become part of public debate. It also never became an important issue that the conditions attached to the government support were not systematically followed. As the lending statistics revealed, the total credit expansion for the five major banks was between 2.5 and 2.7 percent rather than the 3–4 percent the banks had committed to.[59] Moreover, the restrictions imposed on executive pay soon revealed limitations. Signing up to the AFEP-MEDEF code of conduct happened on a voluntary basis with few formal consequences and covered only a limited number of bank executives. Still, following public outcry when the size of bonus payments became known in French press in February 2009, several leading bank executives renounced their bonuses voluntarily.[60] According to the Court of Audit the executive pay commitment was generally followed, but it was unclear whether these were temporary arrangements or commitments meant to become institutionalized.[61] Indeed, the French president and finance minister judged the situation unsatisfactory in the summer of 2009, after it had become known that BNP had provisioned €1 billion as bonus payments for its traders.[62]

In sum, the French support scheme was judged successful by both the government and the banks. Despite some criticism, what mattered was that the French banking sector had withstood the financial market difficulties of 2008–9 and that the government had managed to intervene in an appropriate manner.

Germany

One might have expected a similar type of private coordination in Germany, where collective action by the banking sector has a long tradition. Indeed, the government initially sought to maintain its arm's

---

58. Interview, 15 April 2011.

59. Cour des Comptes, *Les concours publics aux établissements de crédit: bilan et enseignement à tirer*, 39.

60. Jabko and Massoc, "French Capitalism under Stress."

61. Cour des Comptes, *Les concours publics aux établissements de crédit: bilan et enseignement à tirer*, 92.

62. Dong, "Bonus."

length relationship and encourage the banks to find a solution among themselves. Only when it became clear that private initiatives would be insufficient to avert a crisis did the government engage in negotiations with the banking sector representatives and propose a government-led plan. Yet contrary to the forced recapitalization in the United States and the collective banking industry plan in France, the German plan was voluntary and thus stigmatizing, which soon led to a clash. Trying to respond to these imbalances revealed by the German plan, the government therefore decided to invest heavily in reregulation and effectively abandoned its bank-friendly approach in favor of a more intrusive supervisory regime and a preventive bank levy for future bailouts. The following discussion reviews these three phases—(1) private sector solutions, (2) public-private bailout scheme negotiations and (3) reregulatory turn toward more intervention.

Private-Sector Solutions

Much of the favorable financial regulation in the 2000s had to do with the German government's desire to establish a financial center that could rival London or even New York. This affected in particular decisions concerning accounting standards and supervisory issues that varied from country to country, so that banks could respond by moving abroad.

> Banks can threaten to leave. The regulators only handled them with kid gloves. It was a completely different mindset from today. The finance minister at the time continued to declare that finance has surpassed Germany's automobile industry and had to be supported. We joked that it was finance-Stalinism.[63]

With respect to individual bank bailouts, the government involved the representatives of the financial industry from very early on and asked them to contribute to the rescue. This began most notably with the rescue of IKB, where the government met with banking representatives in a weekend session on 28–29 of July 2007. The meeting and telephone sessions included representatives from government, the Bundesbank, BaFin, and all three banking pillars: Josef Ackermann representing the commercial banks, Christopher Pleister for the cooperative banking association Bundesverband der Volks- und Raiffeisenbanken (BVR), Karl-Peter Schackmann-Fallis for the Deutscher Sparkassen- und Giroverband (DSGV). In addition, the board of the Kreditanstalt für Wiederaufbau (KfW), a public agency charged with the financing of infrastructure and industry and principal stockholder of

---

63. Interview, 10 December 2011.

IKB, participated and even some of the members of the administration of KfW participated through by conference calls.[64] A described by a participant, "IKB was supposed to be saved by the private sector. The meeting was dominated by the banking associations. The saving banks announced that they were willing to contribute €1 billion. Then the KfW joined in."[65]

At the end of the weekend, the IKB rescue package of €3.5 billion was carried at 70 percent by the KfW, while other banks with stakes in IKB assumed the remaining 30 percent. During the following months, IKB's situation continued to deteriorate. By February 2008, the banks and the KfW agreed to two more bailout packages, in KfW's case state backed, which ended up increasing KfW's participation in IKB to 90.8 percent. In August 2008, KfW sold its part in IKB to the US investor Lone Star, at a very low price and after transferring a considerable amount of IKB's risky assets into its own books or into a special purpose vehicle.[66]

HRE's rescue began in a similar way, as an attempt to stabilize the bank through a private banking consortium. On 23 September, HRE sent a letter to the German finance minister to request that he and Josef Ackermann approach the banking sector to ask for a special credit line. In an informal meeting on 25 September with the heads of several major German banks, banking associations, the financial regulator, and the central bank, it was agreed "to find a solution for HRE's difficulties without the state."[67] During the first crisis session on 26–29 September, the banking sector agreed on a private sector contribution of €8.5 billion for the rescue of HRE. Negotiations were formally organized between the banks themselves and the government. Jörg Asmussen, head of the Treasury, only arrived at the room on Sunday night at 5:00 p.m., which was "surprisingly late" according to the banks and maybe "tactical" but "quite dangerous."[68] For the banks, €8.5 billion was a substantial contribution "beyond the limit of pain," according to the president of the commercial bank association Bundesverband deutscher Banken (BdB) Klaus-Peter Müller, who emphasized that his member institutions were really upset about the amount.[69]

Yet within only four days, it became clear that the liquidity need of HRE had to be adjusted upward from €35 billion to €50 billion. Faced with such changes in the context, the previous agreement had to be renegotiated on Sunday, 5 October. Banks agreed to increase their contribution to €15 billion, but this second rescue offer would also just buy time. A regulator summarizes, "Solutions in Germany have traditionally been funded within the private sector. IKB and HRE both had rescue commitments from the

64. Steinbrück, *Unterm Strich*, 197.
65. Interview. 10 December 2011.
66. The finance ministry estimates the net losses at €10 billion for the public budget and €1.4 billion for the bank associations.
67. Steinbrück cited in Krüger et al., *Beschlussempfehlung und Bericht*, 120.
68. Ackermann cited in ibid., 135.
69. Cited in ibid., 126.

financial sector. And then the taxpayer began to contribute more and more money." This is partially a matter of size, he adds: "Can Deutsche Bank keep IKB from failing? Maybe, but supporting HRE is already another dimension. Then add the Landesbanken. At some point, it just becomes too much and the state has to ask itself whether it is time to intervene."[70]

But not only financial institutions kept encountering difficulties, the real economy began to feel the crisis as well. "Peer Steinbrück said until very late that we are not affected and that we will not react," remembers one observer.[71] Indeed the Mittelstand, Germany's small- and medium-sized enterprises, had signaled that they did not feel the financial turbulences. But when access to credit effectively tightened, "[the Mittelstand] literally went amok. That's when the political awareness began." At that point, a government official remembers, "We had to change our discourse from one day to the next."[72]

Negotiating a National Bailout Plan

On 5 October, just before midnight and after reaching an agreement on HRE, the government began to openly discuss a systemic national bank support scheme. Participants in this meeting included Josef Ackermann (Deutsche Bank), Klaus-Peter Müller (BdB), Martin Blessing (Commerzbank), Paul Achleiter (CFO of Allianz AG), and on the government side Finance Minister Peer Steinbrück and Deputy Finance Minister Jörg Asmussen, the governor of the Bundesbank Axel Weber, and Jens Weidmann from the Federal Chancellery.[73] Based on a proposal developed by the Bundesbank, the group agreed on a national scheme that would become the Finanzmarktstabilisierungsgesetz only twelve days later. During the talks and the negotiations that preceded and followed it, three topics were noteworthy: (1) the lack of a collective commitment from the industry and the voluntary nature of the aid arrangement, (2) the degree of sanctions the government sought to tie to the proposed aid, and (3) the difficulties in setting up a publicly run rescue fund.

Collective recapitalization, which would have avoided stigmatizing individual banks, was debated heavily, but eventually discarded. Nobody felt comfortable having the government inject capital even into healthy banks and impose interests on everybody. "All bank associations were against forced recapitalization," remembers a close observer.[74] The resistance of the banking sector led a lack of political will in a context where government still had faith that the sector knew best how to organize its own rescue.

---

70. Interview, 24 March 2011.
71. Interview, 15 November 2011.
72. Interview, 10 December 2011.
73. Steinbrück, *Unterm Strich*, 211.
74. Interview, 17 February 2012.

More important, it also reflected the complexity of the German situation, which was broken up into different administrative levels and pillars. In Germany, the saving banks had a well-functioning deposit insurance fund. Interbank solidarity existed within the pillar, but not beyond. Discussions to merge or extend these insurances across the pillars were forcefully opposed by the savings banks: "even before we could ask, they said 'Do not even think about it.' "[75] "They refused to use their insurance to bail out banks with a completely different risk portfolio," said another participant, concluding that it would have been impossible to design a sectorwide solution.[76] In addition, the government was equally divided between the federal and the *Länder* levels. Some public savings banks were rescued by their *Land*, others jointly: "It was unorganized muddling through, . . . with much kicking and screaming, both from politics and from the banks."[77]

Interestingly, Germany did not face this issue for the first time. Following the Herstatt failure, the banking sector and the government agreed to found a privately funded Liquiditäts-Konsortialbank (LikoBank) in 1974, which was supposed to act as a lender of last resort to ailing financial institutions. Yet the rescue bank was not at all used during the financial crisis! Because the LikoBank held "only" €6 billion, the government feared that it would have quickly been depleted.[78] The deposit insurance fund was more important, but already used up through IKB. The commercial banks could not keep up, and the saving banks, which had paid their contributions, refused to pay for the gamblers. An alternative solution on the side of the commercial banks was equally difficult to image because of the heterogeneity in size: "Deutsche Bank is huge, Commerzbank weak, HRE small. How should they support each other collectively? Yes, we had solidarity among the saving banks. But the commercial banks chickened out, because of their huge imbalances."[79]

While the saving banks blocked an industrywide FDIC-like deposit insurance mechanism, the commercial banks refused to be treated in the same way through some form of collective recapitalization, which necessarily came with costs and conditions. The biggest bank was not among those most badly hit: why should it accept a collective recapitalization? Had Deutsche Bank had the size of Crédit Mutuel in the French landscape, the result might have been different. Or alternatively, had Josef Ackermann been as interested in a collective scheme as Michel Pébereau, he might have persuaded others that solidarity was in their best interest.

Without such efforts, the rational for accepting collective recapitalization was not evident. The conditions attached to the aid were uncomfortable, and the government did seek to insert sanctioning mechanisms to discourage

75. Interview, 24 January 2012.
76. Interview, 17 February 2012.
77. Interview, 10 December 2011.
78. Interviews, 10 December 2011 and 24 January 2012.
79. Interview, 24 January 2012.

reliance on public support. Concerning the public guarantees to increase liquidity, for example, public actors had long discussions on the best pricing. One suggestion was to link the pricing of aid to credit default swaps (CDS), in order to include variation according to the creditworthiness of the different institutions and sanction poor judgment in the past. As one participant noted, "Aid was supposed to be unattractive. But the CDS had skyrocketed during the crisis. If we had taken them as a guideline, we would have simply induced a collapse of the banks in difficulty. We thus began to smooth the CDS movements, to at least take out the peeks."[80]

Insisting on proper behavior in unusual times was difficult. Solvency requirements, for example, reflected the ratings attributed to the different institutions, which also dropped because of the crisis. One participant noted that "one bank, once it had been downgraded, saw its capital requirement jump from €250 million to €4.5 billion. Overnight!"[81]

Despite a general agreement that banks should not receive favorable conditions, decision makers struggled to determine the appropriate measures. Everything had to go quickly and the government had to invent much from scratch, with a very small staff at SoFFin. Once the law had been put into place, the Bundesbank emptied out a building in Frankfurt and put some of its staff at SoFFin's disposition. But a public agency working on bank bailouts is not an easy task to design. On the one hand, attracting specialists who could go through the books of the banks in trouble and make detailed recommendation required aligning itself with the salaries of the financial sector. As one government official observed, "A mergers and acquisitions specialist earns between €300,000 and €500,000. For the ministry in Berlin, that kind of salary was unimaginable. Not even the head of the Treasury earned as much."[82]

In addition, a public agency needs to make a call for tender before working with a law or audit firm on a project. How is that possible when a bank calls for support on Friday and needs a response when markets open on Monday? Many of these issues had to be resolved in record time. In sum, one public official argues, it was not the individual conditions, but the overall dependence that led only banks in great difficulties to apply for aid through SoFFin: "If I was the CEO of a bank, I would never go to SoFFin, because you lose you autonomy. It will drive you to ruins, make you totally dependent."[83]

Josef Ackermann of Deutsche Bank confirmed this judgment when he announced publicly in 2008 that "it would be a shame if we had to admit that we would need money from the tax payer." By presenting Deutsche Bank as healthy, in comparison to those that actually needed help, he created the

---

80. Interview, 10 December 2012.
81. Interview, 24 January 2012.
82. Interview, 24 January 2012.
83. Ibid.

schism in the industry that the government had sought to avoid and that is always the great risk of a voluntary plan. Chancellor Angela Merkel and Finance Minister Peer Steinbrück were furious: after all, the declaration came from one of the founding negotiators of the German bailout scheme. The *Frankfurter Allgemeine Zeitung* cited Ackermann's declaration as "quote of the year," because of its potentially hurtful effect on the German plan. Even if Josef Ackermann had always agreed to participate in collective negotiations and had called for government intervention as early as March 2008, he was not willing to participate fully with the German finance industry during the turbulent times in the fall of 2008.

Without the support of the major banks, the associations were unable to move. A international observer confirms: "You never hear from the BdB. It sometimes feels like an association of grocers. They are so many of them. . . . It is really, really difficult to get them to take a position. They are even more stuck in their different statutes than before, they never managed to become more homogenous."[84]

At that time, it had become clear that, first, the size of aid needed was much larger than initially expected, and second, that the private sector was too heterogeneous and therefore both unable and unwilling to provide a collective solution.

Reregulation

The lessons the German government took out of the fall of 2008 were that it could not count on the financial industry to support itself and that it was going to be on the losing side if it only had the choice to intervene once the collapse of a potentially systemic institution had become inevitable. Feeling that the 2008 bailout attempts had been too soft on the banking sector and too painful for the taxpayer, the government shifted its strategy in 2009 and invested much effort in designing new oversight mechanisms and preventing future bailouts.

Most important, starting in 2011, banks were obliged to contribute a bank levy in order to underwrite a restructuring fund governed by the FMSA. The fund, which was designed to contain about €70 billion, aims to support the reorganization and restructuring of ailing financial institutions that are considered to be systemically important. Banks can apply to be supported, but the regulatory agency can also intervene and force the orderly resolution of institutions that threaten the stability of the sector. In such cases, the healthy assets of the institution will be transferred into a bridge bank and the troubled assets have to be sold off. The losses that can result from such sales will have to be carried by the owners and bondholders of the bank in order to

84. Interview, 3 May 2011.

avoid burdening the taxpayer, while the FMSA manages the bridge bank and supports it with guarantees.

A government-induced resolution of a bank is considered by several observers as "paradigmatic change," compared to the voluntary bank participation in the 2008 bailout.[85] Within Europe, the solution is described as quite progressive, since European talks on a similar bank levy were difficult to bring forward. "It took until the restructuring law to develop a systematic approach to the obligations of the banking sector," one observer has pointed out.[86] Unlike France, the German government was unable to develop a systematic bailout solution jointly with the banking industry. Like the United Kingdom, Germany therefore insisted on constraining reregulation afterward.

Comparative Assessment

Initially, the French government had made €360 billion available for the different elements of the French bank support plan: €265 billion for the SFEF, €40 billion for recapitalization through the SPPE, and €55 billion guarantees for the Dexia rescue. The actual amounts needed were much lower. The SFEF only issued state-backed securities for €76.9 billion, the SPPE used €20.75 billion to inject capital into French banks (including €1 billion for Dexia), and the guarantees needed for Dexia-FSA were €22 billion at the end of 2009. The costs associated with the creation of a bad bank for Dexia in 2012 are still uncertain.

By the end of March 2011, all banks had bought back their securities from the SPPE, which in addition provided €800 million to the public budget through dividends. Likewise, the loans granted to French banks through the SFEF are paid back according to schedule with an interest rate of 2.75 percent plus a risk premium that varies according to the benefiting banks financial health.[87] A complete evaluation of the SFEF financing mechanism will have to be executed after the final reimbursement in 2014, but only a bank failure and severe problems with the collateral provided would block a complete reimbursement of the €77 billion. In addition, interest revenue in May 2011 was at €1.4 billion. The only part of its support plan in which the French government clearly lost money is Dexia: by the end of 2009, the registered latent losses of French public support for Dexia were €1.9 billion.[88]

In May 2011, Christine Lagarde announced that, excluding Dexia, the French bank plan had actually brought a benefit of €2.7 billion to the

85. Interviews, 22 February and 23 March 2011.
86. Interview, 22 February 2011.
87. 95 percent of the loans went to the principal five French banks and an additional €2.2 billion to seven other French financial institutions.
88. Cour des Comptes, *Les concours publics aux établissements de crédit: bilan et énseignement à tirer*, 23.

government budget, thanks to the interest rates and divides paid for the support, but mainly also to the fact that no French bank ended up going bankrupt.[89] For all of these reasons, the French bank support plan ranks among the most profitable ones in Europe, according to Eurostat.[90]

The initial commitment of the German government covered €80 billion for recapitalization and allowed guarantees for €400 billion, for which it budgeted €20 billion in case of default. In July 2009, €200 billion were made available for the transfer of toxic asset, although this should be considered as a guarantee rather than a purchasing facility. The actual outlays for guarantees peaked in October 2010 at €174 billion.[91] Capital injections in HRE, WestLB, Commerzbank, and Aareal Bank amounted to €29.28 billion at the end 2010.[92]

It is very difficult to evaluate the precise costs of the German bailout package, because the government participation in the capital of ailing banks has only been partially reimbursed as of mid-2011. The guarantee scheme seems rather stable, as no default has occurred that would impose costs on the federal budget. Evaluating the costs of the transfer of toxic assets is much more difficult and can only be done once the liquidation institutions EEA and FMS-WM have finished their tasks. However, it is already clear that the deficit of the German bank support plan is high in international comparison, because the losses of financial institutions (IKB, WestLB, SachsenLB and HRE Bank) have been born by the government.[93] In European comparison, the German plan ranks as the second most expensive in absolute terms with a net loss of €17 billion, topped only by Ireland (€35 billion). In terms of GDP, the German bank bailout increased the public deficit by 0.7 percent (cumulated over 2008–10), ranking as the sixth most expensive in Europe.[94]

Despite its comparatively good performance some observers criticized the French plan, arguing that revenue might have been higher had the conditions granted to banks been somewhat more ambitious. Moreover, all government revenue consists of interest payments and dividends, while the government had not demanded a share of the capital gain of the supported banks.[95] The Court of Audit also criticized the second tranche of SPPE financing, arguing

89. Anonymous, "Le plan de soutien aux banques a rapporté 2,7 milliards d'euros à l'Etat."

90. European Commission, *Eurostat Supplementary Table for the Financial Crisis: Background Note*, 7.

91. FMSA, *Zwischenbilanz der Bundesanstalt für Finanzmarktstabilisierung*.

92. Panetta et al., "An Assessment of Financial Sector Rescue Programmes; Zimmer et al., *Strategien für den Ausstieg des Bundes aus krisenbedingten Beteiligungen an Banken*.

93. Ibid.

94. European Commission, *Eurostat Supplementary Table for the Financial Crisis: Background Note*, 7.

95. Zimmer et al., *Strategien für den Ausstieg des Bundes aus krisenbedingten Beteiligungen an Banken*, 38.

that it might not have been necessary, since banks could have raised capital on financial markets.[96]

In addition, the monitoring of loan availability necessitated a *médiateur du credit*, an ombudsperson, which small- and medium-sized enterprises could call if they had trouble obtaining bank loans. With more than sixteen thousand cases handled by mid-2011, about two-thirds were closed with a successful loan negotiation, benefiting about eighty-five hundred firms.[97] Since this complaint service is free of charge for the firms, the costs of €20 million are currently covered by the French Central Bank. These additional costs are not listed as bailout expenditures, even if they remain relatively small compared to the overall expenditures.

In an international comparison, the International Monetary Fund (IMF) describes the German package as "sizeable" but "far more hands off" than the US and the UK plans, since authorities "rely on banks' assessments in seeking public assistance." Concerning the conditions attached, "the FMSA's assistance appears milder than in the UK, but more stringent than in the US."[98] Unlike the French plan, but similar to the UK, the German conditions applied to banks with solvency issues. The situation of the four banks covered by SoFFin—Commerzbank, HRE, WestLB, and Aareal Bank—thus required a restructuring plan and comes with a considerable loss of autonomy and changes in the bank management. But as in France, some German participants wonder whether silent participations were the right choice for recapitalization, rather than asking for ordinary stock.[99]

Overall, the French bailout plan was characterized by tight cooperation between the French government and the six, later five, major banking groups. This is also responsible for the weaknesses of the plan, in particular the favorable conditions that some public officials regretted later on, and that Massoc and Jabko criticize as proof of the undue weight of the financial industry on public decisions.[100] But the close network of finance and the state in France also represented an advantage in terms of coordination and collective action capacity. Collective plans have the benefit of mutual oversight among the banks, where competitors are attentive not to let others benefit disproportionately. The French government was also able to delegate the expertise and costs of running the liquidity provision of the SFEF to the banking industry, which avoided creating the difficulties SoFFin experienced in the first days. To be sure, the final costs depend crucially on the health of the sector, but the collective French plan may have helped at least one bank to avoid sliding into insolvency, which could have imposed additional costs

96. Ibid.
97. Information video on www.mediateurducredit.fr, consulted on 25 July 2011.
98. Jabko and Massoc, "French Capitalism under Stress."
99. Interview, 17 January 2012.
100. Jabko and Massoc, "French Capitalism under Stress."

on the government had it then organized a bailout of the financial institution in question.

In Germany, where bank failures were more sizeable than in France, the government has made a concerted effort to avoid future public expenditures with its restructuration law. The new institutional capacities of the banking supervisors are more extensive than regulatory reform initiatives in other countries. In particular the bank levy to fund future bailout measures is pioneering, as it was pushed through despite adamant opposition from the German banking association and Deutsche Bank.[101]

Hannes Rehm, the head of the German rescue fund explains the reasoning of such preventive regulation with the fatality that characterized the German situation: "unfortunately, bailouts are not a lucrative business," else the banks would not ask the government to step in.[102] Compared to the French plan, the Germans were unable to engineer a collective banking solution, as they had initially wished. Mitchell argues that the German government was comparably weak in the initial negotiations of the scheme.[103] This is certainly true but the initial absence was a conscious decision in order to encourage a private sector solution. When the government realized that this plan was not realistic, it engaged in heavy reregulation in order to even out the imbalances that resulted from the initial crisis management.

Conclusion

The German negotiations show that the government counted steadily on the collective action capacity of the financial sector. When the industry divisions became apparent, it was left with no other options than to pick up the bill if it wanted to avoid a complete collapse of its banking sector and possibly the entire economy. The French industry cooperation was helped by the fact that banks had rather similar difficulties and were not as badly shaken as some of their German counterparts. But more important, an industry agreement was possible because the number of large banks was small and coordination manageable. In early crisis management, even banks that were not affected by the crisis went along with the collective plan, both for liquidity provision and for recapitalization.

In all countries, the influence of the financial industry was criticized and created an outcry in public opinion. Germany and France were no exceptions. A close study of business-government interaction in France does confirm the tight cooperation and the personal favoritism that can result from the links between senior bank management and the administration. In

101. "Die Krise but Not La Crise?" 1023.
102. Landgraf and Drost, "SoFFin: Weiteres Jahr mit hohen Verlusten."
103. Mitchell, "Saving the Market from Itself."

the end, however, all French banks decided to participate collectively, and although they received favorable conditions, their cooperation helped the government to obtain what it wanted: a strong signal about government intervention that did not weigh heavily on the public budget. Moreover, collective oversight from the banks gave the administration important signals about the utility of their aid and the necessity to close the scheme after the second recapitalization initiative in 2009.

The power of the French financial industry appears thus more balanced: it takes the form of mutually beneficial complicity. In Germany, the government was unable to engage the financial industry collectively in the same way. The weakness of the government was made into a spectacle by Josef Ackermann's self-interested comments, which illustrated how much the government depended on the goodwill of its major financial institutions during the crisis management. The restructuring law needs to be understood as an attempt to correct these imbalances, which had dire consequences not only for the public budget.

7

Ireland and Denmark

The cheapest bailout in the world so far.
—Brian Lenihan, Irish minister for finance

The final analysis pairs two small European countries with substantial financial development, a homegrown housing market bubble, and a great dependence on international wholesale markets for bank funding. Ireland and Denmark were among the first European countries to announce that the government would step up to support the banking sector, issuing a public guarantee on all deposits on 30 September and 5 October respectively, as the panic swept over the two open economies. Both Ireland and Denmark were outliers in Europe by guaranteeing existing unsecured bank bond debt as well.

While the fate of Ireland has garnered much attention, little is known of the equally difficult situation in Denmark. OECD data show that the Danish housing market was more inflated than the Irish and that export markets suffered a more substantial plunge as a consequence of the crisis.[1] The assets of the financial industry were much larger than GDP in both countries: twice the GDP in Denmark and three times GDP in Ireland, if one considers only onshore banking and not the international fund industry based in Dublin as well, as mentioned above. Supporting their financial industry was therefore potentially devastating for both small open economies.

Indeed bank failures in the months that followed illustrate the trying times. While the Irish government was forced to nationalize Anglo Irish and become a major stakeholder in most Irish banks, Denmark experienced

---

Epigraph: The Lenihan statement compares the Irish bank guarantee scheme with rescue proposals in the United States and the United Kingdom on 10 October 2008, before it became clear that the insured losses would drive Ireland to the brink of bankruptcy and lead it to seek a sovereign bailout in 2010.

1. OECD, *OECD Economic Surveys: Denmark 2009*, 18.

a dozen bank failures, including some of its largest banks. According to several observers, the substantial number of failures in Denmark reflects "the country's status as the worst hit by the economic turmoil apart from Iceland."[2]

Unlike the last two comparisons, however, Ireland and Denmark did not have comparable monetary policy options. While Ireland is a member of the Eurozone, Denmark is not, but maintains a fixed exchange rate regime with the euro. It could thus attempt to coordinate its government's efforts with intervention through the Danish central bank (Nationalbank). Inversely, Denmark knew it would not be sheltered from a crash through an effective lender of last resort. Given the size of its financial sector, relative to the size of the country, both Ireland and Denmark had only a limited fiscal spare capacity to save failing banks. But Denmark was particularly vulnerable, according to Buiter and Sibert, because it had its own currency and could not fall back on the European Central Bank in case of illiquidity.[3] Autonomous monetary policy for small countries is thus a mixed blessing: it offers additional options for intervention but considerably increases the risks linked to financial sectors that had grown larger than the national economies, because the lender of last resort in the national currency can be quickly exhausted. The Icelandic example glaringly proved that point in the fall of 2008.

Besides the difference in monetary policy, the management of the bank support schemes was strikingly different between Ireland and Denmark. While the Irish government was torn between denial and panic, the Danish government negotiated a sectorwide rescue scheme based on substantial participation by the financial industry. Even if the Danish solution needed frequent updating, it committed the banking sector collectively through considerable fees for guarantees and contributions to a fund covering losses from bank failures, which effectively ring-fenced the Danish financial industry and protected the public budget.

To understand the parallels between the Irish and Danish cases, it is necessary to begin with the structure of the two financial industries and their exposure to the crisis. This will prepare the presentations of the two bank support schemes and an analysis of the contributions of the financial sector.

Financial Systems in Ireland and Denmark

Denmark is often described as a corporatist country and Ireland as a liberal market economy, but their banking sectors began to look rather similar in the mid-1990s after a period of deregulation in Denmark. Still

2. Milne, "Danish Banks Set Off Alarm Bells."
3. Buiter and Sibert, *The Icelandic Banking Crisis and What to Do About It.*

the initial regulatory approach was different, rooted in quite distinctive traditions.

In many aspects, the Irish banking industry reflected the British banking and regulatory philosophy—a relatively liberal regulatory model with light oversight—due its close ties and historical linkages with the United Kingdom. A late developer, the Irish financial sector only gained autonomy in the last four decades. From 1973 to 1995 the Irish Stock Exchange was part of the London Stock Exchange. An independent monetary regime was only developed after Ireland left the sterling monetary union in late 1978. After joining the EMU, a genuine financial regulator was established in 2003: the Irish Financial Services Regulatory Authority, which operated with great autonomy as a new division of the Irish Central Bank.[4]

Danish banking resembled in parts the organization of banks in Germany: characterized by a substantial presence of savings banks, a modest number of commercial banks and mortgage associations, which used to have a monopoly on housing finance since 1850. The industry was organized into strong industrywide organizations, with a tradition of collective bargaining. However, the strong ties between financial and industrial companies, characteristic of the German financial sector, were formally prohibited in Denmark by the Banking Act of 1930 in the aftermath of a profound banking crisis. Like Ireland, Denmark is a member of the EU since 1973, but it refused to join the monetary union after a popular referendum against the Maastricht Treaty in 1992. It has nonetheless maintained a fixed exchange rate with the euro, making it in many ways de facto member of the Eurozone.[5]

During the 1970s and 1980s, the Danish banking industry was deregulated, and housing finance was liberalized in the 1990s. However, the most incisive experience was the financial crisis that hit the Nordic countries during the late 1980s and 1990s, arguably one of the five biggest financial crises in world history.[6] Between 1987 and 1995, 102 Danish financial institutions ceased to exist, most often through mergers with sound institutions. Eight banks passed into bankruptcy. Nonetheless, Denmark was least affected among all Nordic countries, and unlike in Sweden or Finland, no nationwide government rescue plan was put into place.[7]

As a result of deregulation and the crisis, the 1990s were marked by consolidation of the Danish financial industry, and a number of financial institutions merged across the sectoral divides between savings and commercial banks, mortgage institutions, and insurance companies. This profoundly

4. The Central Bank could in principle issue directives to the financial regulator in case of conflict, but none were ever issued.

5. Goul Andersen, "From the Edge of the Abyss to Bonanza—and Beyond," 95.

6. Reinhart and Rogoff, *This Time Is Different.*

7. Mayes, "Did Recent Experience of a Financial Crisis Help in Coping with the Current Financial Turmoil?" 999.

reorganized the landscape. To begin with, savings banks were absorbed by the commercial banking sector. While 231 banks had operated in Denmark in 1989, the Financial Regulator counted 138 financial institutions in 2008 at the outbreak of the crisis.[8] In addition to consolidation, the bond market on the Copenhagen Stock Exchange had become huge compared to the size of the Danish economy by the mid-2000s. Housing finance boomed, creating a considerable bubble on the Danish property market.[9]

The Irish financial industry experienced a similar growth during the 1990s and 2000s, as part of the Irish economic miracle. With the establishment of the International Financial Service Center (IFSC) in 1987, Dublin became a major center for financial activities, attracting foreign institutions to Ireland for international trading activities, in particular fund management. With a GDP growth rate between 6 and 11 percent between 1994 and 2000, Ireland earned the nickname "Celtic Tiger" because of it rapid output, employment, and productivity increases. Irish banks such as Allied Irish Bank and Bank of Ireland, which had traditionally been conservative high street banks, began to enter into competition with new market players and developed aggressive strategies, in particular in the mortgage market.

In 2001, the international recession marked a turning point: although growth resumed in Ireland in 2003, it was driven by a construction boom rather than foreign direct investment and productivity growth. Expansion of property investment was fueled by rapid credit expansion, which in turn was provided by local banks that relied extensively on international wholesale markets for funding.[10]

The explosion of mortgage lending through cheap funding that banks could obtain on international wholesale markets was very similar in Denmark. Between 2003 and 2007, there was a very strong credit expansion, with lending accounting for more than 50 percent of annual growth for several Danish banks. Household debt increased from 106 percent of GDP to 132 percent and debt of nonfinancial institutions from 89 percent to 106 percent during this period.[11]

The landscape of the financial industry is also largely comparable. Despite a total number of about 140 financial institutions operating in Denmark, only 5 had an operating capital of over DKK50 billion, with Danske Bank and Nordea as the market leaders. An additional 12 had over DKK10 billion in 2008, followed by a large group of medium-sized and small banks, according to the classification of the Danish Financial

---

8. Finanstilsynet, "Markedsudviklingen i 2008 for Pengeinstitutter," 21.
9. Mortensen and Seabrooke, "Housing as Social Right or Means to Wealth."
10. See Honohan, *The Irish Banking Crisis*; Lane, *The Irish Crisis*.
11. Østrup, "The Danish Bank Crisis in a Transnational Perspective," 82.

regulator.[12] Moreover, Danish banks have expanded internationally through acquisition of retail banks, in particular Nordea, which is a true pan-Nordic bank based in Finland and Sweden as well, and Danske Bank, which has acquired retail banks in Sweden, Finland, Norway, the Baltic Republics, Ireland, and the UK.

Similarly, the landscape in Ireland is characterized by the presence of a great number of foreign financial institutions in a variety of sectors such as investment banking and fund management. It is therefore useful to distinguish between the onshore banking sector and the offshore sector, which accounts for almost half of Ireland's financial sector. The domestic sector is dominated by Allied Irish Bank and Bank of Ireland, who held over 70 percent of the market in 2006.[13] Altogether thirteen retail banks offered personal account services and small-business lending in Ireland, six of which were Irish-owned. In both cases, only roughly a dozen institutions proved central to the stability of the financial system, with several heavyweight institutions at the center. In Irish banking, these institutions had privileged personal and individualized ties with the public authorities, while banking association organizations and collective bargaining played a much more crucial role in Denmark.

As a result of the rapid expansion of the financial industries relative to the size of their economies, the structural power of finance was very high in both countries. Both governments had put financial development at the center of their growth strategies and put great emphasis on facilitating innovation and on letting the sector develop. However, due to the experience of the Scandinavian financial crisis and the early timing of financial deregulation, the Danish oversight was somewhat more established than in Ireland, which was in many ways a late developer. The productive power of the financial industry in Denmark thus appears to be lower than in Ireland and somewhat similar to Germany. In Ireland, it was very high.

Exposure to the Crisis

By 2006, there were clear signs in Ireland that the boom in the property market was over. As the housing market bubble deflated, the construction industry was severely hit. The property slowdown in turn affected the Irish banking system, which had lent roughly two-thirds of the gross national product to property developers for the financing of building projects and land purchases.[14] The international financial crisis provided the final trigger for collapse, as commercial funding for the Irish banks dried up. Bank share prices dropped rapidly from March 2007 to September 2008.

---

12. Finanstilsynet, "Markedsudviklingen i 2008 for Pengeinstitutter," 21.
13. Goddard, Molyneux, and Wilson, "Banking in the European Union."
14. Kelly, *Whatever Happened to Ireland?*

In Denmark, the downturn started also with a sharp fall in housing prices in the third quarter of 2007. By way of international comparison, the drop in Danish property prices has been among the largest in industrialized countries, topping both Ireland and Spain.[15] This, in turn, caused losses on loans for property projects. In addition, Danish banks started to experience difficulties in raising funds on international markets. In late 2007, two banks began to stumble: bankTrelleborg and Roskilde Bank. In response, the Danish Nationalbank provided liquidity support, but bankTrelleborg was unable to meet solvency requirements and announced that it would be taken over by Sydbank in January 2008.

Roskilde Bank suffered a similar fate due to its high-risk lending to real estate developers but was unable to find a buyer. In July 2008, the Danish government intervened and organized a bailout to prevent a contagion to the rest of the Danish financial industry. The Danish Nationalbank provided liquidity and issued a guarantee on most debt obligations. At the same time, the Danish banking industry declared that it would collectively cover losses up to DKK750 million and the government guaranteed additional losses. In August, the assets and liabilities (excluding equity and subordinated debt) of Roskilde Bank were transferred to a new company jointly owned by the Danish government and banking industry.[16] Still the collapse of Roskilde Bank was interpreted as a sign that the US subprime crisis had reached Europe and made it very difficult for Danish banks to continue funding themselves through international wholesale markets. After the collapse of Lehman Brothers in September 2008, the liquidity requirements of Danish banks were met by loans made available by the Danish Nationalbank.

In Ireland, among the hardest hit were the banks that had intensive ties to the property market. Both Anglo Irish Bank and Irish Nationwide Building Society had roughly 75 percent of their loans in the construction and property sector in 2006, compared to 32 percent for Allied Irish Bank and 16 percent for Bank of Ireland.[17] In March 2008, the share price for Anglo Irish fell by 18 percent over one week due to concerns about property exposure. By September, the government began to consider nationalizing Anglo Irish.[18] To reassure depositors, it raised deposit protection from €20,000 to €100,000. Although this might have prevented a run on the bank, it did not stop Ireland from slipping officially into recession on 24 September 2008.

15. OECD, *OECD Economic Surveys: Denmark 2009*, 18.
16. See Østrup, "The Danish Bank Crisis in a Transnational Perspective."
17. Regling and Watson, *A Preliminary Report on the Sources of Ireland's Banking Crisis*, 32.
18. Honohan, *The Irish Banking Crisis*.

National Bank Support Schemes

The Irish Bailout Plan

The banking crisis jumped to an unprecedented scale in late September 2008. While Anglo Irish's situation seemed to have stabilized, Depfa, an Irish subsidiary of the German bank Hypo Real Estate, faced severe liquidity pressures on Sunday, 28 September. Fearing a collapse of Anglo Irish, which might draw the entire Irish banking system with it, Bank of Ireland and Allied Irish Bank requested government intervention. To avoid a collapse of the Irish financial sector, the government, the Central Bank, and the Financial Regulator decided to issue a general guarantee on the deposits and most liabilities of Irish-owned banks for two years: Allied Irish Bank, Anglo Irish Bank, Bank of Ireland, Irish Life and Permanent, Irish Nationwide Building Society, and the Educational Building Society. The gross amount of liabilities amounted to €375 billion, more than twice the gross national product of Ireland.[19] It passed parliament as the Credit Institution Bill 2008 on 30 September.

The blanket guarantee on deposits was one of the first comprehensive measures in the global financial crisis and raised many concerns. To begin with, Ireland did not consult with its European counterparts or the European Central Bank.[20] By protecting deposits in Irish banks, the government created conditions that would attract investment and move funds from other troubled countries, which earned bitter criticism from British authorities as well as the EU on state aid grounds. Moreover, foreign banks complained about the coverage of the scheme. Danske Bank, owner of National Irish Bank, which was not covered by the guarantee, experienced a massive withdrawal of Irish deposits.

From an Irish perspective, the guarantee scheme was initially rather successful in stemming the most immediate pressures. Funds flowed in and the question of Anglo Irish's nationalization evaporated. Still, worries persisted, and in the weeks that followed the government asked the Financial Regulator to work with two private consultancies, PricewaterhouseCoopers (PwC) and Merrill Lynch, to check the health of their financial institutions and examine the need for recapitalization. In late November, the government decided to make public funds available and announced a recapitalization package of €10 billion on 14 December 2008. Under the plan, the government initially bought preference shares in Bank of Ireland and Allied Irish Bank for €2 billion each and for €1.5 billion in Anglo Irish Bank.

The recapitalization measures had little success in restoring market confidence as their announcement was drowned by revelations of a circular loan

19. Nyberg, *Misjudging Risk*, 77.
20. Brown, *Beyond the Crash*, 51.

scandal at Anglo Irish. As a measure to keep the bank afloat, the CEO admitted to have hidden €87 billion of loans to ten wealthy businessmen referred to as the "golden circle" in return for buying shares. The scandal led to a series of resignations in the management of Anglo Irish, the Financial Regulator, as well as Irish Life and Permanent and Irish Nationwide, which were found to have made deposits under the government guarantee scheme as exceptional support to Anglo Irish Bank.

In the light of these revelations, the government finally decided to announce the full nationalization of Anglo Irish on 15 January 2009. Shortly after, further capital injections increased the control of the Irish state in Allied Irish and Bank of Ireland, gave it full control over two building societies, and made it the largest shareholder in all the major banks. The only bank to refuse government participation was Irish Life and Permanent.

By then, the focus shifted from containment to the resolution of insolvent banks, which implied assessing the value of remaining assets and proposing unwinding solutions. On 7 April 2009, the government announced its intention to set up a National Asset Management Agency (NAMA) by late 2009 for the transfer of toxic assets. NAMA currently covers all six Irish-owned banks and acts as a bad bank: risky property assets are removed from the banks' books through a special purpose vehicle. NAMA will finance the purchase of the troubled assets through government bonds and is run as an independent agency with management services provided through the National Treasury Management Agency.[21] In addition, a Prudential Capital Assessment Review (PCAR) was set up in early 2010 to assess each bank's recapitalization needs.

Initially, the Irish guarantee scheme contained no provision outlining bank obligations. However, the covered institutions committed to paying a quarterly charge to the exchequer in exchange for the guarantee. The charge is based on the increased debt service costs borne by the government as a result of the guarantee. The conditions for capital injections were negotiated on an individual basis with each bank and included lending, executive pay, and changes in corporate governance. However, it soon became evident that the Irish state would become a majority shareholder, which implied important changes in senior management and greatly undermined political autonomy of banking industry. The recapitalization of Allied Irish Bank and Bank of Ireland, for example, gave the government the right to appoint 25 percent of the banks directors, ownership of 25 percent of total ordinary voting shares, a say on the strike price of selling shares, and the receipt of a dividend payment of 8 percent; the banks offered a commitment to increase lending and reduce executive pay by at least 33 percent.[22]

21. For further information, see www.nama.ie.
22. Department of Finance, "Recapitalisation of Allied Irish Bank and Bank of Ireland."

One of the consequences of the Irish bank bailout was its impact on government debt, which ended up throwing the state into a sovereign debt crisis. Losses in Anglo Irish alone were responsible for roughly half of the total costs of the Irish bank rescue.[23] On 21 November 2010, Taoiseach Brian Cowen announced that the government had requested support from the EU and the IMF. On 28 November, the Irish government, the EU, and the IMF agreed on an €85 billion rescue package.[24] The EU/IMF rescue package contained a substantial amount of aid to the Irish banking system. Of the €85 billion support, €50 billion was set aside to provide funding to the Irish government, so it would not need to rely on bond markets to fund its fiscal deficit or roll over existing debt for three years; €10 billion were provided for the banking system: €8 billion to provide additional capital and €2 billion to fund credit enhancements that could allow Irish banks to sell packages of risky loans to private investors. The final €25 billion of the rescue package were a safety cushion should the Irish banking system require support beyond the initial €10 billion.[25]

The stated aim of the package was to "de-risk" Irish banking. In order to do so, the deal specified that capital injections should go to increasing tier 1 capital ratios to 12 percent. Second, risky loans held by banks were to be reduced through transfer to NAMA and selling off as loan packages to private investors. Third, banks were encouraged to downsize through sale of affiliates and noncore assets. Fourth, the deal explicitly called for the unwinding of the two banks that are no longer viable: Anglo Irish and Irish Nationwide Building Society.[26]

During the negotiations of the EU-IMF deal, it was envisioned that holders of subordinated debt would not be repaid in full. However, no agreement was reached for restructuring the nonguaranteed senior bonds, and disagreement persisted between the different lenders.[27] The EU and the IMF also insisted on more extensive loan book assessment by third parties, not just the Irish Central Bank. Indeed, the Central Bank and the Financial Services Authority of Ireland were blamed to have failed in their banking oversight in the years leading up to the crisis as well as their crisis management. Starting in October 2010, the Central Bank Reform Act created a new more centralized body—the Central Bank of Ireland—which replaced the previous two-pillar arrangement.[28] The institutional reform was accompanied by major personnel changes as well.

23. McCarthy, *Ireland's European Crisis*, 5.

24. Contributors to the package were the European Financial Stability Mechanism and the the European Financial Stability Facility (€22.5 billion each), the IMF (€22.5 billion) and the Irish National Pension Reserve Fund (€17.5 billion), as well as the UK, Denmark, and Sweden, which provided bilateral loans.

25. Lane, *The Irish Crisis*, 19.

26. Ibid., 21.

27. Kelly, *Ireland's Future Depends on Breaking Free from Bailout.*

28. For further information, see www.irishstatutebook.ie/2010/en/act/pub/0023/index.html.

The Danish Bank Rescue Plan

Despite the turbulent times, Denmark had several policy instruments to fall back on during the outbreak of the crisis that were lacking in other countries. To begin with, the memory of the financial crisis of the 1990s was still vivid in the Nordic countries in the 2000s, even if one can debate how much previous lessons were heeded.[29] Bank resolution was an important concern and a public guarantee fund for depositors and investors (Garantifonden for Indskydere og Investorer, GII) had been established in 1994 to provide guarantees for distressed financial institutions and help with their unwinding if need be. When the public deposit insurance was judged to be contrary to EU state aid rules, the Danish banking industry collectively established a private alternative in 2007, the Private Contingency Association for distressed banks (Det Private Beredskab).[30]

The Roskilde Bank failure was the first test for the Private Contingency Association, who took ownership of the bank jointly with the Nationalbank. However, the size of Roskilde Bank, the seventh largest in Denmark, and its massive losses soon exhausted the fund and clarified the need for government backing and the Nationalbank's leading role.[31] Still the Private Contingency Association became the backbone of the Danish bailout plan that the government and the Danish Bankers Association (DBA) began to negotiate as confidence faltered in September 2008.

The Danish bailout scheme became known as "Bank Bailout Package I" and specified that all members of the Private Contingency Association were covered by an unlimited deposit guarantee until 30 September 2010. In return, the combined contribution of private banks to the fund amounted to DKK35 billion (approximately €4.7 billion). The government committed to set aside the money paid by the fund to cover potential bank losses stemming from bank failures and to guaranteed all deposits beyond the depositor insurance scheme in case the funds of the private scheme were exhausted. In particular, the government and the Private Contingency Association established the unwinding company Financial Stability (Finansiel Stabilitet A/S), which could secure the payment of creditor claims to distressed institutions and handle the controlled dismantling of financial institutions that no longer met solvency requirements. The Bank Bailout Package I was passed by the Danish parliament on 10 October, following an agreement between the government, political parties, and the Danish Bankers Association five days earlier.

29. Mayes, "Did Recent Experience of a Financial Crisis Help in Coping with the Current Financial Turmoil?"

30. *Det Private Beredskab* is also sometimes translated as "Private Reserve Fund."

31. Kluth and Lynggaard, "Explaining Responses in Danish and Irish Banking to the Financial Crisis," 786.

Although the bailout scheme helped to avoid a run on Danish banks and prepare the orderly resolution of troubled institutions, funding difficulties continued throughout the remainder of 2008 and many feared the collapse of even the largest banks, including Danske Bank. To avoid a generalized crisis and credit squeeze, the Danish parliament adopted an additional law to address solvency difficulties through recapitalization on 3 February 2009. Known as Bank Package II, the new legislation gave banks access to capital through preferred shares acquired by the government, for a total of potentially up to DKK100 billion (€14 billion). The recapitalization scheme administered by the Danish Ministry of the Economy was open until 30 June 2009 for banks wishing to apply. Moreover, Bank Package II introduced a guarantee scheme for loans until the end of 2013.[32]

A third package known as the Exit Package (or Bank Package III) was introduced in March 2010. Bank Package III sought to prepare an end to government support by replacing the initial state guarantee that was set to end in September 2010. The new package ended the full coverage extended previously to depositors and unsecured creditors and limits the deposit guarantee to DKK750,000 (€100,000) per customer. However, financial markets reacted quickly when the failure of two banks—Amagerbanken and Fjordbank Mors—under the new scheme imposed losses on senior creditors.

To respond to this dilemma and encourage private takeovers of struggling banks, the Danish government passed a fourth bank package in August 2011, known as Consolidation Package, or Bank Package IV. Bank Package IV enables Finansiel Stabilitet S/A and the Guarantee Fund for Investors and Depositors to provide a dowry to private institutions willing to take over a distressed bank or its risky assets. Finally, a Development Package of March 2012 opened up the possibility for banks to transfer commercial real estate to Finansiel Stabilitet S/A on a case-by-case basis and established instruments to support the agricultural sector and export financing.

The coverage of the bank support schemes extends to all institutions that contribute to the Private Contingency Association. This is effectively 99 percent of the Danish banking industry, in terms of market share, despite the high costs involved. Only fourteen banks have decided that they prefer not to be covered.[33] Unlike schemes in countries such as France or Ireland, where coverage was extended on a voluntary or statutory basis to national financial institutions only, the Danish guarantee scheme does not exclude foreigners. Foreign banks registered in Denmark, including subsidiaries of foreign banks, may join the scheme, which is also open to foreign branches of banks operating in Denmark. In addition, debt obligations of banks to foreign nationals are covered.[34]

32. Østrup, "The Danish Bank Crisis in a Transnational Perspective," 84–85.
33. Gry Braad, "Fakta."
34. Østrup, "The Danish Bank Crisis in a Transnational Perspective," 100.

Besides the contributions paid to the fund, conditions for the public guarantee scheme specified that no dividends shall be paid to shareholders and no new stock option plans must be implemented during the duration of the package. The costs for the recapitalization aid for participating banks were dividend payments between 9 percent and 12 percent, a commitment to publishing biannual reports on the evolution of lending, and restrictions on executive pay.[35]

Credit institutions furthermore had to publish their individual need for solvency and the Financial Supervisory Authority was granted greater control of financial institutions. On balance, the control of the government over individual credit institutions participating in the schemes has been lighter than elsewhere and the banking sector has succeeded in preserving operational autonomy. The appointment of public representatives to the board of financial institutions, for example, only happened in exceptional cases.

Collective Action by the Financial Industry

Ireland

The Irish bank rescue scheme was government-led and rather uncoordinated, as many analysts have pointed out. The banking industry was not a key player in initial meetings and entered into contact on an individual basis or sometimes in pairs, but never as an entire sector. Not only was the government not able to rely on an industry-led solution, it also spent considerable time trying to obtain information about the bank's activities that it did not have at hand. The following sections examine the lack of collective engagement of the Irish banking industry by analyzing the role banks played in the initial setup of the bank rescue package. It then analyzes the weakness of Irish crisis management and examines the relationship between the Irish government and the European Central Bank. As the discussion will highlight, both bank and government initiatives appear to have been sidelined in the multilevel negotiations over Ireland's sovereign bailout in 2010.

Business-Government Relationships in the Initial Support Scheme

Ireland had been the first European country to announce a bailout of its banks. The decision to guarantee virtually all of the liabilities of the Irish-owned banking system was taken overnight and in a clear state of panic. The discussions on Sunday, 28 December 2008, leading up to the announcement involved a small group of public officials and was driven by the Department

35. Ibid., 102. However there are no conditions imposing the maintenance of lending specifically to Danish residents or companies.

of Finance rather than the Central Bank and Financial Services Authority of Ireland (CBFSAI).[36] The main participants in the series of meetings were Taoiseach Brian Cowen, Finance Minister Brian Lenihan, Secretary General of the Finance Minister David Doyle, Head of the Banking Division in the Finance Ministry Kevin Cardiff, Governor of the Central Bank John Hurley, and Financial Regulator Patrick Neary. Other senior government officials, including officials from the National Treasury Management Agency, were also present at some of the meetings.

The two main banks, Bank of Ireland and Allied Irish Banks, had coordinated to ask for a meeting with the government that afternoon, fearing that the imminent collapse of Anglo Irish would result in a contagion that could be catastrophic for both. Represented by their CEOs and chairs—Brian Goggin and Richard Burrows for Bank of Ireland and Eugene Sheehy and Dermot Gleeson for Allied Irish Bank—the two banks were called in twice. In the initial meeting, they indicated that they favored both an immediate general guarantee, including subordinated debt, or the nationalization of Anglo Irish Bank and possibly Irish Nationwide Building Society. Either solution promised to signal that the government backed the Irish banking sector. The government asked them whether they would be available to provide a liquidity facility to Anglo Irish, for which they consulted with their staff. In a second meeting, later that evening, the government officials announced to the bank representatives that it would provide a general guarantee. The banks confirmed that they could each make a facility of €5 billion available to Anglo Irish.[37]

All participants confirm that the banks were not present when the guarantee decision was taken. In fact, the decision itself appears to have been based on a memo produced by the Merrill Lynch team, which had been hired as consultants by the Department of Finance in September 2008. Their memo, sent at 6:43 p.m. to Kevin Cardiff, outlines the different options available to the government and provides pros and cons.[38] It is a more detailed discussion than a similar paper considered by the Department of Finance in mid-2008.[39] The memo emphasized that the scope of such a guarantee could be up to €500 billion and that the market would doubt its credibility, knowing that the Irish government could not cover the full amount. It suggested that such an option would be best taken in coordination with other European governments. In the extreme urgency of the situation, no such coordination was undertaken on Sunday night or in the first hours of Monday morning, when

36. Irish Independent, "John Hurley."

37. Honohan, *The Irish Banking Crisis*, 124.

38. The e-mail and PDF attachment are now available online at www.ritholtz.com/blog/2011/02/irish-bank-memo-merrill-lynch-9-28-08/.

39. Honohan, *The Irish Banking Crisis*, 117–18. The Central Bank and the Financial Regulator had discussed crisis management and bankruptcy proceedings ever since the failure of Northern Rock. However, neither the Emergency Liquidity Assistance available through the Central Bank nor the "black book" developed in Ireland for such crisis management were actually used during the crisis, because it was considered too "cumbersome."

it proved already difficult to gather the cabinet members for approval.[40] In the aftermath, analyses of the night of 28–29 September describe the government as paralyzed, which was later confirmed, among other sources, by government insiders through a Wikileaks's cable.[41]

To be sure, Allied Irish and Bank of Ireland had been consulted during the meetings at their request. However, no industry body was invited, none of the smaller banks were consulted, and more generally no policy experts outside the inner circles of government nor foreign counterpart or officials from the European institutions were contacted. More surprisingly, however, nobody thought to involve representatives from Anglo Irish, Irish Nationwide Building Society, or Irish Life Permanent in the discussion.[42] These three banks were clearly in the most difficult situation and the government had appointed PwC accountants to investigate their loan books.

The government had sought to engage Allied Irish and Bank of Ireland through their short-term liquidity facility to Anglo Irish of €5 billion each, in addition to €4 billion available for an asset swap through the Central Bank and Financial Regulator. But when funds began to flow into Ireland as a result of the general guarantee, both provisions were not drawn on. Anglo Irish seemed to have gotten off the hook—at least for a short while.

Irish Government in Crisis

Two elements were noteworthy about the Irish guarantee: first, its coverage of only Irish-owned banks, and second, its rather generous extension to not only depositors, but also unsecured bondholders. Indeed, the government primary maxim during the bailout was that "no Irish bank should fail." What might appear as arbitrary coverage indicates the importance of local relationships in Irish banking, since insiders "knew perfectly well which banks were regarded as 'local' and which as 'foreign.' "[43] Be it a small country phenomenon or an Irish sense of "family," the decision was nonetheless reversed in the face of international pressure a week later, when the government invited five foreign-owned banks with a substantial presence in the market to join the scheme.[44] With the exception of Postbank Ireland, a joint venture between the Irish postal services and Fortis bank, all declined when they saw the terms of the guarantee.[45]

40. Boyle, *Without Power or Glory*, 108–9.
41. Doran and Keenan, *Revealed*.
42. Honohan, *The Irish Banking Crisis*, 124.
43. Honohan, "Resolving Ireland's Banking Crisis," 220.
44. These five banks were Ulster Bank, First Active, Halifax Bank of Scotland, IIB Bank, and Postbank Ireland.
45. Honohan, "Resolving Ireland's Banking Crisis," 221. By late 2011, three of the foreign banks closed their operations: First Active Bank, Halifax Ireland, and Postbank Ireland. Kluth and Lynggaard, "Explaining Responses in Danish and Irish Banking to the Financial Crisis," 772.

Many analysts of Irish politics have highlighted the very tight relationship between domestic business interests and governments, which resulted in a series of scandals in areas such as beef production, broadcasting, or construction. As Hardiman observes, foreign-owned industries in Ireland have not been the subject of corruption investigations.[46] In the financial industry, it appears that domestic firms have benefited from particularly light oversight and some authors accuse the government of having fallen prey to bank lobbying and clientelism in the decade prior to the crisis, due to a lack of public accountability and an insufficient tradition of policy evaluation and economic expertise.[47] Many accounts of the Irish crisis management underline the personal ties between political and financial elites, in particular a much-publicized golf meeting in the summer of 2008 between Taoiseach Brian Cowen and Sean FitzPatrick, at the time chairman of Anglo Irish bank, but also a personal friendship between the Taoiseach and Fintan Drury, an Anglo director.[48] Although the government and administration deny that political connectedness of senior bank management or corruption directly affected their work, the investigation reports criticize the "unwarranted complacency" of the regulator and the "unduly deferential approach to the banking industry."[49] In many cases, concerns expressed by the Central Bank or regulatory staff took the form of informal recommendations, which were simply set aside by senior bank management.[50] However one wishes to describe the bank-government relationships in the period leading up to the crisis, it is fair to say that domestic banks had a rather privileged position.

Contrary to US discussions about institutions that are too big to fail, the scope of the Irish scheme was motivated not so much by consideration about the systemic importance of individual banks, but rather by the fear of contagion if the Irish banking sector would have been identified as fragile. This view was held by both the Irish government and the European Central Bank.[51] Still a parliamentary inquiry report notes that Anglo Irish had proposed to the Department of Finance on 18 September 2008 to acquire Irish Nationwide Building Society. Kevin Cardiff stated in a hearing that he suspected that the struggling bank sought "to maneuver itself into a position of being 'too big to fail'" so that the market would be persuaded that it was going to be supported by the government through any difficulties.[52] The

46. Hardiman, *Irish Governance in Crisis*, 5.
47. Barrett, "The EU/IMF Rescue Programme for Ireland: 2010–2013."
48. Lyons and Carey, *The Fitzpatrick Tapes*, 136.
49. Honohan, *The Irish Banking Crisis*, 8–9; Nyberg, *Misjudging Risk*, 62–72.
50. Honohan, *The Irish Banking Crisis*, 96–97.
51. Interview, 16 February 2012.
52. House of the Oireachtas, *Report on the Crisis in the Banking Sector*, 130. In a second hearing, the assistant secretary general responsible for banking revisiting his initial declaration and could not confirm whether this meeting had taken place.

takeover never went through and nobody would have argued that Anglo Irish was too connected to fail. According to one observer:

> Anglo Irish Bank had only six branches in Ireland, no ATM's, and no organic relationship with Irish business except the property developers. It lent money to people to buy land and build: that's practically all it did. It did this mainly with money it had borrowed from foreigners. It was not, by nature, systemic.[53]

The guarantee decision appears thus to have been based on the principle of not letting an Irish bank fail and on rather incomplete information. The assurances provided by the government agencies and the auditors PwC and Merrill Lynch led the government to affirm that Irish banks were fundamentally sound and solvent and that the difficulties were merely due to a liquidity crush.[54] This implied that the guarantee served only to reassure markets but would not be called on. On 10 October 2008, Brian Lenihan therefore affirmed having put into place "the cheapest bailout in the world so far."[55] This would prove to be a colossal misjudgment.

Anglo Irish actively played on the government's ignorance, as a taped telephone call revealed by the *Irish Independent* demonstrates.[56] In the conversation, an Anglo Irish executive explained to a colleague that they had misrepresented their situation in September 2008 in order to obtain an initial €7 billion loan from the government. The amount was entirely arbitrary, "big enough to be important" but small enough to appear manageable, determined with the sole purpose of making sure the government had "skin in the game" and would be required to "support their money," once the real situation of Anglo Irish became apparent.[57] The deception resulted in a public takeover of Anglo Irish in January 2009 and demonstrated that the government was unable to judge the quality of the information given by the Anglo Irish executives.

Misjudgment about the severity of the solvency problems of Irish banks also marked the management of recapitalization and decision to transfer toxic assets through. During the initial negotiations of the recapitalization scheme, the government proposed that the financing necessary for capitalization were to come from equity funds, including sovereign wealth funds from the Middle East, but Irish banks strongly opposed this.[58] A private solution was thus abandoned. The level of capital injections were negotiated

---

53. Lewis, "When Irish Eyes Are Crying."
54. Cowen, "The Euro: From Crisis to Resolution?"
55. The Irish Times, "Irish Bailout Cheapest in World, Says Lenihan."
56. Williams, "Tapes That Reveal What Really Led to National Collapse."
57. Ibid.
58. Kluth and Lynggaard, "Explaining Responses in Danish and Irish Banking to the Financial Crisis," 783.

individually with the banks on terms set unilaterally by the government. It appears that at the time, the government felt that it could shoulder the recapitalization. Brian Lenihan affirmed on Irish television at the announcement of the recapitalization package that "there will be no exposure to the taxpayer on this [€10bn support fund for banks]."[59]

By the time NAMA was set up, it became increasingly clear that the government was committing more and more substantial amounts of public money, possibly with considerable losses. The NAMA arrangement shows how fluid the boundaries between public and private expenditures had become as a result of the crisis. The special purpose vehicle created for removing risky assets from the balance sheets of the banks is on paper owned jointly by NAMA (at 49 percent) and private investors (51 percent). The private investors are the pension fund managers Irish Life Investment Managers; New Ireland Assurance; and Clients of Allied Irish Banks Investment Managers, which are part of Irish Life Permanent, Bank of Ireland, and Allied Irish Banks respectively. Banks thus did agree to contribute to NAMA. However, since all three of these banks had been under government control and guarantee by 2011, the debt of NAMA is now considered as government debt entirely.[60]

In sharp contrast to Brian Lenihan's earlier declaration, Patrick Honohan, who became governor of the Irish Central Bank in September 2009 after having researched banking crises during his prior work as a professor of economics, described the Irish case as "one of the most expansive banking crises in world history."[61]

Ireland and the European Central Bank

Overall, the decision to give a blanket guarantee to banks on 29 September 2008 not only for senior bonds, but also for subordinated debt compromised the capacity to allocate some part of the bank losses to bondholders and put severe stress on the Irish taxpayer.[62] Although this decision might be attributable to a series of failures and malfunctioning of information and oversight, it is important to understand why this fateful decision was not reversed.[63] University College Dublin economist Morgan Kelly argued that the reason for Ireland's financial ruin was not the initial decision, "the real error was sticking with the guarantee long after it had become clear that the bank losses were insupportable."[64]

59. Six One News, 14 December 2008, cited in http://thestory.ie/2010/11/22/talking-points-in-time.

60. European Commission, *State Aid N725/2009—Ireland: Establishment of a National Asset Management Agency (NAMA), Asset Relief Scheme for Banks in Ireland.*

61. Cited in Browne, *Let's Own Up to Our Part in the Burst Bubble.*

62. Nyberg, *Misjudging Risk.*

63. Brigid Laffan and Niamh Hardiman's close reading and helpful comments have contributed significantly to the following section.

64. Kelly, *Ireland's Future Depends on Breaking Free from Bailout.*

According to informal statements by a series of policymakers, the decision to renew the guarantee for unsecured bondholders of Irish banks, rather than letting them take haircuts, was due to pressure exerted on Ireland from the European Central Bank.[65] Irish economist Colm McCarthy goes as far as blaming the ECB under Jean-Claude Trichet for the fact that the banking crisis turned into a sovereign debt crisis: its "no-bank-bondholder-left behind policy" was imposed on Ireland by the ECB and "the principal source of the sovereign debt crisis."[66]

Irish banks had depended on liquidity facilities from the ECB throughout the crisis. In September 2010, members of the board of the ECB had grown frustrated with the crisis management in several member countries, requiring the ECB to continue offering unconventional measures to support banks.[67] The threat of reducing liquidity support gave the ECB an important sway over the Irish government. When it had to turn to the ECB and the IMF in late 2010 to negotiate a sovereign bailout, the ECB's position was crucial and seems to explain why the guarantee of unsecured senior bondholders of Irish banks was upheld. As Whelan argues in a report to the European Parliament:

> In fact, there is no mention of senior debt whatsoever in the official programme conditionality, which suggests that this requirement is more of a "backroom" agreement. Irish officials and politicians have pointed to the ECB as also insisting that all senior bank bonds be repaid, so this backroom agreement most likely involves the ECB in some capacity, suggesting that repayment of senior bank bonds is somehow a *quid pro quo* for the ECB's agreement to continue providing funding to the Irish banks.[68]

This accusation has not been refuted by European authorities. When Brian Lenihan defended the sovereign bailout package in the Irish Parliament, he emphasized that "there is simply no way that this country, whose banks are so dependent on international investors, can unilaterally renege on senior bondholders against the wishes of the ECB."[69] Similarly, Brian Cowen insists,

> At no stage during the crisis would the European authorities, especially the European Central Bank, have countenanced the dishonoring of senior bank bonds. The euro area policy of "No bank failures and no burning of senior bank creditors" has been a constant during the crisis. And as a member of the euro area, Ireland must play by the rules.[70]

---

65. See McCarthy, *Ireland's European Crisis*; O'Callaghan, *Did the ECB Cause a Run on Irish Banks?*.
66. McCarthy, "Colm McCarthy."
67. The Irish Times, "Banks Must Be 'Weaned Off ECB Funds.' "
68. Whelan, *Bank and Sovereign Debt Resolution*," 6.
69. Cited in Lewis, "When Irish Eyes Are Crying," 7.
70. Cowen, "The Euro: From Crisis to Resolution?"

To summarize, the extensive public costs incurred during the Irish bank bailout were the result of a complex mix of inappropriate regulation prior to the crisis, incomplete oversight, misjudged risk, deception and flawed crisis management, to which one needs to add the institutional relationships within the Eurozone. Domestic banks used their ties to the government to request support and avert solutions they considered inappropriate. They did not, however, engage collectively with the government in any significant way or devise schemes to support one another. On the contrary, executives from Anglo Irish judged support from within the Irish banking sector as counterproductive since markets would not judge such support as sound financial investment. They believed that it would appear that the bank executives had "just met them in the pub" and that "we are all in each other's pockets."[71] Indeed, the only ties among Irish banks that became apparent during the crisis period was the circular loan scandal at Anglo Irish, a rather inglorious attempt at finding a collective solution to the public crisis.

Denmark

Despite its comparable size and structure, the Danish financial industry negotiated collectively rather than individually with the government. Much of this resulted from the government's proactive stance, since it was eager to engage the industry to avoid repeating the early mistakes, in particular in the management of the Roskilde failure. To understand the striking features of the collective arrangement, it is helpful to consider the context of early intervention, the nature of industry commitments, and the cohesion even in contexts where specific institutions benefited in particular.

Early Intervention: Beyond Support from the National Bank

Traditionally, the Danish Nationalbank had supported struggling banks through liquidity provision, acting as a lender of last resort for both bankTrelleborg and Roskilde Bank in late 2007 and early 2008. When liquidity support was insufficient, the government tried to find a healthy institution willing to take over their competitor. When no such solution could be found for Roskilde Bank, the Danish Nationalbank negotiated with the financial industry to acquire the failing bank. At the time, the industry contributed DKK750 million and the Danish government guaranteed that it would cover all additional losses. It became clear very quickly that the government's responsibility would be far above the industry's contribution, reaching DKK6.6 billion in 2009 and well over DKK9 billion in 2012.[72]

---

71. Williams, "Tapes That Reveal What Really Led to National Collapse–Clip 26: Irish."
72. Carstensen, "Projecting from a Fiction"; Finansiel Stabilitet, *Annual Report 2009*, 30–31.

In contrast to the United States or the United Kingdom, monetary policy instruments used by the Danish central bank were not central to supporting the banking industry. To be sure, the Nationalbank used a series of instruments to provide greater liquidity at the height of the interbanking market freeze in September 2008, in particular temporary credit facilities and an expansion of collateral rules. However, these instruments were much less used than the support given through the bank packages.[73]

An important reason for this was that Danish banks had a high demand for euro liquidity and also dollar liquidity. Not being a euro member with a fixed exchange rate regime proved to be a particular challenge.[74] High demand for euro and dollar liquidity by Danish banks led to increasing pressure on the Danish krone. When rumors spread that the Nationalbank had limited foreign reserves and was approaching the maximum allowed deviation in its fixed exchange rate regime, some foreign investors began speculating against the krone. The currency crisis reached an unprecedented level in the first weeks of October, where "we could literally see our reserves pouring out of our coffers," as Nils Bernstein, the governor of the Nationalbank remembers: "I felt like driving a car without brakes."[75] In his view, swap lines established with the Federal Reserve Bank and the ECB, as well as the issuance of thirty-year government bonds help avoid a crash, but also the government guarantee for deposits and loans to Danish banks. By creating confidence in the Danish financial sector, the government intervention was important for Denmark's Nationalbank "to keep the krone stable."

Unlike monetary policy in the United States, which was said to have been more important than government intervention through TARP, the stability of the national currency in Denmark actually depended in part on the bank rescue scheme. Moreover, not being a member of the Eurozone was a challenge rather than an advantage. Nationalbank governor Nils Bernstein underlines, "When you are a small open economy and a storm of this magnitude sweeps through the markets—you would rather not have your own currency to worry about."[76]

Similarly, the CFO of Denmark's leading Danske Bank referred to the euro as a "safe harbor" the Danish financial industry would have needed.[77] With a national currency, but fixed exchange rates, the Danish economy was in the worst of both worlds. It had to manage a currency crisis in the midst of a banking crisis and maintained relatively high interest rates to prevent capital outflows, which aggravated the funding difficulties of Danish banks on international markets.

73. Carstensen, "Projecting from a Fiction."
74. Bernstein, "The Danish Krone during the Crisis."
75. Ibid.
76. Ibid.
77. Quoted in Dougherty, "No Quick Solution to Financial Crisis, Denmark Shows."

Collective Commitments

Both the Danish public authorities and the Danish industry drew their lessons from these early experiences and especially the Roskilde Bank failure. For the government, getting the financial industry to contribute to the rescue schemes became central. For the financial industry, assuring their continued access to international financial markets was an increasingly pressing concern. If Danish banks would end up failing rather than being taken over by competitors as had happened in the past, confidence in the Danish financial industry would falter further and increase their funding costs substantially. These funding difficulties were confirmed when markets froze in reaction to the fall of Lehman Brothers on 15 September and the Irish guarantee on 30 September, which led to a massive deposit withdrawals from the Irish branches of Danske Bank.[78]

The Danish Bankers Association believed it would need to send a strong signal and was eager to work with the government on a solution. Within a very short time frame, the negotiating parties agreed to the arrangement that would underpin the Danish guarantee scheme at the heart of Bank Package 1. The Private Contingency Association established in 2007 served as a backbone for the plan. In terms of commitment, the Danish government guarantee covered existing unsecured bank bond debt, like in Ireland, potentially up to two and a half times the Danish GDP and comparable to the Irish guarantee. However, the financial industry participated in the scheme both by paying the government in return for the guarantee (DKK15 billion) and by contributing another DKK10 billion and an additional pledge of DKK10 billion as a collective guarantee. The contribution of the Danish financial sector is managed through the Private Contingency Association, and all its members are covered by the government package. Put differently, Bank Package I was an industry-financed scheme where the government would only come in when losses exceed DKK35 billion.[79]

The Danish government and the Private Contingency Association also set up Finansiel Stabilitet S/A, a public company charged with the unwinding of insolvent banks. The financial sector will finance the losses of the state-owned company up to a limit of 2 percent. All additional losses are covered by a state guarantee. Through this mutual agreement, the financial industry contributed both directly and had incentives to find private sector solutions that can help avoid having Finansiel Stabilitet S/A take over an insolvent institution.

The Danish Banking Association was an important negotiating partner in the preparation of Bank Package II as well, despite the fact that the capital injections benefited in particular Danske Bank. According to its former

---

78. Østrup, "The Danish Bank Crisis in a Transnational Perspective," 84.
79. Kickert, "How the Danish Government Responded to Financial Crises," 56.

director, Peter Straarup, Danske Bank would not have survived without the capital injections.[80] The capital injections were voluntary, but banks needed to have a 12 percent tier 1 capital reserve after recapitalization and had to accept an interest payment of roughly 10 percent.

Participation in both schemes was useful during the crisis, but also very costly for Danish banks. It was difficult to know *ex ante* to what extend Finansiel Stabilitet S/A would incur losses, which were shared by Danish banks according to the size of their guaranteed volume. Danske Bank, for example, paid a quarterly fee of DKK625 million for the guarantee coverage and DKK3.4 billion for losses incurred through unwinding other banks. The cost in participating only in bank package I was thus DKK8.4 billion in two years.[81]

Danish banks were eager to move beyond the initial schemes and participated in the design of the so-called exit scheme, bank package III. In order to avoid overburdening the Danish financial industry and the taxpayer, creditors and depositors would not longer be guaranteed full coverage, but creditors would have to accept haircuts, and depositors would be exposed to losses for deposits over DKK750,000. The deposit insurance up to this amount was financed by a Guarantee Fund, jointly owned by the financial industry. The agreement also entails a standard setup for dismantling distressed financial institutions and is financed through a contribution of DKK3.2 billion from the banking industry to the public unwinding company Finansiel Stabilitet S/A.

However, the return to "normal failures" was quickly punished by international financial markets.[82] When Amagerbanken, at the time Denmark's fifth largest bank, and later Fjordbank Mors failed, senior creditors—for the first time in Europe—suffered haircuts of 41 percent and 26 percent respectively. Citing the lack of government support for failing banks, the credit rating agency Moody's downgraded six Danish lenders, including Danske Bank, making funding costs soar for the Danish industry.

It was of little consolation that the *Financial Times* commended Denmark for imposing costs on bondholders, contrary to Ireland, where "Irish taxpayers bail out German, French and UK investors in private Irish banks."[83] For Danish banks and the government, it became important to signal that unwinding could happen without such haircuts, preferably through private takeovers. This was the motivation behind Bank Package IV and its reinforced dowry scheme. Again, the dowry given to the buyer of a struggling financial institution was funded through Finansiel Stabilitet S/A and the financial industry's Guarantee Fund.

Put differently, at all different stages of the bailout negotiations, the Danish financial industry contributed massively not only in helping to design

80. Cited in Carstensen, "Projecting from a Fiction," 18.
81. Barsøe Venshøj, "The Financial Crisis and the Danish Banking Sector," 10.
82. Carstensen, "Projecting from a Fiction: The Case of Denmark and the Financial Crisis."
83. *Financial Times*, "Danish Lessons."

the public responses, but also by committing funds and engaging each other collectively through formalized institutions such as the Private Contingency Association and the Guarantee Fund. As Pedersen has highlighted, this interaction is at the heart of the Danish model, which has been described as a "negotiated economy":

> Whereas both mixed and market economies are based on a clear division of labor between the sovereign state and an autonomous market, a negotiated economy entails political and economic relations that are neither strictly public nor private. . . . The country remained committed to policy-making through negotiations and trust in collective solidarities.[84]

This trust in collective solidarities is intact even in times of crisis. To be sure, as everywhere, Danish government officials complained about the scandalous lack of competence and professionalism in bank management as one of the reasons for the extent of the crisis. However, Brian Mikkelsen, minister of economics and business affairs since 2009, argues that these individual shortcomings were not representative for the banking sector in general.[85] Confidence in the industry's ability to save itself remained high, and the government continued to encourage private sector solutions for failing banks.

This is illustrated further by the mutual respect the public authorities and banking representatives pay to one another. Nils Bernstein, governor of the Danish Nationalbank closed his speech at the annual convention of the Danish Bankers Association in 2009 with special thanks to the outgoing chairman for the "good cooperation" during the crisis.[86] What may seem like an insignificant gesture of politeness is tellingly absent from any of Irish governor John Hurley's speeches at industry events.

Comparative Assessment

The Irish and the Danish bank bailout schemes exposed their countries to substantial risks through an initial extensive guarantee of both depositors and creditors. With banking sectors well above the size of the national economies, these commitments and the subsequent instruments constituted between 2.5 and 3.5 times the size of GDP. According to Eurostat, only 67 percent of GDP was actually extended in Denmark through public authorities, compared to 270 percent in Ireland. Considering the evolution of government investment in the banking sector and the different sources of

---

84. Pedersen, "Corporatism and Beyond: The Negotiated Economy," 202.
85. Cited in Carstensen, "Projecting from a Fiction," 17.
86. Bernstein, "Overview of Developments in Denmark."

revenue, Eurostat ranks the Danish bank rescue plan as the most profitable in Europe in 2011, helping the Danish government to reduce its fiscal deficit by 0.3 percent of GDP over 2008–10.[87] This is equivalent to €0.7 billion in absolute terms, topped only by Spain and France, which made a net benefit of €1.5 billion and €2.4 billion, or 0.1 percent of their respective GDPs. In the same study, Ireland holds the last place in Europe, with a 22.7 percent deficit increase, equivalent to €36 billion.

The estimation of total costs depends on a series of assumptions about contingent liabilities and evolves very much over time. However, it appears that the total fiscal costs of the Irish bailout are probably underestimated by the Eurostat comparison. According to the Irish House of the Oireachtas, the direct costs to the state in 2012 were estimated at €64 billion (41 percent of GDP).[88] According to Lane, "while the public capital injections into Bank of Ireland and AIB may be viewed as financial investments that may ultimately yield return, the capital poured into Anglo Irish Bank and Irish Nationwide Building Society are effectively write-offs."[89] Worldwide, only Iceland appears to have suffered a higher impact on sovereign debt.[90]

However, the case studies show that the difference in costs of the bank bailout is not due to the general health of the Danish banking sector, as one could have argued for the case of France, for example. Only a small minority of Danish banks chose not to be covered by the unlimited guarantee scheme. Concerning recapitalization, a total of fifty banks and mortgage lenders applied for capital contributions before the closing date on 30 June 2009 for a total of DKK63 billion.[91]

From the summer 2008 to the summer of 2012, the Financial Stability Company took over and unwound a dozen Danish banks, including Amagerbanken, the country's fifth biggest listed lender, in February 2011; Fjordbank Mors in June 2011; and assets of FIH Erhvervsbank, Denmark's six largest bank in March 2012.[92] In 2013, the Danish Financial Stability Company continues to manage the resolution of the two banks through subsidiaries (i.e., bad banks). Even the Danish government, which tried to remain as distant as possible from the actual bank management, was thus forced to take over two banks. But this is little compared to the Irish government, which today effectively owns all of the domestic Irish banking sector.

---

87. European Commission, *Eurostat Supplementary Table for the Financial Crisis: Background Note.*

88. House of the Oireachtas, *Report on the Crisis in the Banking Sector,* 13.

89. Lane, *The Irish Crisis,* 17.

90. Laeven and Valencia, "Resolution of Banking Crisis."

91. See www.philip.dk/en/news/bank-bailout-packages-i-and-ii.html.

92. Hansen and Sandstrom, *Danish Government Readies New Bank Sector Plans.* For details on the individual bank asset transfers and the subsidiaries created by Finansiel Stabilitet S/A for their unwinding, see www.finansielstabilitet.dk. The last bank to fail was Tønder Bank in November 2012. Milne, "Danish Banks Set Off Alarm Bells."

It is difficult to argue that Irish intervention in the banking sector, however late it may have come, was a "gift to the bankers." As banks were taken over, senior management changed and became the target of public outrage. Not only did the senior management of the troubled banks find it difficult to not be heckled in public, the downturn also had financial and legal consequences,

> Action by Irish Bank Resolution Corporation, the former Anglo Irish Bank, which is winding down Irish Nationwide, has already led to the bankruptcy of former chairman Seán Fitzpatrick, while former chief executive David Drumm is being pursued by the bank in the US.[93]

This situation differed from other countries: "In America the banks went down, but the big shots in them still got rich; in Ireland the big shots went down with the banks."[94] In terms of moral hazard, it is difficult to imagine that Irish bankers would consider repeating this experience.

Conclusion

Denmark and Ireland did not struggle with exactly the same challenges. While Denmark had to avoid a currency crash, Ireland's policy autonomy was severely constrained through the European institutions, in particular in the context of the sovereign bailout in 2010. When the crisis broke in 2008, the governments also found themselves facing very different regulatory legacies, with a rather well-functioning regime in Denmark, bearing the memory of the banking crisis in the 1990s, and an excessively lax and complacent one in Ireland. Still much about these trying times is comparable. In both cases, the financial sector had invested heavily in the domestic housing market, relying excessively on international wholesale funding for short-term liquidity. In both, the housing market bubble burst and financial institutions found themselves unable to access these previously available international markets. Governments responded, almost simultaneously, by issuing a guarantee on deposits and bank debt to reassure markets. With time, however, the liquidity crisis revealed severe solvency problems in several important banks, so that recapitalization and other measures became necessary.

The objective of this last comparison is not to argue that Ireland could look like Denmark today; too many factors explain the entire evolution and outcome. The comparison has sought to demonstrate, however, that part of the discrepancy in crisis management is linked to the way in which governments were able to commit the financial sector collectively to participating in

---

93. *Irish Times*, "Cantillon."
94. Lewis, "When Irish Eyes Are Crying," 4.

their own rescue. Had the Danish industry not rolled up its sleeves, Denmark might have looked more like Ireland.

Both Ireland and Denmark are small countries, where public officials, regulators, and senior bank management know each other well. In Denmark, this connectedness was institutionalized within the banking sector through well-functioning associations, in particular, the Danish Bankers Association, which allowed the Private Contingency Association to be endowed with a crucial role during the crisis.

Denmark avoided Ireland's fate, but the situation was just as risky. Pedersen insists that a central aspect of the Danish negotiated economy is "gambling":

> First, the survival of an entire nation, including the population's economic growth and welfare is at stake. Second, decision-making depends upon the capacity of the elite to interpret contemporary economic and other conditions for action, and to do so in a manner that will lead to successful national strategies.[95]

Interpreting economic conditions for action in 2008 required concerted action and mutual surveillance within the financial industry, rather than top-down support or regulatory constraints. In the recent banking crisis, the Danish experiment withstood the test, even if twelve banks had to be unwound and regulatory responses had to be frequently adjusted.

In Ireland, connectedness implied mainly that individual banks relied on their privileged relationships with public officials, but not that they invested into strong ties with their competitors to respond jointly to the crisis. The collective inaction of the domestic Irish banking industry added to the paralysis of the government. Both parties might have hoped that the other side was stronger than it eventually turned out to be. The financial tsunami swept away both, as each was unable to turn their fate around. This highlights the fuzzy border between unwillingness and incapacity to act. To return to the images of our initial negotiation game, Ireland appears like a game of chicken in which the two cars collided, crashed, and burned. We can be certain that both the government and the domestic banking industry had wished for a different outcome.

---

95. Pedersen, "Corporatism and Beyond"; see also Obinger et al., *Transformations of the Welfare State.*

Lessons Learned

The market can stay irrational longer than you can stay solvent.
—John Maynard Keynes

The banking crisis of 2008 took even the best-prepared governments by surprise. In weekend meetings and overnight sessions around the world, public officials and financial industry representatives tried to find the most appropriate responses to an evolving set of problems. Evaluating the precise consequences of individual decisions, policy choices, and rescue arrangements will consume the time of economists, historians, and policy analysts for years to come. This study seeks to contribute to the debate by focusing on the nature of business-government relationships in a variety of countries. In particular, it has demonstrated that the participation of the financial industry in their own rescue varied significantly across countries and that the government's approach was in many ways dependent on the commitments made by the private sector. Moreover, the discussion explores how the nature of the bailout arrangements is partially linked to the costs of the banking rescue, although this relationship is by no means straightforward, since many different factors affect the fiscal impact of bank support.

Most clearly, the comparison across countries helps us evaluate the autonomy of the government vis-à-vis their financial sector, or inversely, the influence the industry has on government choices during crisis management. The power of the financial sector depended in great part on structural aspects such as the role and size of the financial sector and had produced distinct systems of meaning enshrined in regulatory approaches in the years leading up to the crisis. Within these settings, however, the power of the financial industry can be gauged by the extent of their collective contribution to their own rescue. The collective action of the financial sector was one of the most central concerns of governments negotiating with ailing banks during the crisis.

In the following, we will review the different interactions and analyze the logics of business-government relations comparatively. This summary underscores the fact that even those governments that have appeared to handle the crisis well were left with a bitter aftertaste of impotence in the face of financial turmoil. One series of responses therefore sought to correct governmental capacity by imposing tighter regulation once the most immediate concerns had been attended to. Another approach relied on international cooperation and European integration of competences that were previously guarded as matters of sovereign policymaking. As a result, the power struggles during banking crises at the domestic level led to sometimes profound transformations of government capacity in the long run.

This conclusion reviews the comparative lessons, first, by summarizing how business-government relations affect bank support schemes. Second, it returns to the question of power in business-government interactions. A final section considers the current attempts to introduce regulatory reforms at the national and international level, in order to discuss the moral hazard consequences of the bank bailouts in the long run more fully.

Bank Bailouts in Comparison

The paired comparisons have demonstrated that there is no such thing as an Anglo-Saxon or liberal market economy solution to banking crises, no bank-based system or coordinated market solution, and no small open economy approach. Within every pair that we would have expected to be marked by structural features such as the role of banks in the economy, the reliance of domestic banks on international markets, or the availability of monetary policy options at the domestic level, we have seen that divergence in approaches is often more striking than convergence.

The governments in the United States and the United Kingdom did not deal with their struggling banks in the same manner. The US government was stringent with deposit-taking institutions but rather lenient with large financial institutions, which it supported with favorable conditions during the TARP program and unconventional facilities of the Federal Reserve. The United Kingdom, by contrast, adopted a constraining approach to bank support, both in terms or pricing and conditions, even if this applied only to the financial institutions that specifically sought help. In the two liberal market economies, collective industry action was not well established, and bailouts eventually had to rely on government intervention. The first comparison therefore gives us little leverage to gauge the heuristic value of the central argument in this book: in both countries collective inaction by the industry forced the government into a position they would have preferred to avoid. And yet, government responses in the face of industry inaction were strikingly different. The UK government quickly acknowledged the incapacity of the financial industry to contribute collectively to a solution and decided to press ahead without them, imposing conditions that were hard to swallow for the struggling institutions. In the United States, the negative connotation attached to government intervention in the economy led public authorities to try for too long to push the industry to devise a private sector solution. By trying to rely on collective action from the industry in a country that had no real tradition of coordinated decision making, the US government exposed its vulnerability and ended up designing a support scheme that was much more bank friendly than in the United Kingdom. In many aspects, crisis management in the United States was the most deferential to its large financial institutions, compared to all the countries examined in this book, which is reflected in public opinion's uneasiness about the continued dominance of the financial sector over the US government. In the United Kingdom, by contrast, all policy observers concur that the days of liberal regulation of banking activities are over, and the Brown government has received rather favorable ratings for its management of failing institutions, despite the considerable costs the bailouts have imposed on the public budget.

France and Germany both have a high level of bank intermediation and a tradition of public-private coordination on economic issues. However, Germany, the archetypical coordinated market economy, was unable to come up with a bank support plan carried by the private sector. Despite the attempts of the government to encourage such an industry-led solution, the banking crisis proved too massive for the three-pillar structure of the German financial sector. Parts of the industry were unwilling to extend support schemes that existed within their pillars to other institutions, and the commercial banking sector contained firms that were too heterogeneous in size to allow for a coordinated collective response. Faced with these institutional legacies and bargaining difficulties, the German government was obliged to step in and intervene much further than it had wished. In France, by contrast, the small number of financial institutions of somewhat comparable size and the strong ties between public officials and bank representatives allowed a very well-coordinated response that was partially carried by the private sector.

A similarly negotiated response emerged in the Danish case. Thanks to earlier experiences and a strong tradition of coordinated economic responses, the Danish financial industry was able to overcome a heterogeneous financial structure comparable to Germany and produce an innovative public-private arrangement supported to a great extent by the Danish financial industry. The Danish arrangement allowed for the unwinding of a series of financial institutions in a rather orderly fashion and enabled the government to adjust its approach over time. This coordination stands in stark contrast to the paralysis of the Irish government and the absence of substantive engagement of the Irish financial industry. By attempting to support the struggling banking sector single-handedly, the Irish government completely overextended itself and lost control over its economy entirely. In the process of the Irish collapse, banks lost their autonomy as well. If one thinks of Irish business-government relations as a power struggle, the victory of the financial industry was too short-lived to be worth mentioning. In the end, both parties lost.

The comparison across the six cases also helps to put into perspective the importance of monetary policy instruments for supporting the banking sector, summarized in table 8.1. The first two country pairs had equivalent monetary policy settings, with the United States and the United Kingdom being able to rely on facilities from their central banks to support the financial sector, while France and Germany both had to abide by the collective policy decisions of the Eurozone, which required a more central role of direct fiscal commitments. Within each of these two pairs, monetary policy cannot explain the different approaches, because the conditions were largely comparable.

In the Danish and Irish comparison, the role of central banks differed. Denmark had to manage the stability of its currency while supporting the financial sector, which meant that interest rates determined by the Nationalbank during the crisis were a response to currency imbalances rather than the need for liquidity of the Danish banks. Ireland was sheltered through EMU, but had to deal with policy instructions from the European authorities, in particular in 2010, where some argue that Ireland should have required senior bondholders of Irish banks to accept haircuts. However, the Danish experience, where haircuts were imposed on the bondholders of Amagerbanken and Fjordbank Mors in 2011, shows that these decisions did have consequences for the credit ratings and the access to liquidity of the Danish banking sector, and Danish banks were eager to move to a system that signaled stronger government support for the industry. It is difficult to hypothesize what would have happened in the Irish case. Haircuts for senior bondholders might have alleviated some of the public budget commitments, but it is overly optimistic to argue that Ireland could have avoided seeking a sovereign bailout in 2010. Whatever the precise consequences of Eurozone membership were in the two countries, the case studies have demonstrated that monetary union is a mixed blessing for small open economies in the midst of a banking crisis. In either

TABLE 8.1
The role of central banks

| | | National fiscal spare capacity | |
		Limited	Sufficient
Monetary Policy Authority	Autonomous	Iceland	United States, United Kingdom
	Fixed	Denmark	
	Collective	Ireland	France, Germany

case, monetary tools where not available to offset the burden placed on direct fiscal intervention. The nature of the bank support scheme and the contribution from the private sector is therefore all the more central.

Concerning the net fiscal impact of bank bailouts, we have seen in the initial overview that French and Danish bailout schemes were among the most profitable in Europe, while the United Kingdom, Germany, Ireland, and the United States were among the most costly in absolute terms. In relative terms, however, the fiscal impact of the US bailout is rather small. The estimated $150 billion net costs listed by the bailout watch website ProPublica constitute less than 1 percent of GDP, while Laeven and Valencia estimate the US net costs to be 2.1 percent.[1] A significant part of this variation results from the size of the balance sheets and the exposure of the troubled banks in which the government still holds stakes.

However, there is reason to believe that the industry participation in rescue scheme helps to manage the costs the taxpayer is exposed to. First of all, a part of the burden of support mechanisms is shouldered by the industry directly, as in Denmark, where a portion of the government funds used to stabilize the banking sector was contributed by the industry directly in return for the public guarantee. Second, banks have a collective incentive to monitor each others' behavior and development and can influence the degree of support each one of them will be able to benefit from. As in all collective solutions, such an arrangement limits free riding through the control of peers. Since financial institutions share information about market evolutions, they can more easily identify if one of their competitors appears to rely unduly on the collectively financed support scheme without reducing risky behavior. Finally, collective arrangements incentivize their members to exit a scheme that is no longer necessary in order to reduce the costs linked to participation. Rather than relying on the government to determine the most appropriate moment to cut of public support, private actors will be likely to signal their preferred moment for phasing out governmental support. This has been the case in both France and Denmark, even if some banks in France appeared to have benefited longer than necessary from government recapitalization.

Comparing the Power of the Financial Industry

The central objective of this study was to gauge the power of the financial industry by comparing its role in the design of the bailout arrangements across countries. Contrary to popular writings, which focus on the lobbying of the financial sector, this study insists that these activities are not the most telling indicator of financial power. Rather, the structural importance

1. Laeven and Valencia, "Systemic Banking Crises Dataset: An Update."

of finance for the functioning of a nation's economy enables it to benefit from policies in its favor, even when financial industry representatives have not specifically asked for them. Because of their structural importance, the financial elite in all advanced economies everywhere is well connected with the government and will be consulted in some way or another in periods of crisis. In addition, governments, the financial sector, and other actors have produced interpretations of financial activities that further structure their interactions and define their relationships and interests. These narratives determined the starting point and challenge of crisis management, which in some countries was heavily tilted in favor of the industry, in particular the Anglo-Saxon countries—the United States, the United Kingdom, and Ireland, but increasingly also Germany.

Studying crisis management, however, requires examining agency. This book has argued that the industry's capacity to refrain from contributing to their own rescue is more revealing of business power than lobbying or tight networks. Governments everywhere have tried to encourage such participation. Indeed the justification for government intervention to support failing banks was based on the collective consequences of individual failure. It would thus seem only logical that avoiding such collective effects should come at a price for individual firms. Given the severity of the crisis, however, the financial industry could attempt to avoid contributing collectively by insisting on their individual health, hoping that the government would nonetheless intervene to support the sector.

In the six cases, we have been able to study different kinds of such power struggles between the public authorities and the financial industry. In most countries, the financial industry has been unwilling or incapable of collective action to support each other. In both the United States and Germany, this inaction was all the more determining because both governments pushed for collective commitments of the financial industry, hoping to be able to rely on their industries rather than on public intervention. But the financial sector eventually pulled out and the government was left to pick up the pieces. In the United Kingdom and Ireland, the financial industry also did not engage collectively, but neither government had much hope that they would do so. Rather, both decided to take a proactive and interventionist stance very early on. Although this proactivity had the benefit of putting the financial sector back into its place and dictating a governmental roadmap, the choice was ultimately unwise for Ireland, because it had taken on a financial sector that had previously grown too large in size. Proactivity in the face of a reluctant financial industry is only a good solution when the government actually has the spare fiscal capacity to follow up on its ambitious plans. Put more theoretically, the structural and productive power of the banking sector in Ireland had been so substantial in the past that the government room for maneuver was limited and ultimately doomed. The final set of interactions occurred in France and Denmark, where governments solicited and relied on the collective action of the financial industry. Although this cooperation may seem to indicate a power relationship built on mutual dependence, it is actually more balanced than a power relationship marked by unequal burden sharing. For a small open economy with an overextended financial sector like Denmark, it was certainly the best possible solution for managing the banking crisis.

Explaining Collective Inaction during Crisis Management

The question therefore becomes: What explains when collective action will succeed or fail? We know from collective action theory that larger heterogeneous groups are more difficult to mobilize than small homogenous ones. This seemingly applies to the French example, where the financial industry was a small group of like-minded firms. But it does not do a good job of explaining Denmark, where the industry comprised a rather diverse set of financial institutions, similarly to Germany. It also does not explain why the US government was trying to go out of its way to make the US bailout favorable for the industry for fear they would not accept it otherwise. After all, there were only nine major US financial institutions gathered by the administration in a room on 13 October 2008.

To understand the industry dynamics we need to move beyond the simple shape of the industry and also understand the stakes and alternatives for the individual firms. In particular, one variation stands out across cases, and it lies in answering the following question: Which firms were healthy and which in bad shape?[2] As in all collective action issues, if the most important players have no interest in participating and/or can shift their activities elsewhere, the joint enterprise will fall apart. Inversely, if the most important players have to manage their own difficulties, they might be interested in pursuing or even organizing a joint rescue effort.

In the United States, the healthy financial institutions that the public authorities wished to include in the TARP recapitalization scheme were Wells Fargo and JP Morgan. Wells Fargo's CEO Dick Kovacevich was visibly not pleased to be forced to accept government capital, but Well Fargo was a Wall Street outsider. It was much more crucial for the industry dynamic to have the support of JP Morgan's Jamie Dimon, who quickly acknowledged the importance of the scheme.[3] Had the US government not integrated the interests of a big player like JP Morgan, their plan might have failed. In the United Kingdom, HSBC, Barclays, and Standard Chartered had been in sufficiently good shape to raise capital privately. Standard Chartered had even agreed in the run up to serve as a test case for government planning. In addition, as Culpepper and

---

2. Bell and Hindmoor, *Masters of the Universe but Slaves of the Market*.
3. Bair, *Bull by the Horns*, 2–8; Sorkin, *Too Big to Fail*, 528.

Reinke argue, HSBC had significant operations abroad and could credibly threaten to exit if government intervention was to constraining.[4] The healthy UK banks were thus spared from the British bailout and in particular the punitive conditions. In France, the bank that clearly did not need a nationwide rescue scheme was Crédit Mutuel. One of the smallest French financial institutions, it had no clout in the collective negotiations. Things were different in Germany, where Deutsche Bank was among the healthiest German institutions. Overshadowing all other German banks, Deutsche Bank would have also been the most important contributor to a collective agreement, even if the Sparkassen would have agreed to share their sector's deposit insurance. The heterogeneity of German banking thus combined with the fact that the pivotal player had little interest in an industrywide arrangement. Denmark might have looked like Germany had Danske Bank been in good health. But it was not, to a point were some speculated that the Danish recapitalization was even just put into place to bail out Danske Bank. The diversity of the Danish banking sector thus did not weigh heavily because the biggest player had no incentive to walk away from the table. In Ireland, finally, Allied Irish Bank and Bank of Ireland, the most important high street banks, did take an initial leadership role and offered to open up liquidity to Anglo Irish. This initial agreement was not followed up on through a more formal collective agreement, first because it was no longer deemed necessary and later because the health of the two leaders had deteriorated considerably as well.

Collective action thus depends on the dynamics between the different stakeholders and their individual motivations for participating in joint arrangement. The structure of the financial sectors—homogenous or heterogeneous—matters, as do repeated interactions between the different participants. These are enabling conditions only, however. What is pivotal is the health of the leading financial institutions. If the most significant ones or a significant portion of a country's financial industry has no need for government support, individually, this is likely to lead to collective inaction. The healthy institutions can simply walk away from the negotiation table, all the more if they do not depend on just one government. They may agree on the benefits of a rescue scheme, in general, but can afford to gamble with the government in the hope that the government will pay for the bailout rather than the industry.

Regulation and Future Moral Hazard

Understanding the power relations during crisis management only gives us a snapshot. Once bailout arrangements were in place, governments in most countries quickly worked to correct what they had experienced

---

4. Culpepper and Reinke, *Structural Dependence of Capital on the State.*

as unbalanced relationships with finance. We therefore need to examine whether issues that have led to the crisis in the first place have been addressed. An analysis of both the power relationships in the early crisis and of the fiscal impact of the bailout arrangements needs to consider how these choices affect their future relationship and whether governments may risk repeating the experience. In economic terms, how do bailout schemes score with respect the moral hazard they create? To move toward an answer, we need to consider the signals sent to the financial industry, and this requires considering reregulation in the aftermath of the crisis as well.

Chapter 4 underlined that both the degree of constraint imposed through the bailout scheme and the extent of reregulation need to be considered. When both are absent, we can speak of a "free bailout" for the financial industry; when both are present, we see a "discourage and punish" approach, respectively in the upper left and lower right quadrant of table 4.1. Constraints without reregulation discourage the financial industry from relying on government support (lower left quadrant) and favorable bailouts with stringent reregulation constitute a "rescue now, pay later" approach.

In all of the cases studied, governments have been aware of the moral hazard problem of bank support. Both liquidity provision through central banks and direct government intervention will encourage financial institutions to count on public support in the future. It is therefore important to make this support costly somehow, to create the incentives for financial institutions to adjust their behavior in order to avoid repeating similar experiences.

The empirical studies have shown that the costs of bank support schemes for the financial sector as a whole have been high in Ireland, Denmark, and the United Kingdom. In Denmark, financial institutions voluntarily accepted a scheme to pay a substantial part of the costs of their own rescue. In the United Kingdom, failing banks had the choice to accept governmental support, which was both expensive, stigmatizing, and which had important consequences for corporate governance and senior management changes, in particular when the government became a majority stakeholder. In Ireland, banks ended up under government control, which meant that they had to completely sacrifice their autonomy. Although initiatives have been put forward in all countries, some have argued that they are not going far enough in countries such as

TABLE 8.2
Overview of bank accountability

		Reregulation	
		No	Yes
Bailout constraints	No		United States, France, Germany
	Yes	Ireland, Denmark	United Kingdom

Denmark and Ireland,[5] but have been quite ambitious in the United Kingdom. Whether this is an accurate impression or not needs to be confirmed with time. What is certain, however, is that in all three cases, the incentives for financial institutions to avoid repeating this experience are strong.

The bank support schemes in the United States, France, and Germany were less constraining than the other three. Although fees and conditions applied, the consequences of government support were not as discouraging. To respond to the perceived imbalance, governments in all three countries were eager to move toward stricter banking regulation, greater oversight powers, and more interventionist approaches to early resolution and unwinding of struggling institutions. In their attempt to govern the financial industry through tighter regulation, these three governments are quite similar to the United Kingdom, which had put into place the Banking Act of 2009 and the Vickers Commission proposals that aim to make banks safer. In the United States, reregulation happened most notably through the Wall Street Reform and Consumer Protection Act, known as the Dodd-Frank Act. In Germany, it took the form of the *Restrukturierungsgesetz* and the bank levy of 2011. In France, several proposals have been made by the new Socialist government of François Hollande, in particular to ring-fence some speculative market activities, thus echoing the Volcker rule contained in the Dodd-Frank Act and the UK Vickers' Commissions' proposals.

A definite judgment on the influence of finance over public authorities will depend on the scope and implementation of these regulatory efforts. Although many observers acknowledge that the Dodd-Frank Act is an ambitious effort to rationalize and improve financial regulation, doubts remain about the actual effects and the difficulties of implementation.[6] The French reform efforts appear to be somewhat of a compromise between ambitious political declarations of a newly elected government, the European initiatives, and an adherence of the French public administration to its domestic financial industry model. In French banking circles, the proposal was tellingly called "Volvic reform," a reference to elements of the Volcker and Vickers proposals, which indicates its similarity to the pleasant and easily digestible spring water from the Auvergne region.[7] If reregulation turns out to be ineffective, France and the United States risk moving into the upper left corner of the table, the "free bailout" quadrant, which has the highest moral hazard consequences and is thus the worst of all bailout configurations. The difference between France and Denmark, the two cases where governments negotiated rather constructively a public-private bailout solution, is thus that France risks maintaining a financial sector that is overly confident on future government support with comparably low costs. France has done rather well

---

5. E.g. Carstensen, "New Financial Regulation in Denmark after the Crisis."
6. *The Economist*, "The Dodd-Frank Act: Too Big Not to Fail."
7. Rollard, "Les opposants à la réforme bancaire donnent de la voix."

through the crisis of 2008, but it cannot be certain it will be able to repeat the experience without reliance on taxpayers' money the next time around.

However, regulatory reform at the domestic level is not the only consequence to the difficulties in crisis management experienced since 2008. One of the most remarkable developments is the increasing integration of competences that were previously core activities of national states at the international or European level. To be sure, the banking crisis initially triggered a breakdown of international financial cooperation, in particular in Europe, where existing coordination mechanisms proved insufficient to respond to the challenges in 2008. Yet over time, international coordination returned and is likely to shape the future of support mechanisms given to the financial industry. This is in particular true within the EU. On the one hand, the European competition authorities reviewed and harmonized national responses during the crisis, as part of their state aid review. More important, however, governments recognized that they only had a limited capacity to respond to the problems posed by financial integration and instability. The integration of bank supervision and possible support through a European banking union, agreed to on 13–14 December 2012, could thus mitigate unresolved issues and counterbalance the moral hazard issue created by the bank support schemes at the national level.

In either case, it is useful to prepare for the next bank bailouts—be it at the domestic or at the international level. Although international finance is generally marked by great uncertainty about future developments, one thing remains certain: the next financial crisis will happen, sooner or later.

Acknowledgments

Just like most of the governments studied in the book, I have accumulated many debts since 2009. To begin with, I would have never have undertaken this study without Emiliano Grossman, who got me interested in banking and who coauthored a first comparative study with me, which informs much of the research design in this project and has been integrated into the comparative overview. His encouragement and insights were crucial throughout the project. Mark Blyth gave feedback at numerous occasions and supported the project both professionally and through his excellent cooking on many evenings during my stay in Boston.

I had the privilege of meeting Hans-Helmut Kotz early in my research. He patiently discussed his experience in Germany and provided guidance for the organization of my inquiry elsewhere. Likewise, Marco Mazzucchelli was also available for repeated discussions. More generally, I would like to thank all the policymakers, bank representatives, and experts who shared their time and insights on a topic that most people prefer not to discuss anymore. I have learned tremendously during these conversations, in particular about the genuine search for solutions to rather intractable problems. I realize that all of the participants would have much preferred designing bank bailouts in a time frame that resembled the one I had to reflect on their actions and write this book.

Many colleagues have read and commented on parts of the manuscript or discussed my thoughts and individual cases with me: Suzanne Berger, Martin Carstensen, Pepper Culpepper, Quoc-Anh Do, Arthur Goldhammer, Peter Gourevitch, Niamh Hardiman, Nicolas Jabko, Juliet Johnson, Desmond King, Mareike Kleine, Brigid Laffan, Philip Lane, Patrick Le Galès, Charles Maier, Philip Manow, Cathie Jo Martin, Andy Martin, Daniel Mügge, Will Phelan, Michael Piore, Raphael Reinke, Leonard Seabrooke, Daniel Seikel, Matthias

Thiemann, Eleni Tsingou, Nicolas Véron, Etienne Wasmer, Meredith Wilf, Jonathan Zeitlin, and Nick Ziegler. Their remarks were incredibly helpful and have considerably influenced this book. In addition, the core of the argument has taken shape during presentations at a series of conferences: the political economy series at MIT in April 2010, a conference at the IIIS at Trinity College Dublin in February 2011, at the Max Planck Sciences Po Center Launch Conference in December 2011, at the Center for European Studies of Harvard University in February 2012, at the IGIS Research Seminar of the Elliott School of George Washington University in February 2012, at the CES Conference and the SASE Conference in Boston in March and June 2012, at the Institute for Political Sciences at the University Bremen in July 2012, at the LIEPP–MaxPo Seminar and at the Transformation of the State conference in Sciences Po in October and December 2012, at the annual meeting of the International Studies Association in San Francisco in April 2013, and finally at a workshop at the Copenhagen Business School in May 2013. I thank all participants for helpful discussions, and Erik Jones, Philippe Martin, Daniel Mügge (once more), and Chris Mitchell for detailed comments as discussants.

At the universities of Bremen and Göttingen, Susanne Schmidt, Stephan Leibfried, and Andreas Busch have supported this project, and I thank them for their interest. All three have provided exceptionally close readings and many useful comments on the entire book. I hope to have responded to their queries and concerns in the revisions, at least partially.

At Cornell University Press, Peter Katzenstein and Roger Haydon have encouraged me with their unique mix of enthusiasm, helpful interrogations, and a critical eye to the most important shortcomings. It is a privilege to work with them. This book has gotten much better under their guidance and thanks to the close reading and excellent remarks of the anonymous reviewers.

Portions of this manuscript have appeared as journal articles. The initial coauthored study has been published as Emiliano Grossman and Cornelia Woll, "Saving the Banks: The Political Economy of Bailouts," *Comparative Political Studies* 47, no. 6 (2014). Parts of the chapter on France and Germany have been integrated in Cornelia Woll, "The Power of Finance in Continental Europe: A Comparative Study of Bank Support Schemes," *Government and Opposition* 49, no. 3 (2014). I thank the publishers for allowing me to use these materials.

The research has been funded by Sciences Po, the Max Planck Society through an Otto-Hahn research group, and later through the funding of the MaxPo Center on Coping with Instability in Market Societies, as well as Harvard University during my visit at the Center for European Studies in 2011–12. I have also benefited from the ANR funding of the Interdisciplinary Center for the Evaluation of Public Policy (LIEPP). Moreover, I acknowledge excellent research assistance from Helene Blanche Naegele, Anna Györy, and Shantelle Williams. Elsa Massoc has been a research assistant to Emiliano Grossman on our coauthored article.

Throughout the writing of this book, I have benefited from the support and friendship of the colleagues who enabled me to work in excellent intellectual conditions: Jens Beckert, Marion Fourcade, Michel Gardette, Christine Musselin, Bruno Latour, Patrick Le Galès, Wolfgang Streeck, and Etienne Wasmer. Special thanks also go to Patricia Craig at Harvard and Vincent Morandi, Bénédicte Barbe, Alexandre Biotteau, as well as Marina Abelskaïa-Graziani and Christelle Hoteit at Sciences Po for keeping my working hours (almost) hassle free.

Finally, my parents and sister have patiently encouraged me and cheered me on. My husband and daughter have accompanied me on two continents and have never grown tired of discussing financial regulation with me (albeit at different levels of expertise). Without their support and enthusiasm, this book would not have been written. It is dedicated to them.

Appendix

List of Interviews

The semidirected interviews were conducted between November 2009 and May 2013. Each interview lasted between thirty minutes and two hours and was held in English, French, or German. All material is dealt with anonymously, so that citations cannot be linked to the authors or their institutions. Translations for French or German quotations are my own. To allow situating individual quotations in time, the date of the interviews appears in the text, not in the list below. Anonymous transcripts containing longer portions of the quoted text are available on request.

- Henner Asche, head of Market Analyses, Deutsche Bundesbank
- Lorenzo Bini-Smaghi, member of the Executive Board of the European Central Bank, 2005–11
- Giacomo Caviglia, principal financial stability expert, Financial Stability Policy Division, European Central Bank
- Christoph Crüwell, head of unit Organization, Division of Bank Supervision, Bundesanstalt für Finanzdienstleistungsaufsicht (BaFin)
- Derek Dunne, Euro Preparations Unit, Her Majesty's Treasury
- Stephan Evans, deputy director, Financial Stability and Contingency Planning, Her Majesty's Treasury
- Barney Frank, congressman (D-MA) 1981–2013; chair of the House Committee on Banking and Financial Services, 2007–11
- Martina Garcia, deputy director, Banking and Financial Sector Analysis, Her Majesty's Treasury
- Heiko Hofer, central unit Markets, Deutsche Bundesbank
- Alexander Jochum, senior advisor, Division of Bank Supervision, BaFin

- Robert Steven Kaplan, professor at Harvard Business School; former vice chairman of Goldman Sachs with oversight responsibility for the investment banking, 2002–5
- Donald Kohn, Brookings Institute; former vice chairman of the Board of Governors of the Federal Reserve System, 2006–10
- Hans-Helmut Kotz, former board member of the Deutsche Bundesbank, 2002–10
- Françoise Malrieu, president of the Société de Financement de l'Economie Française
- Sylvie Matherat, director for Financial Stability, Banque de France; Basel Committee
- Marco Mazzucchelli, investment banker; former deputy CEO—global head of banking at Royal Bank of Scotland Global Banking & Markets, 2009–11
- Günther Merl, president of the German Banking Stabilization Fund SoFFin, 2008–9
- Philippe Mongars, deputy director of the Financial Stability Directorate, Banque de France; Basel Committee
- Patrick Montagner, director of Controlling General and Specialised Credit Establishments, Autorité de Contrôle Prudentiel
- David Moss, professor at Harvard Business School, affiliated with the work of the Congressional Oversight Panel for the Troubled Asset Relief Program
- Ulrich Müller, executive director of Lobbycontrol
- Michel Pébéreau, former chairman of BNP Paribas, 2003–11
- Nicola Pesaresi, head of Unit State Aid Case Support, DG COMP, European Commission
- Jesper Rangvid, professor at Copenhagen Business School; chairman of the Danish inquiry report commissioned by the Ministry for Business and Growth
- Imène Rahmouni-Rousseau, head of unit, Office of Financial Stability and Markets, Banque de France; Financial Stability Board since 2010
- Antoine Saintoyant, chief of office Banking and Credit Institutions, French Ministry of the Economy, Finances, and Industry
- Damon Silvers, deputy chair of the Congressional Oversight Panel of TARP; General Counsel, American Federation of Labor and Congress of Industrial Organizations
- Peer Steinbrück, former finance minister of Germany, 2005–9
- Jean-Claude Trichet, former governor of the European Central Bank, 2003–11
- Jean Tricou, director of the Department for Investment Banks and Market, Fédération Bancaire Française
- Vincent Vignale, financial advisor at Citigroup Investment Banking
- Mario Wandsleb, SoFFin, Bundesanstalt für Finanzmarktstabilisierung

Bibliography

Abdelal, Rawi. "Writing the Rules of Global Finance: France, Europe, and Capital Liberalization." *Review of International Political Economy* 13, no. 1 (2006): 1–27.

Acemoglu, Daron, Simon Johnson, Amir Kermani, James Kwak, and Todd Mitton. *The Value of Political Connections in the United States.* Unpublished manuscript. Harvard University, 2010.

Acharya, Viral V., Matthew Richardson, Stijn van Nieuwerburgh, and Lawrence J. White. *Guaranteed to Fail: Fannie Mae, Freddie Mac, and the Debacle of Mortgage Finance.* Princeton, NJ: Princeton University Press, 2011.

Admati, Anat R., and Martin Hellwig. *The Bankers' New Clothes: What's Wrong with Banking and What to Do about It.* Princeton, NJ: Princeton University Press, 2013.

Allen, Franklin, and Douglas Gale. *Comparing Financial Systems.* Cambridge, MA: MIT Press, 2001.

Andrianova, Svetlana, Panicos Demetriades, and Anja Shortland. "Is Government Ownership of Banks Really Harmful to Growth?" Discussion Paper. DIW Berlin, 2010.

Anonymous. "Good Sport: Banks Are Getting By, A Pity about the Customers." *The Economist,* December 3, 2009. www.economist.com/world/britain/display story.cfm?story_id=13278900.

———. "Hubris to Nemesis: How Sir Fred Goodwin Became the 'World's Worst Banker.'" *The Times,* January 20, 2009.

———. "Le nouveau fiasco à 5 milliards de la Société Générale." *Libération.* April 27, 2009. Available at http://www.liberation.fr/economie/0101564129-le-nouveau-fiasco-a-5-milliards-de-la-societe-generale.

———. "Le plan de soutien aux banques a rapporté 2,7 milliards d'euros à l'Etat." *La Tribune,* May 18, 2011. Available at www.latribune.fr/entreprises-finance/banques-finance/banque/20110518trib000622649/le-plan-de-soutien-aux-banques-a-rapporte-27-milliards-d-euros-a-l-etat.html.

Arrow, Kenneth J. "The Economics of Agency." In *Principals and Agents: The Structure of Business,* edited by J. W. Pratt and Richard Zeckhauser, 37–51. Cambridge, MA: Harvard Business School Press, 1985.

Augar, Philip. *The Death of Gentlemanly Capitalism: The Rise and Fall of London's Investment Banks.* London: Penguin Books, 2000.

Autorité de la concurrence, "Collusion in the Banking Sector." Press release, September 20, 2010. Available at www.autoritedelaconcurrence.fr/user/standard.php?id_rub=368&id_article=1472.

Bachrach, Peter, and Morton S. Baratz. "Decision and Non-Decisions: An Analytical Framework." *American Political Science Review* 57, no. 4 (1963): 632–42.

———. "Two Faces of Power." *The American Political Science Review* 56, no. 4 (1962): 947–52.

Bagehot, Walter. *Lombard Street: A Description of the Money Market.* New York: John Wiley, 1873.

Bair, Sheila. *Bull by the Horns: Fighting to Save Main Street from Wall Street and Wall Street from Itself.* New York: Free Press, 2012.

Baker, Andrew. "Restraining Regulatory Capture? Anglo-America, Crisis Politics, and Trajectories of Change in Global Financial Governance." *International Affairs* 86, no. 3 (2010): 647–63.

Baker, Tom. "On the Genealogy of Moral Hazard." *Texas Law Review* 75 (1996): 237–92.

Bank of England. *Market Notice: Special Liquidity Scheme,* 2009. Available at www.bankofengland.co.uk/markets/Documents/marketnotice090925sls.pdf.

Banque de France. *De la crise financière à la crise économique: documents et débats.* Paris: Banque de France, January 1, 2010. Available at www.banque-france.fr/publications/documents-economiques/documents-et-debats/documents-et-debats-n-3.html.

Barnett, Michael, and Raymond Duvall. *Power in Global Governance.* Cambridge: Cambridge University Press, 2004.

———. "Power in International Politics." *International Organization* 59, no. 1 (2005): 39–75.

Barofsky, Neil. *Bailout: How Washington Abandoned Main Street While Rescuing Wall Street.* New York: Free Press, 2012.

Barrett, Sean D. "The EU/IMF Rescue Programme for Ireland: 2010–2013." *Economic Affairs* 13, no. 2 (2011): 53–57.

Barsøe Venshøj, Simon. "The Financial Crisis and the Danish Banking Sector: An Analysis of Danske Bank." BA Thesis, Aarhus University, 2012. Available at http://pure.au.dk/portal-asb-student/files/45242518/Bachelor_thesis.pdf.

Barth, James R., Gerard Caprio Jr., and Ross Levine. "Bank Regulation and Supervision: What Works Best?" *Journal of Financial Intermediation* 13, no. 2 (2004): 205–48.

Baumgartner, Frank R., Jeffrey M. Berry, Marie Hojnacki, David C. Kimball, and Beth L. Leech. *Lobbying and Policy Change: Who Wins, Who Loses, and Why.* Chicago: Chicago University Press, 2009.

Baumgartner, Frank R., and Beth L. Leech. *Basic Interests: The Importance of Groups in Politics and in Political Science.* Princeton, NJ: Princeton University Press, 1998.

Baxter, Thomas C. *Too Big to Fail: Expectations and Impact of Extraordinary Government Intervention and the Role of Systemic Risk in the Financial Crisis.* Testimony before the Financial Crisis Inquiry Commission. Washington, DC, September 1, 2010. Available at http://www.bis.org/review/r100903f.pdf.

Beck, Thorsten, Asli Demirgüç-Kunt, and Ross Levine. "Financial Institutions and Markets across Countries and over Time-data and Analysis." World Bank Policy Research Working Paper Series No. 4943 (2009).

——. "A New Database on the Structure and Development of the Financial Sector." *World Bank Economic Review* 14, no. 3 (2000): 597–605.

——. "Finance, Inequality and the Poor." *Journal of Economic Growth* 12, no. 1 (2007): 27–49.

Becker, Gary S. "A Theory of Competition among Pressure Groups for Political Influence." *Quarterly Journal of Economics* 98, no. 3 (1983): 371–400.

Bell, Stephen. "The Power of Ideas: The Ideational Shaping of the Structural Power of Business." *International Studies Quarterly* 56, no. 4 (2012): 661–73.

Bell, Stephen, and Andrew Hindmoor. *Masters of the Universe but Slaves of the Market. The Great Financial Meltdown … And How Some Bankers Avoided the Carnage.* Unpublished book manuscript, 2014.

——. "Taming the City? Structural Power and the Evolution of British Banking Policy amidst the Great Financial Meltdown." *New Political Economy* (forthcoming).

Benston, George J., and George C. Kaufman. "The Intellectual History of the Federal Deposit Insurance Corporation Improvement Act of 1991." In *Reforming Financial Institutions and Markets in the United States*, edited by George C. Kaufman, 1–17. Dordrecht: Kluwer Academic, 1994.

Bermeo, Nancy, and Jonas Pontusson, eds. *Coping with Crisis: Government Reactions to the Great Recession.* New York: Russell Sage Foundation, 2012.

Bernanke, Ben S. *The Federal Reserve and the Financial Crisis.* Princeton, NJ: Princeton University Press, 2013.

Bernhagen, Patrick, and Thomas Bräuninger. "Structural Power and Public Policy: A Signaling Model of Business Lobbying in Democratic Capitalism." *Political Studies* 53, no. 1 (2005): 43–64.

Bernstein, Nils. "Overview of Developments in Denmark." *BIS Review*, no. 156. Speech at the Annual Meeting of the Danish Bankers Association (November 30, 2009).

——. "The Danish Krone during the Crisis." *BIS Review*, no. 35. Speech at the Copenhagen Business School (March 22, 2010). Available at www.bis.org/review/r100325c.pdf.

Bhagwati, Jagdish. "The Capital Myth: The Difference between Trade in Widgets and Dollars." *Foreign Affairs* 77, no. 3 (May 1998): 7–12.

Blinder, Alan S. *After the Music Stopped: The Financial Crisis, the Response, and the Work Ahead.* New York: Penguin Press, 2013.

Block, Fred. "The Ruling Class Does Not Rule." *Socialist Revolution* 7, no. 3 (1977): 6–28.

Blyth, Mark. "Structures Do Not Come with an Instruction Sheet: Interests, Ideas, and Progress in Political Science." *Perspectives on Politics* 1, no. 4 (2003): 695–706.

Bonse, Eric, and Hannes Vogel. "Bankenrettung: Eurostat weist Vorwürfe zurück." *Handelsblatt*, July 30, 2009, International edition. Available at www.handelsblatt.com/politik/international/bankenrettung-eurostat-weist-vorwuerfe-zurueck/3229690.html.

Borio, Claudio. "Implementing the Macroprudential Approach to Financial Regulation and Supervision." *Financial Stability Review* 13, no. September (2009): 31–41.

Boyle, Dan. *Without Power or Glory: The Greens in Government.* Dublin: New Island, 2012.

Braun, Matias, and Claudio Raddatz. "Banking on Politics: When Former High-Ranking Officials Become Bank Directors." *World Bank Economic Review* 24, no. 2 (2010): 234–79.

Bronnec, Thomas, and Laurent Fargues. *Bercy au cœur du pouvoir? Enquête sur le ministère des Finances.* Paris: Editions Denoël, 2011.

Brost, Marc, Mark Schieritz, and Arne Storn. "Hypo Real Estate: Die Mutter aller Pleiten." *Die Zeit*, September 8, 2009. Available at www.zeit.de/2009/26/HRE.

Brown, Gordon. *Beyond the Crash: Overcoming the First Crisis of Globalization*. New York: Free Press, 2010.

Browne, Vincent. "Let's Own Up to Our Part in the Burst Bubble," *Irish Times*, April 6, 2011.

Brunnermeier, Markus, Andrew Crocket, Charles Goodhart, Avinash Persaud, and Hyun Song Shin. *The Fundamental Principles of Financial Regulation*. Geneva Report on the World Economy. Geneva: International Center for Monetary and Banking Studies, 2009.

Buiter, Willem H., and Anne Sibert. *The Icelandic Banking Crisis and What to Do About It: The Lender of Last Resort Theory of Optimal Currency Areas*. CEPR Policy Insight, 2008. Available at www.cepr.org/pubs/policyinsights/PolicyInsight26.pdf.

Burchell, Graham, Colin Gordon, and Peter Miller, eds. *The Foucault Effect: Studies in Governmentality*. Chicago: University of Chicago Press, 1991.

Busch, Andreas. *Banking Regulation and Globalization*. Oxford: Oxford University Press, 2009.

Callon, Michel, Pierre Lascoumes, and Yannick Barthe. *Agir Dans Un Monde Incertain—Essai Sur La Démocratie Technique*. Paris: Seuil, 2001.

Callon, Michel, Yuval Millo, and Fabian Muniesa, eds. *Market Devices*. Malden, MA: Blackwell, 2007.

Calmes, Jackie. "Audit Finds TARP Program Effective." *New York Times*, December 10, 2009. Available at www.nytimes.com/2009/12/10/business/economy/10audit.html.

Calomiris, Charles W., Daniela Klingebiel, and Luc Laeven. "Financial Crisis and Resolution Mechanisms: A Taxonomy from Cross-Country Experience." In *Systemic Financial Crisis: Containment and Resolution*, edited by Patrick Honohan and Luc Laeven, 25–75. Cambridge: Cambridge University Press, 2005.

Carey, David. "Iceland: The Financial and Economic Crisis." OECD Economics Department Working Papers, 2009.

Carpenter, Daniel, and David A. Moss, eds. *Preventing Regulatory Capture: Special Interest Influence and How to Limit It*. Cambridge: Cambridge University Press, 2013.

Carstensen, Martin. "New Financial Regulation in Denmark after the Crisis—Or the Politics of Not Really Doing Anything." In *Danish Foreign Policy Yearbook*, edited by Nanna Hvidt and Hans Mouritzen, 106–29. Copenhagen: DIIS Book, 2011.

———. "Projecting from a Fiction: The Case of Denmark and the Financial Crisis." *New Political Economy* 18, no. 4 (2013): 555–78.

Cassidy, John. "Anatomy of a Meltdown." *The New Yorker*, December 1, 2008. Available at www.newyorker.com/reporting/2008/12/01/081201fa_fact_cassidy.

Cerny, Philip G. "Globalization and the Erosion of Democracy." *European Journal of Political Research* 36, no. 1 (1999): 1–26.

Cetina, Karin Knorr, and Alex Preda, eds. *The Sociology of Financial Markets*. Oxford: Oxford University Press, 2006.

Chang, Ha-Joon. "The Hazard of Moral Hazard: Untangling the Asian Crisis." *World Development* 28, no. 4 (2000): 775–88.

Cohan, William D. *House of Cards: A Tale of Hubris and Wretched Excess on Wall Street*. New York: Anchor Books, 2010.

Committee of European Banking Supervisors. *Analysis of the National Plans for the Stabilisation of Markets*, February 5, 2009. Available at www.eba.europa.eu/documents/10180/16151/CEBS+2008+202+rev+2+_Analysis+of+measures+under+national+rescue+plans_.pdf.

Congleton, Roger D. "On the Political Economy of the Financial Crisis and Bailout of 2008–2009." *Public Choice* 140 (2009): 287–317.

Congressional Oversight Panel. *Assessing Treasury's Strategy: Six Months of TARP*, April 7, 2009. Available at www.gpo.gov/fdsys/pkg/CPRT-111JPRT48565/pdf/CPRT-111JPRT48565.pdf.

———. *The Final Report of the Congressional Oversight Panel*, March 16, 2011. Available at www.gpo.gov/fdsys/pkg/CHRG-112shrg64832/pdf/CHRG-112shrg64832.pdf.

Cour des Comptes. *Les concours publics aux établissements de crédit: premiers constats, premières recommandations*. Rapport public. La documentation française, 2009.

———. *Les concours publics aux établissements de crédit: bilan et enseignement à tirer*. Rapport public. La documentation française, 2010.

Cowen, Brian. "The Euro: From Crisis to Resolution? Some Reflections from Ireland on the Road Thus Far." Georgetown University, Washington, DC, March 21, 2012. Available at www.corkeconomics.com/wp-content/uploads/2012/03/3.21.12-Cowen-Speech.pdf.

Crouch, Colin. "Privatised Keynesianism: An Unacknowledged Policy Regime." *British Journal of Politics and International Relations* 11, no. 3 (2009): 382–99.

Crouch, Colin, and Wolfgang Streeck, eds. *The Political Economy of Modern Capitalism: Mapping Convergence and Diversity*. London: Sage, 1997.

Culpepper, Pepper D. *Quiet Politics and Business Power: Corporate Control in Europe and Japan*. New York: Cambridge University Press, 2011.

Culpepper, Pepper D., and Raphael Reinke. *The Structural Dependence of Capital on the State: Explaining Bailout Policies in the UK and US*. Unpublished manuscript. Florence: European University Institute, 2013.

Dahl, Robert A. "The Concept of Power." *Behavioral Science* 2, no. 3 (1957): 201–15.

Danielson, J. "The First Casualty of the Crisis: Iceland." In *The First Global Financial Crisis of the 21st Century*, edited by A. Felton and Carmen M. Reinhard, 9–14. Brussels: CEPR, 2008.

Darling, Alistair. *Back from the Brink: 1,000 Days at Number 11*. London: Atlantic Books, 2011.

Davies, Howard. *The Financial Crisis: Who Is to Blame?* Oxford: Polity, 2010.

Dean, Mitchell. *Governmentality: Power and Rule in Modern Society*. London: Sage, 1999.

Deeg, Richard. "Change from Within: German and Italian Finance in the 1990s." In *Beyond Continuity: Institutional Change in Advanced Political Economies*, edited by Wolfgang Streeck and Kathleen Thelen, 160–202. New York: Oxford University Press, 2005.

———. "Industry and Finance in Germany since Unification." *German Politics and Society* 28, no. 2 (2010): 116–29.

Demirgüç-Kunt, Asli, and Enrica Detragiache. "Does Deposit Insurance Increase Banking System Stability? An Empirical Investigation." *Journal of Monetary Economics* 49, no. 7 (2002): 1373—1406.

Demirgüç-Kunt, Asli, Baybars Karacaovali, and Luc Laeven. "Deposit Insurance around the World: A Comprehensive Database." World Bank Policy Research Working Paper, June 2005. Available at http://papers.ssrn.com/sol3/papers.cfm?abstract_id=756851.

Demirgüç-Kunt, Asli, and Ross Levine. "Bank-based and Market-based Financial Systems: Cross-country Comparisons." World Bank Working Paper No. 2143. Washington, DC: World Bank, 1999.

Deneuville, Virginie. "Les Banques Françaises Prêtes à Se Financer Toutes Seules à Compter D'octobre." *L'AGEFI Quotidien.* September 17, 2009, Edition de 7H edition. Available at www.agefi.fr/articles/les-banques-francaises-pretes-a-se-financer-seules-a-compter-d-octobre-1107575.html.

Department of Finance. "Recapitalisation of Allied Irish Bank and Bank of Ireland" (2009). Available at www.finance.gov.ie/viewdoc.asp?DocID=5669.

Deutsch, Karl. *The Nerves of Government: Models of Political Communication and Control.* New York: Free Press, 1963.

Deutsche Bundesbank. "Cornerstones of the Financial Market Stabilization Act." *Monthly Report* 60, no. 11, 2008, 30–31.

Djelic, Marie-Laure, and Joel Bothello. *Limited Liability and Moral Hazard Implications—An Alternative Reading of the Financial Crisis.* Unpublished manuscript. Paris: ESSEC Business School, 2013.

Dong, T. "Bonus? Lagarde continue de faire pression sur les banques." *Le Figaro,* August 17, 2009. Available at www.lefigaro.fr/societes/2009/08/17/04015-20090817ARTFIG00255-bonus-lagarde-continue-de-faire-pression-sur-les-banques-.php.

Doran, James. "US Watchdog Calls for Bank Executives to Be Sacked." *The Guardian,* April 5, 2009. Available at www.guardian.co.uk/business/2009/apr/05/useconomy-regulators.

Doran, Shane, and Brendan Keenan. "Revealed: Total Chaos in Coalition as Economy Collapsed." *Irish Independent,* June 2, 2011. Available at www.independent.ie/irish-news/revealed-total-chaos-in-coalition-as-economy-collapsed-26738594.html.

Dougherty, Carter. "No Quick Solution to Financial Crisis, Denmark Shows." *New York Times,* October 27, 2008. Available at www.nytimes.com/2008/10/27/business/worldbusiness/27iht-denmark.4.17287933.html?pagewanted=all&_r=0.

The Economist. "The Dodd-Frank Act: Too Big Not to Fail." February 18, 2012. Available at www.economist.com/node/21547784.

European Commission. "DG Competition's Review of Guarantee and Recapitalisation Schemes in the Financial Sector in the Current Crisis" (2009).

——. *State Aid N725/2009—Ireland: Establishment of a National Asset Management Agency (NAMA), Asset Relief Scheme for Banks in Ireland,* C(2010)1155 final, 2010.

——. "The Effects of Temporary State Aid Rules Adopted in the Context of the Financial and Economic Crisis." Commission Staff Working Paper. DG Competition, 2011. Available at http://ec.europa.eu/competition/publications/reports/working_paper_en.pdf.

——. *Eurostat Supplementary Table for the Financial Crisis: Background Note.* Brussels: Eurostat, 2011. Available at http://epp.eurostat.ec.europa.eu/portal/page/portal/government_finance_statistics/documents/Background%20note_fin%20crisis_Apr%202011_final.pdf.

Farhi, Emmanuel, and Jean Tirole. "Collective Moral Hazard, Maturity Mismatch and Systemic Bailouts." American Economic Review 102, no. 1 (2012): 60–93.

Farrell, Greg. *Crash of the Titans: Greed, Hubris, the Fall of Merrill Lynch, and the Near-Collapse of Bank of America.* New York: Crown Business, 2011.

FDIC. *History of the Eighties—Lessons for the Future.* Washington, DC: FDIC Public Information Center, 1997. Available at www.fdic.gov/bank/historical/history/vol1.html.

Financial Crisis Inquiry Commission. *The Financial Crisis Inquiry Report: Final Report of the National Commission on the Causes of the Financial and Economic Crisis in the United States.* New York: Public Affairs, 2011.

Financial Times. "Danish Lessons." May 26, 2011. Available at www.ft.com/intl/cms/s/0/a37f3624-87c8-11e0-a6de-00144feabdc0.html#axzz2cbacyfiD.

Finansiel Stabilitet. *Annual Report 2009.* Copenhagen: Finansiel Stabilitet S/A, 2009.

Finanstilsynet. "Markedsudviklingen i 2008 for Pengeinstitutter." May 1, 2008. Available at www.finanstilsynet.dk/upload/Finanstilsynet/Mediafiles/newdoc/statistik/8/MU2008_BANK.pdf.

Fioretos, Orfeo. *Creative Reconstructions: Multilateralism and European Varieties of Capitalism after 1950.* Ithaca, NY: Cornell University Press, 2011.

FMSA. *Zwischenbilanz Der Bundesanstalt Für Finanzmarktstabilisierung—Deutsche Bankenrettung Im Internationalen Vergleich Erfolgreich.* Press Release. Frankfurt, January 28, 2011. Available at www.fmsa.de/de/presse/pressemitteilungen/2011/20110128_pressemitteilung_fmsa.html.

Follorou, Jacques. "La fermeture du consortium de réalisation marque la fin du feuilleton des dérives du crédit lyonnais." *Le Monde.* December 28, 2006. Available at www.lemonde.fr/economie/article/2006/12/28/la-fermeture-du-consortium-de-realisation-marque-la-fin-du-feuilleton-des-derives-du-credit-lyonnais_850057_3234.html.

Forsyth, Douglas J., and Daniel Verdier, eds. *The Origins of National Financial Systems: Alexander Gerschenkron Reconsidered.* London: Routledge, 2003.

Foucault, Michel. *Power/Knowledge: Selected Interviews and Other Writings 1972–1977.* New York: Pantheon Books, 1980.

——. *Sécurité, Territoire, Population. Cours Au Collège de France (1977–78).* Paris: Gallimard/Seuil, 2004.

Fourcade-Gourinchas, Marion, and Sarah L. Babb. "The Rebirth of the Liberal Creed: Paths to Neoliberalism in Four Countries." *American Journal of Sociology* 108, no. 3 (2002): 533–79.

François, Pierre, and Claire Lemercier. *Pulsations of French Capitalism.* Unpublished manuscript. Paris: Sciences Po, CSO/CNRS, 2013.

French, Kenneth R., Martin N. Baily, John Y. Campbell, John H. Cochrane, Douglas W. Diamond, Darrell Duffie, Anil K. Kashyap et al. *The Squam Lake Report: Fixing the Financial System.* Princeton, NJ: Princeton University Press, 2010.

Gandrud, Christopher, and Mark Hallerberg. "Bad Banks as a Response to Crisis: When Do Governments Create Them, and Why Does Their Governance Differ?" Paper presented at the ISA Annual Conference, San Francisco, CA, April 6, 2013.

Gerschenkron, Alexander. *Economic Backwardness in Historical Perspective.* Cambridge, MA: Belknap Press of Harvard University Press, 1962.

Gertler, Mark. "Financial Structure and Aggregate Economic Activity: An Overview." *Journal of Money, Credit and Banking* 20, no. 3 (1988): 559–88.

Giddens, Anthony. *The Constitution of Society: Outline of the Theory of Structuration.* Cambridge: Polity Press, 1984.

Goddard, John, Philip Molyneux, and John O.S. Wilson. "Banking in the European Union." In *The Oxford Handbook on Banking,* edited by Allen N. Berger, Philip Molyneux, and John O.S. Wilson, 807–43. Oxford: Oxford University Press, 2010.

Goldstein, Morris, and Nicolas Véron. *Too Big to Fail: The Transatlantic Debate.* Washington, DC: Peterson Institute for International Economics, 2011. Available at www.iie.com/publications/wp/wp11-2.pdf.

Gorton, Gary B. *Slapped by the Invisible Hand: The Panic of 2007.* New York: Oxford University Press, 2010.

Goul Andersen, Jørgen. "From the Edge of the Abyss to Bonanza—and Beyond." *Comparative Social Research* 28 (2011): 89–165.

Gourevitch, Peter A. *Politics in Hard Times: Comparative Responses to International Economic Crises.* Ithaca: Cornell University Press, 1986.

——. "Afterword: Yet More Hard Times? Reflections on the Great Recession in the Frame of Earlier Hard Times." In *Politics in the New Hard Times: The Great Recession in Comparative Perspective.* Ithaca, NY: Cornell University Press, 2013.

Grant, James. "The Fed's Subprime Solution." *The New York Times,* August 26, 2007. Available at www.nytimes.com/2007/08/26/opinion/26grant.html.

Grant, Wyn, and Graham K. Wilson, eds. *The Consequences of the Global Financial Crisis: The Rhetoric of Reform and Regulation.* Oxford: Oxford University Press, 2012.

Grossman, Emiliano. "Europeanization as an Interactive Process: German Public Banks Meet EU State Aid Policy." *Journal of Common Market Studies* 44, no. 2 (2006): 325–48.

Grossman, Emiliano, and Cornelia Woll. "Saving the Banks: The Political Economy of Bailouts." *Comparative Political Studies* 47, no. 6 (forthcoming 2014).

Gry Braad, Signe. "Fakta: Disse Banker Er Ikke Omfattet Af Statsgarantien." *Børsen* (October 14, 2008). Available at http://borsen.dk/nyheder/bolig_og_privatoekonomi/ artikel/1/142720/fakta_disse_banker_er_ikke_omfattet_af_statsgarantien.html.

Hacker, Jacob S., and Paul Pierson. "Business Power and Social Policy: Employers and the Formation of the American Welfare State." *Politics and Society* 30, no. 3 (2002): 277–325.

——. *Winner-Take-All Politics: How Washington Made the Rich Richer—and Turned Its Back on the Middle Class.* New York: Simon & Schuster, 2011.

Hall, Peter A., and David Soskice. *Varieties of Capitalism: Institutional Foundations of Comparative Advantage.* Cambridge: Cambridge University Press, 2001.

Hansen, Flemming, and Gustav Sandstrom. "Denmark Plans Support Measures for Banks." *Wall Street Journal,* August 12, 2011. Available at http://online.wsj.com/article/SB10001424053111903918104576503771186790318.html.

Hardie, Iain, and David Howarth. "Die Krise but Not La Crise? The Financial Crisis and the Transformation of German and French Banking Systems." *Journal of Common Market Studies* 47, no. 5 (2009): 1017–39.

Hardiman, Niamh, ed. *Irish Governance in Crisis.* Manchester, UK: Manchester University Press, 2012.

Harvey, David. *The Enigma of Capital: And the Crises of Capitalism.* 2nd ed. Oxford: Oxford University Press, 2011.

Hayek, Friedrich A. von. *Denationalization of Money: An Analysis of the Theory and Practice of Concurrent Currencies.* London: Institute of Economic Affairs, 1977.

Herring, Richard J. "Wind-Down Plans as an Alternative to Bailouts." In *Ending Government Bailouts as We Know Them,* edited by Kenneth E. Scott, George P. Shultz, and John B. Taylor, 125–62. Stanford, CA: Hoover Institution Press, 2010.

Herring, Richard J., and Jacopo Carmassi. "The Corporate Structure of International Financial Conglomerates: Complexity and Its Implications for

Safety and Soundness." In *The Oxford Handbook of Banking*, edited by Allen N. Berger, Philip Molyneux, John Wilson, and Jacopo Carmassi, 197-228, Oxford: Oxford University Press, 2010.

HM Treasury. *Budget 2010*. Budget Redbook, London: House of Commons, 2010.

Honkapohja, Seppo. "The 1990s Financial Crisis in Nordic Countries." Bank of Finland Research Discussion Paper no. 5 (2009).

Honohan, Patrick. "Resolving Ireland's Banking Crisis." *Economic and Social Review* 40, no. 2 (2009): 207–31.

——. *The Irish Banking Crisis: Regulatory and Financial Stability Policy 2003–2008*. Report to the Minister for Finance. Dublin: Central Bank, 2010.

Honohan, Patrick, and Daniela Klingebiel. "The Fiscal Cost Implications of an Accommodating Approach to Banking Crises." *Journal of Banking and Finance* 27, no. 8 (2003): 1539–60.

Honohan, Patrick, and Luc Laeven. *Systemic Financial Crises: Containment and Resolution*. Cambridge: Cambridge University Press, 2005.

Höpner, Martin, and Lothar Krempel. "The Politics of the German Company Network." *Competition and Change* 8, no. 4 (2004): 339–56.

House of Commons. *The Run on the Rock*. Fifth Report of Session 2007–2008. Treasury Committee, 2008.

House of the Oireachtas. *Report on the Crisis in the Banking Sector: A Preliminary Analysis and a Framework for a Banking Inquiry*. Committee of Public Accounts. Dublin: House of the Oireachtais, 2012.

Igan, Deniz, Prachi Mishra, and Thierry Tressel. "A Fistful of Dollars: Lobbying and the Financial Crisis." In *NBER Macroeconomics Annual 2011*, edited by Daron Ac and Michael Woodford. Vol. 26, no. 1, 195–230. Chicago: University of Chicago Press, 2011. Available at http://www.nber.org/chapters/c12416.ack.

International Monetary Fund. *Germany: 2008 Article IV Consultation*. IMF Country Report, 2009. Available at www.imf.org/external/pubs/ft/scr/2009/cr0915.pdf.

Irish Independent. "John Hurley: Last of the Breed." October 3, 2009. Available at www.independent.ie/business/irish/john-hurley-last-of-the-breed-1903360.html.

Irish Times. "Irish Bailout Cheapest in World, Says Lenihan." October 10, 2008.

——. "Banks Must Be 'Weaned Off ECB Funds.'" September 9, 2010. Available at www.irishtimes.com/newspaper/breaking/2010/0917/breaking51.html.

——. "Cantillon." November 8, 2012. Available at www.irishtimes.com/newspaper/finance/2012/1108/1224326308170.html.

Jabko, Nicolas, and Elsa Massoc. "French Capitalism under Stress: How Nicolas Sarkozy Rescued the Banks." *Review of International Political Economy* 19, no. 2 (2012): 562–85.

Jacobs, Lawrence R., and Desmond S. King. "Concealed Advantage: The Federal Reserve's Financial Intervention After 2007." Oxford University, 2012.

Javers, Eamon. "Inside Obama's Bank CEOs Meeting." *Politico*, April 3, 2009. Available at www.politico.com/news/stories/0409/20871.html.

Johnson, Simon, and James Kwak. *13 Bankers: The Wall Street Takeover and the Next Financial Meltdown*. New York: Pantheon, 2010.

Kahler, Miles, ed. *Networked Politics: Agency, Power, and Governance*. Ithaca, NY: Cornell University Press, 2009.

Kane, Edward J. *The S&L Insurance Mess: How Did It Happen?* Washington, DC: Urban Institute, 1989.

Katzenstein, Peter J. *Small States in World Markets: Industrial Policy in Europe*. Ithaca, NY: Cornell University Press, 1985.

Kelly, Kate. "Fear, Rumors Touched Off Fatal Run on Bear Stearns." *Wall Street Journal*, May 28, 2008, sec. Business. Available at http://online.wsj.com/article/SB121193290927324603.html.

Kelly, Morgan. "Whatever Happened to Ireland?" CEPR Discussion Paper No. 7811, 2010.

——. "Ireland's Future Depends on Breaking Free from Bailout. *Irish Times*, May 7, 2011.

Kickert, Walter. "How the Danish Government Responded to Financial Crises." *Public Money and Management* 33, no. 1 (2013): 55–62.

Kiel, Paul. "Behind Administration Spin: Bailout Still $123 Billion in the Red." *ProPublica*, 2011. Available at www.propublica.org/article/behind-administration-spin-bailout-still-123-billion-in-the-red.

Klingebiel, Daniela. "The Use Of Asset Management Companies in the Resolution Of Banking Crises: Cross-Country Experiences." World Bank Policy Research Working Paper No. 2284. Washington, DC: World Bank, 2000.

Klingebiel, Daniela, and Luc Laeven. "Managing the Real and Fiscal Effects of Banking Crises." World Bank Discussion Paper No. 428. Washington, DC: World Bank, 2002.

Kluth, Michael, and Kennet Lynggaard. "Explaining Responses in Danish and Irish Banking to the Financial Crisis." *West European Politics* 36, no. 4 (2013): 771–88.

Krahnen, Jan Pieter, and Reinhard H. Schmidt. *The German Financial System*. Oxford: Oxford University Press, 2004.

Krippner, Greta R. "The Financialization of the American Economy." *Socio-Economic Review* 3, no. 2 (2005): 173–208.

——. *Capitalizing on Crisis: The Political Origins of the Rise of Finance*. Cambridge, MA: Harvard University Press, 2011.

Krüger, Hans-Ulrich, Klaus-Peter Willsch, Nina Hauer, Volker Wissing, Axel Troost, and Gerhard Schick. *Beschlussempfehlung Und Bericht Des 2. Untersuchungsausschusses Nach Artikel 44 Des Grundgesetz*. Berlin: Deutscher Bundestag, 2009.

Kudrna, Zdenek. "Cross-Border Resolution of Failed Banks in the European Union after the Crisis: Business as Usual." *Journal of Common Market Studies* 50, no. 2 (2012): 283–99.

Kwak, James. "Cultural Capture and the Financial Crisis." In *Preventing Regulatory Capture: Special Interest Influence, and How to Limit It*, edited by Daniel Carpenter and David A. Moss. Cambridge: Cambridge University Press, 2013.

Kydland, Finn E., and Edward C. Prescott. "Rules Rather Than Discretion: The Inconsistency of Optimal Plans." *Journal of Political Economy* 85, no. 3 (1977): 473–91.

Laeven, Luc, and Fabian Valencia. "Systemic Banking Crises: A New Database." IMF Working Paper No. 08/224. Washington, DC: International Monetary Fund, 2008. Available at www.imf.org/external/pubs/ft/wp/2008/wp08224.pdf.

——. "Resolution of Banking Crisis: The Good, the Bad, and the Ugly." IMF Working Paper No. 10/146. Washington, DC: International Monetary Fund, 2010. Available at www.imf.org/external/pubs/ft/wp/2010/wp10146.pdf

——. "Systemic Banking Crises Dataset: An Update." IMF Working Paper No. 12/163. Washington, DC: International Monetary Fund, 2012. Available at www.imf.org/external/pubs/ft/wp/2012/wp12163.pdf.

Landgraf, Robert, and Frank Drost. "SoFFin: Weiteres Jahr mit hohen Verlusten." *Handelsblatt*, December 17, 2010. Available at www.handelsblatt.com/ unternehmen/ banken/soffin-weiteres-jahr-mit-hohen-verlusten/3659160.html.

Lane, Philip R. "The Irish Crisis." CEPR Discussion Paper No. DP8287, 2011. Available at http://papers.ssrn.com/sol3/papers.cfm?abstract_id=1794877.

La Porta, Rafael, Florencio Lopez-de-Silanes, Andrei Shleifer, and Robert W. Vishny. "Law and Finance." *Journal of Political Economy* 106, no. 6 (1998): 1113–55.

Latour, Bruno. "The Powers of Association." In *Power, Action and Belief: A New Sociology of Knowledge?* edited by John Law, 264–80. London: Routledge, 1986.

———. *Reassembling the Social: An Introduction to Actor-Network-Theory*. Oxford: Oxford University Press, 2005.

Lavelle, Kathryn C. *Money and Banks in the American Political System*. Cambridge: Cambridge University Press, 2013.

Leeson, Peter T. "Review of Gary Stern and Ron Feldman, Too Big to Fail: The Hazards of Bank Bailouts." *Journal of Economic Behavior and Organization* 56, no. 3 (2005): 448–50.

Lépinay, Vincent Antonin. *Codes of Finance: Engineering Derivatives in a Global Bank*. Princeton, NJ: Princeton University Press, 2011.

Levine, Ross. "Bank-based or Market-based Financial Systems: Which Is Better?" National Bureau of Economic Research Working Paper No. 9138 (2002). Available at www.nber.org/papers/w9138.

———. "Finance and Growth: Theory and Evidence." In *Handbook of Economic Growth*, edited by Philippe Aghion and Steven H. Durlauf, 1:865–934. Amsterdam: Elsevier, 2005.

Lewis, Michael. "When Irish Eyes Are Crying." *Vanity Fair*, 2011. Available at www. vanityfair.com/business/features/2011/03/michael-lewis-ireland-201103.

Lindblom, Charles E. "The Market as Prison." *The Journal of Politics* 44, no. 02 (1982): 323.

Lo, Andrew W. "Reading about the Financial Crisis: A 21-Book Review." *Journal of Economic Literature* 50, no. 1 (2012): 151–78.

Lowenstein, Roger. *When Genius Failed: The Rise and Fall of Long-Term Capital Management*. New York: Random House, 2001.

Lowery, David. "Lobbying Influence: Meaning, Measurement, and Missing." *Interest Groups and Advocacy* 2, no. 1 (2013): 1–26.

Luechinger, Simon, and Christoph Moser. "The Value of the Revolving Door: Political Appointees and the Stock Market." KOF Working Papers No. 310, 2012. Available at http://papers.ssrn.com/abstract=2147674.

Lukes, Steven M. *Power: A Radical View*. London: Macmillan, 1974.

———. "Power and the Battle for Hearts and Minds." *Millennium—Journal of International Studies* 33, no. 3 (June 1, 2005): 477–93.

Lütz, Susanne. "From Managed to Market Capitalism? German Finance in Transition." *German Politics* 9, no. 2 (2000): 149–70.

———. "Convergence within National Diversity: The Regulatory State in Finance." *Journal of Public Policy* 24, no. 2 (2004): 169–97.

Lyons, Tom, and Brian Carey. *The Fitzpatrick Tapes*. Penguin. Dublin, 2011.

MacKenzie, Donald. *An Engine, Not a Camera: How Financial Models Shape Markets*. Cambridge, MA: MIT Press, 2006.

MacKenzie, Donald, Fabian Muniesa, and Lucia Siu, eds. *Do Economists Make Markets? On the Performativity of Economics*. Princeton, NJ: Princeton University Press, 2008.

Malmendier, Ulrike. "Law and Finance 'at the Origin.'" *Journal of Economic Literature* 47, no. 4 (2009): 1076–1108.

Martens, John, and Jim Brunsden. "Dexia to Set Up 'Bad Bank' With Guarantees from France, Belgium." *Bloomberg BusinessWeek*, October 4, 2011.

Martin, Cathie Jo, and Duane Swank. *The Political Construction of Business Interests: Coordination, Growth, and Equality*. Cambridge: Cambridge University Press, 2012.

Mayer, Thomas. "Should Large Banks Be Allowed to Fail?" *Journal of Financial and Quantitative Analysis* 10, no. 4 (1975): 603–10.

Mayes, D. "Did Recent Experience of a Financial Crisis Help in Coping with the Current Financial Turmoil? The Case of the Nordic Countries." *Journal of Common Market Studies* 47, no. 5 (2009): 997–1015.

McCarthy, Colm. "Ireland's European Crisis: Staying Solvent in the Eurozone." UCD Center for Economic Research Working Paper No 12/02. Dublin: UCD School of Economics, 2012. Available at www.ucd.ie/t4cms/WP12_02.pdf.

——. "Only Europe-wide Action Can Help Tackle Debt Crisis." *Irish Independent*. June 3, 2012, Available at www.independent.ie/opinion/analysis/colm-mccarthy-only-europewide-action-can-help-tackle-debt-crisis-3126358.html.

McCollom, James P. *The Continental Affair: The Rise and Fall of the Continental Illinois Bank*. New York: Dodd, Mead, 1987.

McDonald, Lawrence G. *A Colossal Failure of Common Sense: The Incredible Inside Story of the Collapse of Lehman Brothers*. New York: Crown Business, 2009.

McKee, Michael, and Scott Lanman. "Greenspan Says U.S. Should Consider Breaking Up Large Banks." *Bloomberg* (October 15, 2009). Available at www.bloomberg.com/apps/news?pid=newsarchive&sid=aJ8HPmNUfchg.

Merlingen, Michael. "From Governance to Governmentality in CSDP: Towards a Foucauldian Research Agenda." *Journal of Common Market Studies* 49, no. 1 (2011): 149–69.

Mills, C. Wright. *The Power Elite*. New York: Oxford University Press, 1956.

Milne, Richard. "Danish Banks Set Off Alarm Bells." *Financial Times*, November 29, 2012. Available at www.ft.com/intl/cms/s/0/068877d0-3a1a-11e2-baac-00144feabdc0.html#axzz2cbacyfiD.

Mishkin, Frederic S. "How Big a Problem Is Too Big to Fail? A Review of Gary Stern and Ron Feldman's *Too Big to Fail: The Hazards of Bank Bailouts*." *Journal of Economic Literature* 44, no. 4 (2006): 988–1004.

Mishkin, Frederic S., and Philip E. Strahan. "What Will Technology Do to Financial Structure?" National Bureau of Economic Research Working Paper Series No. 6892 (1999). Available at www.nber.org/papers/w6892.

Mitchell, Christopher. *Saving the Market from Itself: Bailouts, Nationalizations, and the Politics of Financial Intervention*. PhD Thesis in Political Science, George Washington University, Washington, DC: 2012.

Mizruchi, Mark S. *The Fracturing of the American Corporate Elite*. Cambridge, MA: Harvard University Press, 2013.

Moran, Michael. *The Politics of Banking: The Strange Case of Competition and Credit Control*. London: Palgrave Macmillan, 1984.

——. *The Politics of the Financial Services Revolution: The USA, UK, and Japan*. New York: St. Martins Press, 1991.

Morin, François. "A Transformation in the French Model of Shareholding and Management." *Economy and Society* 29, no. 1 (2000), 36-53.

Mortensen, Jens L., and L. Seabrooke. "Housing as Social Right or Means to Wealth? The Politics of Property Booms in Australia and Denmark." *Comparative European Politics* 6, no. 3 (2008): 305–24.

Moss, David A. *When All Else Fails: Government as the Ultimate Risk Manager.* Cambridge, MA: Harvard University Press, 2002.

———. "An Ounce of Prevention." *Harvard Magazine* 24 (2009): 25–29.

Moyer, R. Charles, and Robert E. Lamy. " 'Too Big To Fail': Rationale, Consequences, and Alternatives." *Business Economics* 27, no. 3 (1992): 15–26.

Mügge, Daniel. *Widen the Market, Narrow the Competition: Banker Interests and the Making of a European Capital Market.* Colchester, UK: ECPR Press, 2010.

National Audit Office. *Maintaining the Financial Stability across the United Kingdom's Banking System.* Report by the Controller and Auditor General, December 4, 2009.

———. *Maintaining the Financial Stability of UK Banks: Update on the Support Schemes.* Report by the Controller and Auditor General, December 15, 2010.

———. *The Asset Protection Scheme.* Report by the Controller and Auditor General, December 21, 2010.

Nelson, Stephen, and Peter J. Katzenstein. "Uncertainty, Risk, and the Financial Crisis of 2008." *International Organization,* forthcoming 2014.

Nyberg, Peter. *Misjudging Risk: Causes of the Systemic Banking Crisis in Ireland.* Report of the Commission of Investigation into the Banking Sector in Ireland, March 2011.

Obinger, Herbert, Peter Starke, Julia Moser, Claudia Bogedan, Edith Obinger-Gindulis, and Stephan Leibfried. *Transformations of the Welfare State: Small States, Big Lessons.* Oxford: Oxford University Press, 2010.

O'Callaghan, Gary. *Did the ECB Cause a Run on Irish Banks? Evidence from Disaggregated Data.* Irish Economy Note No. 13, 2011. Available at www.irisheconomy.ie/Notes/IrishEconomyNote13.pdf.

OECD. *OECD Economic Surveys: Denmark 2009.* 2009/19. Paris: OECD, 2009.

O'Hara, Maureen, and Wayne Shaw. "Deposit Insurance and Wealth Effects: The Value of Being 'Too Big to Fail.' " *Journal of Finance* 45, no. 5 (1990): 1587–1600.

Olson, Mancur. *The Logic of Collective Action: Public Goods and the Theory of Groups.* Cambridge, MA: Harvard University Press, 1965.

Orléan, André. *Le pouvoir de la finance.* Paris: Odile Jacob, 1999.

Ostrom, Elinor. "Collective Action and the Evolution of Social Norms." *Journal of Economic Perspectives* 14, no. 3 (2000): 137–58.

———. "Crowding Out Citizenship." *Scandinavian Political Studies* 23, no. 1 (2000): 3–16.

Østrup, Finn. "The Danish Bank Crisis in a Transnational Perspective." In *Danish Foreign Policy Yearbook,* edited by Nanna Hvidt and Hans Mouritzen, 75–112. Copenhagen: DIIS, 2010.

O'Sullivan, Mary. "Acting Out Institutional Change: Understanding the Recent Transformation of the French Financial System." *Socio-Economic Review* 5, no. 3 (2007): 389–436.

Pagliari, Stefano, and Kevin L. Young. "Leveraged Interests: Financial Industry Power and the Role of Private Sector Coalitions." *Review of International Political Economy* 21, no. 3 (forthcoming).

Panetta, Fabio, Thomas Faeh, Giuseppe Grande, Corrinne Ho, Michael King, Aviram Levy, Federico Maria Signoretti, Marco Taboga, and Andrea Zaghini.

"An Assessment of Financial Sector Rescue Programmes." BIS Papers No. 48. Basel: Bank of International Settlements, July 10, 2009.

Paulson, Henry M. *On the Brink: Inside the Race to Stop the Collapse of the Global Financial System.* New York: Business Plus, 2011.

Pauly, Louis W. *Opening Financial Markets: Banking Politics on the Pacific Rim.* Ithaca, NY: Cornell University Press, 1988.

——. "The Old and the New Politics of International Financial Stability." *Journal of Common Market Studies* 47, no. 5 (2009): 955–75.

Pedersen, Ove Kaj. "Corporatism and Beyond: The Negotiated Economy." In *National Identity and Varieties of Capitalism: The Danish Experience,* edited by John L. Campbell, John A. Hall, and Ove Kaj Pedersen, 245–70. Montreal: McGill-Queen's University Press, 2006.

Przeworski, Adam, and Michael Wallerstein. "Structural Dependence of the State on Capital." *American Political Science Review* 82, no. 1 (1988): 11–29.

Quaglia, Lucia. "The 'British Plan' as a Pace-Setter: The Europeanization of Banking Rescue Plans in the EU." *Journal of Common Market Studies* 47, no. 5 (2009): 1063–83.

Rajan, Raghuram, and Luigi Zingales. "Financial Systems, Industrial Structure, and Growth." *Oxford Review of Economic Policy* 17, no. 4 (2001): 467–82.

——. *Saving Capitalism from the Capitalists: Unleashing the Power of Financial Markets to Create Wealth and Spread Opportunity.* New York: Crown Business, 2003.

Regling, Klaus, and Max Watson. *A Preliminary Report on the Sources of Ireland's Banking Crisis.* Report to the Minister for Finance, May 31, 2010.

Reinhart, Carmen M., and Kenneth Rogoff. *This Time Is Different: Eight Centuries of Financial Folly.* Princeton, NJ: Princeton University Press, 2009.

Reinhart, Vincent. "A Year of Living Dangerously: The Management of the Financial Crisis in 2008." *Journal of Economic Perspectives* 25, no. 1 (2011): 71–90.

Renick Mayer, Lindsay, Michael Beckel, and Dave Levinthal. *Crossing Wall Street.* Washington, DC: Center for Responsive Politics, November 16, 2009. Available at www.opensecrets.org/news/2009/11/crossing-wall-street-1.html.

Reuters. "Congressional Oversight Panel: TARP Helped Perpetuate A 'Too Big To Fail' System." *Huffington Post,* March 16, 2011. Available at www.huffington post.com/2011/03/ 16/wachdog-tarp-too-big-to-fail_n_836376.html.

Ritholtz, Barry. *Bailout Nation: How Greed and Easy Money Corrupted Wall Street and Shook the World Economy.* Hoboken, NJ: John Wiley, 2010.

Roberts, Sam. "Infamous 'Drop Dead' Was Never Said by Ford." *New York Times,* December 28, 2006, sec. New York Region. Available at www.nytimes. com/2006/12/28/nyregion/28veto.html.

Rogoff, Kenneth. "The Optimal Degree of Commitment to an Intermediate Monetary Target." *Quarterly Journal of Economics* 100, no. 4 (November 1, 1985): 1169–89.

Rollard, Sophie. "Les opposants à la réforme bancaire donnent de la voix." *La Tribune,* December 18, 2012. Available at www.latribune.fr/entreprises-finance/banques-finance/industrie-financiere/20121217trib000737759/les-opposants-a-la-reforme-bancaire-donnent-de-la-voix.html.

Rosas, Guillermo. *Curbing Bailouts: Bank Crises and Democratic Accountability in Comparative Perspective.* Ann Arbor: University of Michigan Press, 2009.

Rose, Nikolas. *Powers of Freedom: Reframing Political Thought.* Cambridge: Cambridge University Press, 1999.

Rowell, David, and Luke B. Connelly. "A History of the Term 'Moral Hazard.'" *Journal of Risk and Insurance* (2012): 1–25.

Schmitz, Stefan W., Beat Weber, and Michaela Posch. "EU Bank Packages: Objectives and Potential Conflicts of Objectives." In Österreichische Nationalbank, *Financial Stability Report* 17: 63–84. Vienna: Austrian National Bank, 2009.

Schwartz, Herman. *Subprime Nation: American Power, Global Capital, and the Housing Bubble.* Ithaca, NY: Cornell University Press, 2009.

———. "Iceland's Financial Iceberg: Why Leveraging Up Is a Titanic Mistake without a Reserve Currency." *European Political Science* 10, no. 3 (2011): 292–300.

Seabrooke, Leonard. *The Social Sources of Financial Power: Domestic Legitimacy and International Financial Orders.* Ithaca, NY: Cornell University Press, 2006.

Seabrooke, Leonard, and Eleni Tsingou. "Power Elites and Everyday Politics in International Financial Reform." *International Political Sociology* 3, no. 4 (2009): 457–61.

———. "Revolving Doors and Linked Ecologies in the World Economy: Policy Locations and the Practice of International Financial Reform." CSGR Working Paper No. 260, June 2009. Available at http://wrap.warwick.ac.uk/1849/1/WRAP_Seabrooke_26009.pdf.

Seybert, Lucia, Stephen Nelson, and Peter J. Katzenstein. "Two Faces of Power Again: Control Power and Circulatory Power in the American Movie Industry." Paper presented at the ISA Annual Convention, San Francisco, CA, 2013.

Shiller, Robert J. *The Subprime Solution: How Today's Global Financial Crisis Happened, and What to Do About It.* Princeton, NJ: Princeton University Press, 2008.

Shin, Hyun Song. "Reflections on Northern Rock: The Bank Run that Heralded the Global Financial Crisis." *Journal of Economic Perspectives* 23, no. 1 (2009): 101–20.

SIGTARP. "Extent of Federal Agencies' Oversight of AIG Compensation Varied, and Important Challenges Remain." *SIGTARP Report* no. 10-002, Washington, DC: Office of the Special Investigator General for the Troubled Asset Relief Program, October 14, 2009.

———. *Quarterly Report to Congress.* Washington, DC: Office of the Special Investigator General for the Troubled Asset Relief Program, June 21, 2009.

———. *Quarterly Report to Congress.* Washington, DC: Office of the Special Investigator General for the Troubled Asset Relief Program, January 26, 2012.

Silber, William L. *When Washington Shut Down Wall Street: The Great Financial Crisis of 1914 and the Origins of America's Monetary Supremacy.* Princeton, NJ: Princeton University Press, 2007.

Sinclair, Timothy J. *The New Masters of Capital: American Bond Rating Agencies and the Politics of Creditworthiness.* Ithaca, NY: Cornell University Press, 2008.

Solomon, Deborah. "White House Set to Appoint a Pay Czar." *Wall Street Journal,* June 5, 2009, sec. Politics. Available at http://online.wsj.com/article/SB124416737421887739.html.

Sorkin, Andrew Ross. *Too Big to Fail: The Inside Story of How Wall Street and Washington Fought to Save the Financial System—and Themselves.* New York: Penguin Books, 2011.

Sorkin, Andrew Ross, Diana B. Henriques, Edmund L. Andrews, and Joe Nocera. "As Credit Crisis Spiraled, Alarm Led to Action." *New York Times,* October 1, 2008, sec. Business Day. Available at www.nytimes.com/2008/10/02/business/02crisis.html.

Steinbrück, Peer. *Unterm Strich.* Frankfurt a.M.: Hoffmann und Campe, 2010.

Stern, Gary H., and Ron J. Feldman. *Too Big to Fail: The Hazards of Bank Bailouts.* Washington, DC: Brookings Institution Press, 2004.

Stigler, George. "The Theory of Economic Regulation." *Bell Journal of Economics and Management Science* 2 (1971): 3–21.

———. "Economic Competition and Political Competition." *Public Choice* 13 (1972): 91–107.

Stiglitz, Joseph E. *Freefall: America, Free Markets, and the Sinking of the World Economy.* Reprint. New York: W. W. Norton, 2010.

Stolz, Stéphanie Marie, and Michael Wedow. "Extraordinary Measures in Extraordinary Times—Public Measures in Support of the Financial Sector in the EU and the United States." Occasional Paper Series No. 117. Frankfurt: European Central Bank, July 2010.

Story, Jonathan, and Ingo Walter. *Political Economy of Financial Integration in Europe: The Battle of the Systems.* Cambridge, MA: MIT Press, 1997.

Strange, Susan. *States and Markets: An Introduction to International Political Economy.* London: Pinter, 1988.

———. *Casino Capitalism.* Manchester, UK: Manchester University Press, 1997.

Streeck, Wolfgang. *Gekaufte Zeit: Die Vertagte Krise Des Demokratischen Kapitalismus.* Frankfurt a.M.: Suhrkamp, 2013.

Sukhdev, Johal, Michael Moran, and Karel Williams. "Post-Crisis Financial Regulation in Britain." In *Crisis and Control: Institutional Change in Financial Market Regulation,* edited by Renate Mayntz, 67-96, Frankfurt: Campus, 2012.

Taleb, Nassim. *The Black Swan: The Impact of the Highly Improbable.* New York: Random House, 2007.

Thiemann, Matthias. *Accounting for Risk: The Regulation of Special Purpose Entities in France, Germany and the Netherlands.* PhD Thesis in Sociology, Columbia University, New York: 2013.

UK Debt Management Office. *The Commissioners of Her Majesty's Treasury Rules of the 2008 Credit Guarantee Scheme.* London, 2008. Available at www.dmo.gov.uk/docs/cgs/press/cgsrules.pdf.

Underhill, Geoffrey R.D., and Xiaoke Zang. "Setting the Rules: Private Power, Political Underpinnings, and Legitimacy in Global Monetary and Financial Governance." *International Affairs* 84, no. 3 (2008): 535–54.

US Department of the Treasury. *Treasury Announces TARP Capital Purchase Program.* October 14, 2008. Available at www.treasury.gov/press-center/press-releases/Pages/hp1207.aspx.

Useem, Michael. *The Inner Circle: Large Corporations and the Rise of Business Political Activity in the U.S. and U.K.* Oxford: Oxford University Press, 1986.

Vogel, David. *Fluctuating Fortunes: The Political Power of Business in America.* Frederick, MD: Beard Books, 2003.

Weber, Beat, and Stefan W. Schmitz. "Varieties of Helping Capitalism: Politico-economic Determinants of Bank Rescue Packages in the EU during the Recent Crisis." *Socio-Economic Review* 9, no. 4 (2011): 639–69.

Wessel, David. *In FED We Trust: Ben Bernanke's War on the Great Panic.* New York: Crown Business, 2010.

Whelan, Karl. *Bank and Sovereign Debt Resolution: "Never Again" Meets "Not Yet."* Briefing Note DG for Internal Policies. Brussels: European Parliament, 2011. Available at www.europarl.europa.eu/document/activities/cont/201103/20110316ATT15718/20110316ATT15718EN.pdf.

White, Lawrence H. *The Theory of Monetary Institutions.* Oxford: Blackwell, 1999.

Wiesmann, Gerrit. "Bank's €55bn Debt Error a 'Misunderstanding.'" *Financial Times,* November 2, 2011. Available at www.ft.com/intl/cms/s/0/c23538f0-056a-11e1-8eaa-00144feabdc0.html.

Williams, Paul. "Tapes That Reveal What Really Led to National Collapse." *Irish Independent,* June 24, 2013. Available at www.independent.ie/business/irish/tapes-that-reveal-what-really-led-to-national-collapse-29366839.html.

Woll, Cornelia. "Leading the Dance? Power and Political Resources of Business Lobbyists." *Journal of Public Policy* 27, no. 1 (2007): 57–78.

——. *Firm Interests: How Governments Shape Business Lobbying on Global Trade.* Ithaca, NY: Cornell University Press, 2008.

——. "The Morality of Rescuing Banks." In "Moral Categories in the Financial Crisis." Discussion forum with Marion Fourcase, Philippe Steiner, Wolfgang Streeck, and Cornelia Woll. *Socio-Economic Review* 11, no. 3 (2013): 601–27.

Young, Kevin L. "Transnational Regulatory Capture? An Empirical Examination of the Transnational Lobbying of the Basel Committee on Banking Supervision." *Review of International Political Economy* 19, no. 4 (2012): 663–88.

Zimmer, Daniel, Werner Brandt, Claudia-Maria Buch, Martin Hellwig, Hans-Hermann Lotter, and Hanno Merkt. *Strategien Für Den Ausstieg Des Bundes Aus Krisenbedingten Beteiligungen an Banken: Gutachten Des von Der Bundesregierung Eingesetzten Expertenrates.* Berlin: Bundesministerium für Finanzen, January 24, 2011.

Zysman, John. *Governments, Markets, and Growth: Financial Systems and the Politics of Industrial Change.* Ithaca, NY: Cornell University Press, 1983.

Index